Examining Modern Economic Anthropology

Bryan Christiansen
Southern New Hampshire University, USA

John D. Branch
University of Michigan, USA

IGI Global
Scientific Publishing
Publishing Tomorrow's Research Today

Vice President of Editorial Melissa Wagner
Director of Acquisitions Mikaela Felty
Director of Book Development Jocelynn Hessler
Production Manager Mike Brehm
Cover Design Jose Rosado

Published in the United States of America by
IGI Global Scientific Publishing
701 East Chocolate Avenue
Hershey, PA, 17033, USA
Tel: 717-533-8845 | Fax: 717-533-7115
Website: https://www.igi-global.com E-mail: cust@igi-global.com

Library of Congress Cataloging-in-Publication Data

Names: Christiansen, Bryan, 1960- editor | Branch, John, 1967- editor
Title: Examining modern economic anthropology / edited by Bryan Christiansen, John Branch.
Description: Hershey, PA : IGI Global Scientific Publishing, [2026] | Includes bibliographical references and index. | Summary: "Modern economic anthropology is a subfield of anthropology that examines how economic systems, behaviors, and practices are embedded in and influenced by cultural, social, political, and environmental contexts. It seeks to understand the diverse ways in which people produce, exchange, distribute, and consume goods and services, going beyond the frameworks of classical economics by emphasizing the interplay of culture, values, and power dynamics"-- Provided by publisher.
Identifiers: LCCN 2025024372 (print) | LCCN 2025024373 (ebook) | ISBN 9798337312606 h/c | ISBN 9798337312613 s/c | ISBN 9798337312620 ebook
Subjects: LCSH: Economic anthropology
Classification: LCC GN448 .E93 2026 (print) | LCC GN448 (ebook) | DDC 306.3--dc23/eng/20250806
LC record available at https://lccn.loc.gov/2025024372
LC ebook record available at https://lccn.loc.gov/2025024373

British Cataloguing in Publication Data
A Cataloguing in Publication record for this book is available from the British Library.

Table of Contents

Detailed Table of Contents

This chapter interrogates the modern myth of scarcity — not as a universal economic truth, but as a theological residue of Western thought, repackaged as scientific reason. The figure of the "economic man," descended from Protestant notions of sin, salvation, and moral failing, now masquerades as a neutral model of rationality. This fiction, universalized through colonial expansion, has shaped development discourse in societies like India, often by displacing indigenous modes of knowing. Rather than reform this model, we argue for its provincialization. Drawing on Indian traditions of dharma, relationality, and experiential action-knowledge, the chapter invites a rethinking — not of how we fit into global economic theory, but of whether that theory ever understood us. It is not "scarcity" that defines the human condition, but the colonial will to describe others as lacking.

This theoretical study examines money as a cultural artifact in the context of planetary boundaries and social inequality. Starting from the assumption that money is more than a neutral medium of exchange, the article analyzes its semiotic, material, and social dimensions. It integrates perspectives from economic anthropology, systems theory, and network theory with ecological economics, proposing six theses that shed light on the tension between abstraction, infrastructure, power, and meaning in modern monetary systems. Methodologically, the study combines an interdisciplinary literature and concept analysis with the design of a theoretically sound research program. It argues that the current monetary system in the Anthropocene has both ecologically destabilizing and socially selective effects. The outlook discusses the potential of alternative monetary architectures—such as indexed, earmarked, or multicentric currencies—to reintegrate economic, social, and ecological goal systems. The study aims to contribute to a transformative monetary theory in the context of global upheaval.

This chapter examines capitalism, socialism, and communism from an economic and anthropological perspective, emphasizing that these systems are culturally defined, historically conditioned, and socially lived. It does so through a detailed overview of each system's history, values, and contradictions, taking advantage of ethnographic case studies from around the world to compare the extremes of labour, resource distribution, and cultural impact. The chapter also explores mixed or hybrid economic systems, digital economies, and emerging alternatives for sustainability and equity. By applying classical theories with present-day issues, the chapter emphasizes the significance of anthropological perspectives to explain the effects of economic systems on human conduct, social ties, and future values.

This paper explores the role of Islamic finance in challenging the dominant capitalist economic system by offering an alternative money ontology, which is based on the principles of social justice, wealth redistribution, and solidarity. This study examines how Islamic finance through mechanisms such as the prohibition of usury, qard hasan (interest-free loans), zakat (obligatory charity), and waqf redefines money not as a commodity for personal gain but as a tool for social responsibility and economic equity. In contrast to conventional finance which emphasizes the accumulation of individual wealth, Islamic finance emphasizes transactions related to real assets and productive activities, which aim to foster social welfare and community welfare. Through this analysis, we argue that Islamic finance presents a viable and ethical alternative to interest-based systems, offering a more equitable and sustainable approach to global economic development.

This chapter provides the framework for critically examining development and economic inequality as cultural marginalization across the globe and in grassroots experiences. Taking the Koch Rajbongshi tribe as a case of systematic oversight, it analyzes the exclusion of indigenous communities by dominant growth paradigms. Using ethnographic accounts, policy reports and theoretical contributions, including (but not limited to) recent work by Sen, Piketty and Fraser, this chapter contends that development needs to articulate social justice, cultural identity and historical recognition alongside its existing GDP-influenced neo-economic character. It compares effective models of literacy-led equity, like those of Kerala and Mizoram, with ongoing exclusion because of bureaucratic inertia. Primary insight and real-time development make the case for a recognition and redistribution-based people-centred development model much stronger.

This chapter examines how digital economies are transforming the lives of marginalized communities in North-East India, a region characterized by socio-cultural diversity and economic vulnerability. It will focus on how digital platforms like gig work applications, e-commerce, and digital micro-entrepreneurship integrate with or disrupt traditional labor practices, such as artisanal crafts and subsistence economies. The study will highlight ongoing socio-economic challenges, including algorithmic biases, digital illiteracy, and labor commodification, which exacerbate existing inequalities. Simultaneously, it will explore how marginalized groups actively adapt to these challenges by leveraging digital tools to preserve cultural identity and create alternative economies. Through ethnographic fieldwork and case studies in Assam, Manipur, and Meghalaya, the chapter will provide insights into the complex interplay between digital inclusion, cultural resilience, and systemic exclusion.

Preface

In recent decades, the study of economics has been dominated by formal models, abstract theories, and quantitative data that often presume a universal logic to human behavior—most notably, that of the rational individual maximizing utility within a market system. While this approach has yielded important insights, it frequently overlooks the intricate and varied social, cultural, and political contexts within which economic activity occurs. *Examining Modern Economic Anthropology* emerges in response to this limitation.

As editors of this volume, we have sought to curate a collection that highlights the rich, multidimensional nature of economic life across time and space. Modern economic anthropology, as a field, interrogates the foundations of what constitutes "the economy," shedding light on how people and communities organize production, exchange, distribution, and consumption not simply to satisfy needs, but to express identities, assert values, negotiate power, and sustain their ways of life.

This book is grounded in the conviction that economic behavior cannot be meaningfully understood without considering its embeddedness in cultural and social contexts. From traditional subsistence economies to digital marketplaces, from communal modes of labor to global trade networks, this volume explores the incredible diversity of economic forms and their implications for contemporary human life.

The chapters in *Examining Modern Economic Anthropology* reflect a broad, critical engagement with the field's most pressing theoretical, cultural, and empirical questions. Together, they provide a mosaic of perspectives that foreground the social embeddedness, cultural specificity, and political significance of economic behavior around the world.

CHAPTER OVERVIEW

In **Chapter 1**, *Rethinking Scarcity: Political Imagination and the Myth of Economic Man*, the authors deconstruct the ideological foundations of scarcity and the "economic man" as Western constructs rooted in theological and colonial legacies. Drawing on Indian philosophical traditions and critiques of development discourse, this chapter challenges the universality of economic rationality and proposes a more pluralistic and relational understanding of economic life.

Chapter 2, *Money as a Cultural Artifact*, repositions money as a deeply cultural and ecological object rather than a neutral facilitator of exchange. Integrating economic anthropology with ecological economics and systems theory, the chapter explores how monetary systems reflect and reproduce power, inequality, and environmental harm. It offers forward-looking perspectives on alternative currencies as vehicles for socio-ecological transformation in the Anthropocene.

In **Chapter 3**, *Capitalism, Socialism, and Communism: Comparative Insights in Modern Economic Anthropology*, classical and contemporary economic systems are reexamined through an anthropological lens. The chapter contextualizes these systems culturally and historically, emphasizing their lived realities and hybrid forms. Ethnographic examples illuminate the effects of economic models on labor, resource distribution, and social relationships—especially as new economic forms emerge in digital and post-capitalist spaces.

Chapter 4, *Islamic Finance and the Anthropology of Money*, explores ethical alternatives to dominant financial systems. Focusing on the principles underlying Islamic finance—including the prohibition of interest and the promotion of wealth redistribution—this chapter argues for a moral reconfiguration of money as a tool for social justice, rather than a commodity for personal gain. The case offers compelling evidence of viable, values-based approaches to economic development.

In **Chapter 5**, *Bridging the Divide*, the authors focus on the Koch Rajbongshi tribe in India to expose how economic development often entails cultural erasure and systemic marginalization. Through detailed ethnographic and policy analysis, the chapter critiques GDP-centric development models and advocates for equity-based, literacy-led, and culturally sensitive frameworks that incorporate social justice and recognition.

Chapter 6, *Digital Economies and Marginalized Communities in North-East India*, explores the impact of digital transformation on communities historically excluded from dominant economic systems. Examining the tension between opportunity and precarity in digital labor and micro-entrepreneurship, the chapter highlights both the vulnerabilities and the resilience strategies of marginalized groups striving to assert identity and economic agency in the digital age.

Finally, **Chapter 7**, *Nonprofit Governance – When the Private Sector Controls*, scrutinizes the blurred lines between nonprofit and for-profit sectors through the case of Club Intrawest. Using longitudinal case analysis, the chapter reveals how corporate governance structures can exploit nonprofit frameworks for private gain, raising ethical and legal questions about ownership, accountability, and consumer protection in hybrid organizational models.

Our contributors examine foundational theories and debates in the field, including the influence of Karl Polanyi and the substantivist tradition, the long-standing formalist-substantivist debate, and the enduring relevance of early anthropologists like Bronislaw Malinowski and Raymond Firth. Beyond theoretical grounding, this book also provides case studies and analyses on topics such as informal economies, environmental and ecological economics, economic inequality, globalization, resistance, commodification, and the rise of digital economies.

The primary objective of this edited volume is to provide a comprehensive, accessible, and contemporary reference source for scholars, graduate students, and practitioners interested in the intersections of culture and economy. Whether one is a newcomer to the field or a seasoned researcher seeking fresh perspectives, this volume offers a holistic overview of where modern economic anthropology stands today and where it may be headed.

In compiling this reference, we have been continually reminded of the field's critical role in challenging economic orthodoxy and expanding the lens through which we view human livelihood. We hope this work contributes meaningfully to that effort, encouraging new conversations, deeper understanding, and more inclusive frameworks in both anthropology and economics.

Chapter 1

Rethinking Scarcity:
Political Imagination and the Myth of Economic Man

Keerthiraj
https://orcid.org/0000-0002-2536-8579
GFGC Punjalakatte, Mangalore University, India

Apoorva Misra
https://orcid.org/0009-0009-0476-8125
Alliance University, India

K. Nizar
https://orcid.org/0000-0003-1104-9750
Presidency University, India

ABSTRACT

This chapter interrogates the modern myth of scarcity — not as a universal economic truth, but as a theological residue of Western thought, repackaged as scientific reason. The figure of the "economic man," descended from Protestant notions of sin, salvation, and moral failing, now masquerades as a neutral model of rationality. This fiction, universalized through colonial expansion, has shaped development discourse in societies like India, often by displacing indigenous modes of knowing. Rather than reform this model, we argue for its provincialization. Drawing on Indian traditions

DOI: 10.4018/979-8-3373-1260-6.ch001

of dharma, relationality, and experiential action-knowledge, the chapter invites a rethinking — not of how we fit into global economic theory, but of whether that theory ever understood us. It is not "scarcity" that defines the human condition, but the colonial will to describe others as lacking.

INTRODUCTION

Modern economics begins with what is widely believed to be a truism: that human wants are infinite, while the resources available to satisfy them are finite. This condition, so the story goes, compels us to make choices—a scientific axiom, we are told, that lies at the foundation of all economic reasoning. But let us suspend this belief for a moment and ask a question that we seldom do: what kind of creature must a human being be for such a picture to even make sense? The races the theological roots of economic scarcity and proposes a culturally grounded alternative drawn from Indian experiential knowledge. The idea that scarcity is a neutral fact of life assumes that we already know what "wants" are, that they are naturally infinite, and that this infinity is somehow an essential feature of human existence. However, this assumption is not the result of scientific investigation into human nature. It is, we want to suggest, a product of a specific historical development within a particular culture—Western Europe—and, more specifically, of a theological narrative that has come to define what counts as "rational" economic behaviour (Love, 2022). Scarcity, then, is not an objective description of reality but a cultural imagination (Ghosh, 2022). It is an imagination born out of Protestant Christian anthropology—of man as fallen, insatiable, and in need of redemption through toil. From this narrative emerges the figure of homo economicus: the rational, self-interested agent whose every action is guided by a calculus of gain and loss. This figure is not a discovery; it is an invention—one that has been secularized and exported worldwide through colonialism, becoming the common sense of modern economic thinking. To call this figure a myth is not to suggest that it is false, but rather to highlight that it performs a political and epistemic function. It enables a certain kind of reasoning about governance, policy, and institutional design. The disciplines that arose in the wake of colonial expansion—economics, political science, sociology—did not merely describe the world; they recreated it in the image of this economic man (Darity, 2022). That India, too, adopted these categories is not surprising. What is remarkable is the extent to which Indian intellectuals and institutions have naturalized them.

While this chapter draws attention to categories like dharma[1], artha[2], kama[3] and mok a[4] as alternate ways of organizing economic life, it is not merely contributing an "Indian case" to the archives of moral economy or substantivist theory. Such frameworks, though critical of neoclassical assumptions, remain tethered to the same conceptual inheritance—the West's theological and philosophical legacy. Our intervention does not seek inclusion within these paradigms but instead calls into question the very intelligibility of "economy" and "rationality" as they appear in modern discourse. In this sense, the chapter is in conversation with postcolonial critiques of universalism, but it goes further: it explores what happens when we take seriously the possibility that Indian traditions never posed scarcity as a fundamental condition of human life.

Let us ask, for instance, whether Indian traditions ever spoke of human beings as creatures driven by scarcity. The answer is a resounding no. Instead, they articulated human motivations in terms of dharma, artha, kāma, and mok a. These are not "needs" to be fulfilled but modes of human life to be understood and cultivated. They presuppose a view of the human being not as a desiring machine, but as someone capable of learning, reflecting, and seeking well-being in relation to others and to the cosmos (Bhinekawati, 2021). This contrast matters, not because one view is superior to the other, but because we have never asked whether these two views are commensurable. Instead, in the name of modernization and reform, we imported one and forgot the other. The consequences are visible everywhere: in the adoption of rational choice models in public policy, in the treatment of economic activity as inherently competitive, and in the design of welfare systems that presume the universal applicability of Western categories. Let us illustrate this with a few cases. Consider Aadhaar, India's massive digital identification system. It was built on the presumption that welfare must be targeted efficiently, that leakages are a form of irrationality, and that recipients must be tracked as individual consumers of state resources. But this presumes a conception of the individual as atomic, self-interested, and devoid of embedded ties. It does not account for the moral economy of the Indian village, where kinship, reciprocity, and honour continue to structure economic relations. Similarly, caste-based reservations assume a model of distributive justice drawn from a particular reading of equality and fairness, ignoring the lived experience of community, dignity, and honour (Ribeiro, 2022). In both cases, the mismatch between imported theories and indigenous practices is stark. Why, then, do we persist in applying these categories? Because, we want to suggest, our academic and policy discourse remains trapped in colonial consciousness. The terms "caste," "religion," "morality," "rationality," and "state" do not describe India; they describe the West's imagination of India. Yet, we continue to measure ourselves against them, often concluding that we are irrational, inefficient, or immoral—precisely because we do not fit.

There is no accusation here. The aim is not to blame "the West" but to diagnose a condition: that our categories of thought are not ours. We have inherited frameworks that do not resonate with our practices, yet we are unable to discard them because we no longer know how to think outside them. This, we submit, is a form of cognitive dependence. It is not merely historical but ongoing. How do we respond? Not by rejecting Western theories outright, nor by glorifying an imagined past. Rather, we must undertake the difficult task of conceptual excavation—of rediscovering and reconstructing our own frameworks (Sun & Teichert, 2022). Indian traditions never spoke of scarcity as a problem. They spoke of Desire (in the singular), which is not to be satisfied but to be gone about with. They never promised happiness as the satisfaction of needs but as the cultivation of wisdom. Happiness was not an object to be acquired but a state of being that could be learnt. The implication is profound: economic models need not begin with scarcity. They could begin with dharma, with relationality, or with the rhythms of life that are structured not by lack but by balance. These are not utopian ideas. They are grounded in experience, in traditions that have sustained communities for centuries (Adams & Mittiga, 2020). To build new economic theories, we must first unlearn the ones we have inherited. And to do that, we must understand their genealogy. Only then can we begin to think from where we stand, rather than where we were made to stand.

To examine this claim, the chapter proceeds in four stages. It first traces the theological and philosophical genealogy of scarcity in Western political economy, revealing its embeddedness in a specific anthropology of the human. Second, it explores how this assumption shaped colonial and postcolonial governance, particularly in India, where institutional designs and welfare systems were premised on a conception of the individual that remains alien to Indian social formations. Third, the chapter introduces Indian categories such as dharma, artha, and svadharma[5]—not as cultural artefacts, but as theoretical resources for a relational economic anthropology. Finally, it reflects on the policy and disciplinary implications of abandoning scarcity as a foundational axiom, arguing for a pluralistic, civilizational approach to economic life.

THE THEOLOGICAL ORIGINS OF HOMO ECONOMICUS

Modern economic theory rests on an implicit anthropology: it presupposes a certain image of the human being. This "economic man" is typically characterized as rational, self-interested, competitive, and endlessly acquisitive. Far from being a neutral description, this figure has deep roots in European intellectual and religious history. Scholars have noted that homo economicus closely resembles the Protestant Christian conception of "fallen" man, secularized and dressed in scientific language (Konnova, 2020). As one analysis puts it, homo economicus is an "appropriate persona of fallen man" – a being who, after the fall from grace, must rely on his own wits to navigate a world of scarcity (Love, 2022). In Christian theology, especially in the Protestant tradition, human nature is tainted by original sin, which manifests as innate selfishness, insatiable desires, and a life of toil outside Eden. The secular economic man inherits these traits: he is assumed to be inward-looking and self-serving, acknowledging others only as means to his own ends (di Somma, 2022). Modern economics, in claiming to be value-free, actually smuggled in this theological anthropology, rebranding sin as self-interest and divine curse as scarcity (Budini, 2024).

It is instructive to recall how foundational Christian narratives frame scarcity. In the Book of Genesis, after Adam and Eve's disobedience, God curses the ground: only "by the sweat of your brow" will humans eat, amidst thorns and thistles – a vivid image of a world of insufficient resources and hard labor. Theologically, scarcity was seen as an ontological condition of a fallen world, not merely a technical problem (Thompson, 2022). Medieval Christian scholars (e.g. Thomas Aquinas) considered scarcity part of the natural order after the Fall, influencing moral teachings on charity and stewardship. The Protestant Reformation, particularly Calvinist thought, intensified the view of humans as depraved and the world as a vale of scarcity where only diligent work and God's grace could bring improvement (Tuniz & Vipraio, 2020). Max Weber famously argued that the Protestant ethic – rooted in asceticism and the notion of proving one's elect status through material success – helped spawn the capitalist spirit of relentless labor and saving (Weber, 1905). Thus, even as economics later presented itself as a science, it was building on culturally specific assumptions about human nature and the inevitability of scarcity.

By the 18th and 19th centuries, early political economists like Adam Smith, Thomas Malthus, and David Ricardo carried these ideas into secular discourse (Ricardo, 1817). Malthus, an English clergyman, explicitly described scarcity in quasi-theological terms: population would always press against food supply, making poverty and competition inescapable – a near paraphrase of the post-Edenic curse (Malthus, 1993; Rela, 2021). Notably, Malthus blamed the suffering of famines on providence and warned against "interference" with divine laws of population – effectively sacralizing scarcity. Adam Smith, while less overtly religious, wrote in an era steeped in Scottish Presbyterian values; his concept of the "invisible hand" can be read as a secularized providence ensuring that individual self-interest (a presumably universal trait) yields social benefits (Smith, 1776). In short, the modern economic agent was never a purely empirical observation of how all humans behave; it was a normative construct grounded in a Euro-Christian vision of mankind's fallen but calculative nature. As O'Boyle (2019) summarizes, orthodox economics constructed homo economicus around four principal traits – individuality, rationality, volitionality,and acquisitiveness. Each of these has a theological echo (Lushch-Purii, 2021). Individuality (an isolated, atomistic self) parallels the Protestant emphasis on individual souls standing alone before God. Rationality and volitionality (the capacity to reason and exercise free will) reflect the Enlightenment's view of man as a reasoning actor – but also the Protestant rejection of external (Church) authority in favor of personal discernment. Acquisitiveness – the pursuit of maximum gain – secularizes the idea of human desires being unlimited due to sin (in Christian terms, man's heart is perpetually restless and greedy without divine orientation).

Crucially, these assumptions were cast as universal truths by economists in the 19th and 20th centuries. By treating economics as analogous to a physical science, early neoclassical thinkers claimed to discover laws of human behavior akin to laws of nature. Students were (and still are) taught that "people have unlimited wants but limited means" as an unquestionable starting point. Yet, this claim hides its cultural genesis. In reality, not all societies have organized their economic life around the principle of maximizing utility under scarcity (Erasmo, 2022). Anthropological studies show many cultures emphasize contentment or balance over endless accumulation; for instance, certain indigenous cosmologies see nature as abundant (provided humans show restraint and gratitude). Classical Indian civilization did not begin its economic thought with the axiom of scarcity at all – its texts speak more of proper allocation (dharma) and prosperity (śreyas) than of an insurmountable gap between wants and means (Bhinekawati, 2021). The very notion of "infinite wants" is arguably a product of modern consumer society; traditional cultures often placed moral or practical limits on wants. By contrast, the Western intellectual tradition – shaped by centuries of theological discourse on desire and sin – conceived of human wants as inherently boundless (since the soul, being fallen, tries to fill a spiritual void with material things). This theology was transmuted into the economic concept of utility maximization.

Furthermore, the portrayal of human cooperation versus competition in economics has theological roots. In Christian thought, humans are inherently prone to selfish conflict (a legacy of sin), requiring divine or institutional intervention for harmony (Mäki, 2021). Hobbes's secular formulation of the "state of nature" – a war of all against all – clearly mirrors this pessimistic view of humanity, albeit without explicit reference to sin. When Ludwig von Mises, a 20th-century economist, wrote that "the natural scarcity of the means of sustenance forces every living being to look upon all others as deadly foes in the struggle for survival," he was echoing a long-standing theological pessimism (Mises, 1949). Mises immediately added that with humans, these conflicts can disappear through the division of labor and cooperation, capturing the classical liberal faith that market exchange reconciles self-interests. But the initial premise – natural scarcity breeding conflict – is presented almost as a metaphysical given, much as Christian doctrine treats human strife as the default without God's grace. Indeed, Christian theology taught that post-Fall, humans could achieve concord only through a higher covenant (first the Church, then for Protestants perhaps the internalized spirit of discipline). In secular economics, the market performs a quasi-redemptive role, turning individual vice (greed) into collective virtue (wealth generation). The invisible hand is a secular stand-in for Providence, ensuring that even in a world of scarce resources and selfish actors, an order and improvement can emerge.

The point here is not to reduce economics to theology, but to uncover the historical contingency of what we take as objective truth. Homo economicus was never a neutral scientific discovery about humans; it was an ideological figure shaped by a specific culture's imagination. The notion of colonial consciousness invites us to see how European theological categories were often universalized through colonial knowledge production. Economic man is one such category: a provincial European understanding of man that masqueraded as universal (Klamer, 2023). When economists claimed their theories were as value-free as physics, they were unaware (or uninterested) that their baseline "economic agent" was carrying heavy cultural baggage – a Protestant-Christian moral psychology laundered into equations of supply and demand.

By recognizing the theological and cultural origins of the scarcity axiom and homo economicus, we create space to question its universality. Is every society doomed to structure itself around managing endless wants with limited means? Or is this a myth – a self-fulfilling prophecy that shapes societies in the image of its assumptions? The next sections explore how this myth became a political reality through institutions, and how it contrasts with Indian conceptions of personhood and economy.

HOMO ECONOMICUS AND THE POLITICS OF STATECRAFT

Suppose we begin not by assuming that the modern state arises from a social contract or the liberal Enlightenment, but by asking a more prior question: what kind of creature must a human being be, for such a state to make sense? What kind of anthropology underwrites its institutions, policies, and justifications? The answer lies in a figure that modern thought has normalized into invisibility: the homo economicus. The political utility of this figure is well known, but rarely interrogated as a product of cultural and theological imagination. If human beings are construed as utility-maximizing agents—rational calculators of costs and benefits—then the state naturally becomes a referee or, at times, a shepherd. This view gives rise to two linked convictions: that individual pursuit of self-interest leads to public good, and that deviations from this logic must be managed or corrected (Braun, 2021). Whether in free-market capitalism or welfare statism, legitimacy is tied to the assumption that human behavior is predictable in response to incentives.

This assumption does not stem from empirical observations of human beings. Rather, it emerges from a theological lineage that secularized itself into modern economics. As Giorgio Agamben has shown, classical Christian theology—particularly Trinitarian debates—generated the concept of divine management (oikonomia), which secularized into notions of providential market order and statecraft (Agamben, 2011; Giraud, 2023). In Christian doctrine, humanity was fallen, prone to sin, and in need of restraint. Over time, this moral anthropology became economic: sin became inefficiency, redemption became productivity. Scarcity, accordingly, became not just a descriptive fact but a moral imperative (Boland & Griffin, 2021). Welfare, then, is not a right but a risk. Aid must be conditional, lest it erode incentives. The poor are not simply unfortunate but are suspected of choosing idleness. These assumptions did not arise from studying the poor, but from a prior image of what human beings should be—a model rooted in theology and carried over into policy via economic abstraction (Minch, 2021). This moral-political anthropology shapes institutions across history. The Victorian workhouse, U.S. work requirements, and contemporary conditional subsidies all reflect the same logic: people must be nudged or coerced into rational behavior (Mäki, 2021). Even the most benevolent state thus casts the citizen as a potential deviant from rational choice, a subject to be optimized.

Colonial policy extended this framework without rupture. Colonized subjects, especially in India, were judged not simply as economic actors but as failed ones. Because they did not privatize land, maximize output, or conform to capitalist time, they were deemed irrational and unfit to govern. This deficit anthropology justified paternalism (Robbins, 2020). Here lies the paradox: colonial scarcity—famines, underdevelopment—was produced by imperial extraction and policy, but explained by invoking "native culture" and failure to behave economically (Isomae, 2022). Post-independence India inherited this paradigm. From Nehru's technocracy to post-1991 liberalization, the figure of the rational actor endured. The tools changed; the anthropology did not.

Consider India's population control programs in the 1970s. Inspired by Malthusian fears, the state incentivized or coerced sterilization, assuming that the poor reproduced from ignorance. The body itself became an object of policy, managed by economic logic. When resistance arose or policies failed, blame fell not on flawed assumptions, but on cultural backwardness. Even today, these models persist. Cost-benefit analysis dominates policy schools. Technology promises to remove "irrational" intermediaries, replacing them with automated compliance systems—Aadhaar, direct transfers, sanitation campaigns—all designed to align society with the rational agent model (Pallesen & Pedersen, 2023). Aadhaar, launched in 2009 as a biometric identity project, presumes that the Indian citizen is an atomized individual, detached from kinship networks, whose behavior can be predicted and regulated through identification and authentication technologies. Yet field studies show that welfare distribution in rural India continues to be mediated by gotra, kinship, and village-level reciprocities that defy the logic of individual entitlement. What fails, then, is not the system per se but the imagination of the subject on which the system is built—a being who does not exist in the Indian context except as an imported abstraction (Chaudhuri, 2022; Nagaraj & Prakash, 2021; Yashodha, 2019). This is not conspiracy or malice. It is the operation of a worldview. Policymakers schooled in Western economics earnestly believe they are designing better systems. But when the underlying anthropology is partial, so too are the outcomes.

What remains unacknowledged is this: homo economicus is not universal. It is a culturally specific product of European experiences with scarcity, governance, and theological reform (Pires, 2024). When imposed on contexts like India, it displaces indigenous logics of trust, cooperation, and relationality. Colonial consciousness is not about rulers but about categories. It is when a society evaluates itself through alien concepts—and inevitably fails. If humans are not utility calculators but relational and moral beings, then policies built on homo economicus will consistently misfire. They will solve problems that don't exist, and create new ones that we cannot see. The challenge is not to reject governance but to reimagine its foundation. What other images of human life are possible? What other beginnings can we envision for law, policy, and economics?

Only when we interrogate the genealogy of our categories can we begin to think otherwise. Until then, we remain in modernity's paradox: building a world for a model of man that does not exist—and wondering why it fails to deliver on its promises.

RATIONAL CHOICE AND THE COLONIAL IMAGINATION: POLITICAL SCIENCE IN THE IMAGE OF ECONOMIC MAN

One of the striking features of post–World War II political science, particularly in its American and European incarnations, has been its emulation of economics—not merely in methodology but in anthropology. The modern discipline increasingly adopted a vision of the political actor as a rational, self-interested individual navigating a world of scarcity and incentives. In this new idiom, now normalized as rational choice theory, voters are said to maximize utility; politicians maximize votes (or rents); bureaucrats maximize budgets; and states, in the field of international relations, maximize power or security (Keerthiraj, Misra, & Vang-Phu, 2025). At each level, political life becomes an arena of strategic choice by rational agents seeking advantage under constraints. The homo economicus is thus not confined to markets; he is transposed wholesale into the polity.

This transplantation, however, is not a neutral move. It is the spread of a particular image of the human being, born out of Western intellectual and theological history, into domains where it neither originates nor fits. Rational choice theory, in this sense, is not merely an analytic tool. It is an anthropological assertion, a vision of human nature posed as universal. And as with other such assertions, its spread to non-Western contexts—such as India—has not simply been academic diffusion. It is a continuation of the imperialism of categories. This is not to suggest conspiracy or bad faith. Rather, it is to reveal how deeply entrenched the colonial consciousness remains within the social sciences. In a society such as India, where notions of duty (dharma), community allegiance, charisma, or spiritual merit often guide political behavior, models assuming individuals as utility-maximizing agents misdescribe what is taking place. A poor villager voting for a leader not on economic grounds but due to caste loyalty or a shared vision of the good life appears "irrational" only within the assumptions of the theory. Yet it is precisely this deviation that political science seeks to explain, rather than questioning whether the framework itself is appropriate.

The colonial consciousness does not simply impose foreign institutions. It imposes a way of seeing—where explanation becomes a matter of fitting diverse practices into pre-given concepts. When those practices resist the fit, the response is not to doubt the concept, but to reform the society. Voter education campaigns that exhort people to vote "rationally" on issues, rather than identities, are one example. Anti-defection laws aimed at disciplining legislators who switch parties are another. These interventions presume that the rational actor model is correct, and that the Indian voter or politician must be corrected until they conform.

What remains unasked is whether these behaviors are in fact guided by other logics—logics unintelligible to the model but meaningful within their own cultural milieu. A politician who distributes resources to his caste group may not be seen by constituents as corrupt, but as fulfilling a moral obligation of dāna. A bureaucrat who favors local networks over formal procedures may not be maximizing personal gain, but responding to embedded ethical codes of loyalty and reciprocity. Yet such nuances are invisible—or worse, classified as dysfunctions—in the lens of economic man. This is not merely an error of theory. It is the consequence of an anthropology masquerading as a science. Rational choice theory presents itself as value-neutral, but it carries within it a normative order. It tells us not just how humans act, but how they should act—namely, in calculative pursuit of interests. This moral order is the secularized remnant of a Protestant ethic that once framed man as a fallen creature in need of regulation. Now repackaged in scientific terms, it is used to design governance systems, institutional checks, incentive mechanisms, and policy interventions across the globe.

India's postcolonial state did not escape this colonization of the political imagination. Its Constitution and institutions were modeled on British and American precedents: the Westminster system, common law judiciary, and federal arrangements. The assumption was that transplanting the form would yield similar function. But as scholars have repeatedly observed, Indian democracy functions differently. Political mobilization occurs through caste, region, and religious networks. Governance is entangled in personal relations. Institutional outcomes diverge from their Western templates. Why should this surprise us? The social world of India is organized around concepts and norms that are not only different from the West but incommensurable with many of its categories. Yet, rather than interrogate the assumptions of theory, most social science has chosen to pathologize Indian practice. This is a conceptual distortion—the result of applying descriptions that originate in one culture to a world they cannot adequately capture.

Consider again the Indian Administrative Service. In theory, it is a rational bureaucracy: neutral, impersonal, objective. But in practice, officers operate in a society that prizes discretion, balance, and relational wisdom. To meet targets is not always to do justice; to follow rules is not always to serve the public. Yet reforms often aim to eliminate discretion—through digitalization, audit metrics, surveillance—as if judgment were the problem and algorithms the solution. The figure of homo economicus again looms large: the official must be incentivized, monitored, and nudged, never trusted to act from virtue or duty.

We may be told that rational choice theory is only a model, that it can be improved by adding cultural variables. But the problem is deeper. It is not merely what is missing, but what is foregrounded. In the rational choice frame, culture becomes a residual factor, a friction to be accounted for. The model remains the center; the rest becomes noise. This is the hallmark of colonial consciousness: the elevation of one culture's description to the status of universal explanation. The nineteenth-century Orientalist painted Indians as mystical and irrational. The late twentieth-century political scientist paints them as strategic actors—yet both see through external categories. Neither grasps Indian behavior on its own terms. One calls it tradition, the other calls it strategy. But both are acts of misrecognition.

If we are to decolonize political science, we must do more than critique models. We must rethink the anthropology upon which they are built. Instead of assuming that voters seek utility, we might ask what values and visions animate their choices. Instead of treating institutions as structures of incentives, we might ask how they embed normative orders. We might design institutions not to enforce behavior through threats and bribes, but to foster moral agency—an administration that calls upon dharma, not just discipline.

This is not a plea for cultural exceptionalism. It is an argument for epistemic humility. Rational choice models are not wrong; they are parochial. They emerged from specific historical contexts and reflect specific moral imaginations. Their mistake lies not in their use, but in their universalization. A truly plural social science would recognize this. It would treat Western theories not as the baseline, but as one of many ways of knowing. And it would draw upon indigenous traditions—not to provide data for foreign theories, but to generate new theories. India does not lack concepts; it lacks the confidence to theorize from them. That is the task ahead.

DHARMA AND THE RELATIONAL ETHIC: INDIAN ALTERNATIVES TO ECONOMIC MAN

Let us begin with a thought experiment. Suppose we ask: how does one describe a human being? The answer, in modern economics, is well known—homo economicus, a solitary individual, driven by insatiable desires, navigating a world of scarce resources. Rational, calculating, self-interested. But suppose this description is not merely mistaken, but misbegotten? That it does not emerge from a reflection on human life as such, but from the theological and cultural trajectory of Western thought—where desire is sin, scarcity a condition of fallenness, and salvation takes the form of productive labor (Dash, 2023; Gibson-Graham, 2006). In contrast to this figure, Indian traditions offer no such anthropology. Here, the human being is not abstracted from society and placed against nature, but is instead constituted by a matrix of relationships, duties, and aims.

To be human is not to possess desires, but to navigate life through a set of pursuits—purusharthas—that structure and orient existence: dharma (duty or right conduct), artha (material well-being), kāma (pleasure or desire), and mok a (liberation) (Badjatya, 2024; Martini et al., 2025). These are not competing claims on the individual. They are not "values" in the Western sense. Rather, they are dimensions of life itself, inseparable from the very experience of being human.

Nowhere is this more apparent than in the way Indian traditions approach economic behavior. Artha—the pursuit of wealth—is not condemned. Nor is kāma—the pursuit of enjoyment—viewed with suspicion. But neither of them is left unregulated or free-floating. They are always seen in relation to dharma, and ultimately subordinated to mok a (Swamy et al., 2021; Sen, 2005). In this picture, wealth is not pursued for its own sake, nor is it an index of utility or success. It is that which sustains dharma, and therefore sukha—a flourishing life. This is not an ethical injunction layered on top of economics. It is a different conceptualization of economic life altogether. The very object of economics in this framework is different. The texts of the tradition—be they the Mahabharata, the Arthashastra, or various smritis—do not separate economics from ethics, or facts from values (Dash, 2023). Nor do they construct a domain called "the economy" that is somehow autonomous from kinship, kingship, ritual, or duty. The pursuit of artha is always contextual—anchored in roles, stages of life, and one's svadharma (situational obligation).

This is not a nostalgic claim about a bygone culture. Rather, it points to a different understanding of what constitutes economic activity. Giving, for instance—dāna—is not an act of charity in the Abrahamic sense, where one's wealth is to be redistributed by divine command. Nor is it a utilitarian "externality" to be priced in or incentivized. Instead, it is an act that arises naturally within the framework of dharma (Roy, 2020). The act of giving—whether to guests, to Brahmins, to temples, or to the poor—is not altruistic. It is appropriate. It is what one does, not in order to be good, but to be human. Likewise, the critique of greed—lobha—is not a call to asceticism. It is a recognition that desires unmoored from dharma lead to disorder. Kāma is not to be destroyed or demonized (Bratoeva, 2024). It is to be fulfilled appropriately. The Kāma Sūtra, far from being a manual of indulgence, is a text of balance. The problem is not pleasure.

The problem is excess—an idea foreign to both the Christian suspicion of desire and the economic celebration of consumption.

What then of scarcity? The Indian texts do not treat scarcity as the fundamental condition of human life (Devi, 2020). Rather, they speak of abundance and moderation, of santu i[6] and maitri[7]. The aim is not accumulation, but sufficiency. The Hitopadesha speaks plainly: "One who is content with what he has owns the world." This is not metaphor. It is an ontological claim about the relation between human beings and the world they inhabit. In this view, scarcity is not the origin of economic life but its deviation. It is in this context that the so-called "positive" nature of modern economics becomes suspect (Martini et al., 2025). What presents itself as a value-neutral analysis of supply and demand is, in fact, a deeply normative project. It takes a theological anthropology, strips it of its religious vocabulary, and reintroduces it as science. Indian texts, by contrast, make no such pretension. They prescribe. They advise. They instruct. They do not claim to be neutral. But they are honest about their assumptions.

Take the Arthashastra of Kautilya (Kautilya, c. 300 BCE). It is a treatise on governance, strategy, and wealth—but always within the frame of Raj Dharma. The king is not a neutral enforcer of law or a provider of public goods. He is a moral agent whose duty is to protect, to nourish, and to regulate—not because market failures require it, but because it is appropriate to his role. The text speaks of tax rates, trade routes, and grain storage. But it also insists on limits to fiscal burden, on charity, on regulation of hoarding. It assumes a state embedded in society, not above it. A state with duties, not merely functions (Mishra, 2022; Dash, 2023). This is not a call to romanticize or restore a golden age. The point is not historical. It is conceptual. If economic man is not the only way to think about human beings, then policy, theory, and governance must begin elsewhere. The Indian traditions offer one such elsewhere—not as an alternative system of economics, but as a different vision of the human altogether (Upadhyay et al., 2024).

To call this "ethical economics" is to miss the point. The traditions do not add ethics to economics. They refuse the separation. They do not ask what is the most efficient way to allocate resources. They ask: what should one do, given who one is? That question cannot be answered by cost-benefit analysis. It requires knowing the self—not the self of psychology or of consumption, but the self that arises in and through one's obligations, relations, and aspirations.

Dharma as Decision-Making: Relational Logics in Action

To even ask how dharma might be "applied" in policy is already to have stepped into a conceptual universe where governance is imagined as rule-making, where decision-making appears as a matter of choosing among outcomes, and where economics becomes the grammar of incentives, contracts, and calculable results. But dharma does not belong to this world. It is not a principle to be enforced, nor a code to be interpreted. It arises in the midst of life—as obligation, not legislation; as relation, not abstraction. What sustains temple economies in South India is not a regulatory framework, but the enactment of duties shaped by varna[8], shraddha[9], and santushti (Gull & Khan, 2023). What allows water to flow in johad systems of Rajasthan is not a model of efficient allocation, but a norm of sufficiency attuned to shared life (Radhakrishnan, 1922; Tsing, 2015). In the chit funds of coastal Karnataka or among Marwari traders, the medium of credit is not collateral, but honor (Chaudhuri, 2022). These are not "cases" of alternative development. They are sites where another anthropology of the human makes itself visible. To operationalizedharma is not to translate it into the language of modern policy, but to unlearn the assumption that there is only one language in which economies must speak.

The modern Indian state, trained in the categories of scarcity, rational choice, and utility, finds this language unintelligible. It misreads tradition as inefficiency, generosity as irrationality, and moderation as backwardness. It seeks to remake society in the image of economic man, believing it to be the only rational way forward. But in doing so, it suppresses another way of being human. A way that does not begin with lack, but with order. That does not posit desire as a problem, but as a possibility. That does not treat wealth as a goal, but as a support. That does not imagine the individual as isolated, but as embedded (Badjatya, 2024; Dash, 2023). If economics is to be meaningful in India—or indeed, anywhere—it must first ask what kind of human being it assumes. The Indian traditions answer this question differently. Perhaps it is time we listened.

EXPERIENTIAL KNOWLEDGE AND ALTERNATIVE ECONOMIC ANTHROPOLOGIES

Amid the epistemic dissonance we have explored—the tension between inherited economic models and Indian societal practices—emerges a possibility: that Indian society, through the sedimentation of centuries, has preserved a form of knowledge that remains largely invisible to our modern disciplines. This is not the knowledge of abstraction or formalization, but what has called experiential or actionable knowledge—knowledge that is lived, transmitted through practice, and embedded in institutions that have not been theorized because they were never meant to be (Gangopadhyay et al., 2020).

Such knowledge does not appear in textbooks. It does not proclaim itself as theory. And yet, it works. Communities know how to manage scarcity, govern commons, sustain trade across generations, and resolve conflicts—without needing to appeal to rational choice theory or formal law (Grafov, 2022; Misra & Keerthiraj, 2025). But because this knowledge does not speak the language of the social sciences, it is dismissed as "informal," "pre-modern," or at best, "local tradition." This, we submit, is a mistake—not merely epistemological, but political. For it reflects the continued dominance of a colonial consciousness that cannot see the world except through its own categories (Shah, 2025).

Trust-Based Trade Networks

What does this experiential knowledge look like? Let us consider not abstractions, but cases. Merchant communities such as the Marwaris or Chettiars built business empires across regions using trust, kinship, and honor. They operated with no written contracts, yet with a higher repayment rate than any formal banking system. In game-theoretic terms, one might speak of "repeated games" and "reputation effects." But that is not how they thought of it. Their trust was not strategic, but moral. It was not game-theoretic, but normative (Grafov, 2022). Similarly, Indian irrigation systems reveal principles of self-governance that modern economists rediscovered only recently through Elinor Ostrom's work. Farmers upstream and downstream shared water according to rotational turns, enforced by social norms and sanctions. There was no Leviathan, no centralized monitor. Yet there was order. Where modern theory sees "the commons," these societies saw dharma—the right conduct appropriate to one's context (Mondal & Choudry, 2024).

Commons and Water: The Logic of Johad

Take caste—not as a rigid hierarchy, but as a network of mutual obligations (jati) that often functioned as economic guilds. A member was not merely a laborer or trader but a participant in a web of reciprocity, reputation, and support (Sunandan, 2022). The concept of bhaichara (brotherhood) illustrates how these networks generated social capital. This is not to deny exclusion or inequality. But to reject caste solely as a vestige of backwardness is to misunderstand its functional role as a bearer of economic and social intelligence. During the COVID-19 crisis, it was caste and community associations that provided food, loans, and medical support when state mechanisms failed (Shah, 2023). Traditional ecological practices offer another example. Indian farmers knew their soils, seeds, and rainfall patterns intimately—not through agronomy but through generations of attentive living. This was not "local knowledge" to be "integrated" into modern policy; it was a different way of knowing. Water tanks in Rajasthan—johads—collected rain, replenished aquifers, and regulated use through community norms (Nigam & Chandra, 2022). Likewise, caste-based reservations are grounded in a logic of individual rights and compensatory justice drawn from liberal theory. But this logic often clashes with how communities perceive honor (maryāda) and obligation. In rural Rajasthan, for example, Jeffrey shows that young men from reserved categories experienced these provisions not as empowerment but as ambiguous sources of stigma, since the category of "backwardness" imposed from above did not match local hierarchies of dignity and worth (Jeffrey, 2010). The problem is not redistribution, but the conceptual language in which redistribution is framed (Bhanot & Verma, 2020; Deshpande, 2017).

Even in the realm of business ethics, Indian traditions offer alternatives. Rather than importing concepts like Corporate Social Responsibility (CSR) as regulatory compliance, one could look to rajadharma—the king's duty to protect and provide—as an analog. Businesses as stewards of social resources is not a metaphor; it is an actionable framework already latent in traditions (Mondal & Choudry, 2024). Gandhi's idea of trusteeship, or the emerging language of "Dharmic capitalism," gestures toward this, though rarely is it institutionalized in business education. Education, too, has been colonized. Today, it serves to produce credentialed individuals, prepared for markets. But in Indian traditions, vidyā was the cultivation of character and consciousness. A guru's role was not to train labor, but to shape being (Gangopadhyay et al., 2020). In politics, too, India's traditions carry wisdom long ignored. Before the colonial state, India practiced polycentric governance: multiple overlapping authorities—village elders, religious heads, caste councils—regulated life (Shah, 2025). This was not chaos; it was a dense ecology of authority. India did not have to "accommodate" diversity. It was diversity.

It is not uncommon, especially within the modern academy, to suspect that any positive account of non-Western traditions must be driven by nostalgia or romanticism. But this suspicion itself rests on a peculiar modern experience—that traditions are things of the past, frozen in time, awaiting revival or critique. The Indian framework presented here is neither a utopia lost nor a system to be "restored." It is not offered as a perfected alternative, but as a living and internally complex way of organizing economic and social life, which continues—despite disruptions—to shape millions of lives today. We are not opposing modernity by resurrecting an idealized past. Rather, we are drawing attention to modes of knowing and acting that remain intelligible within Indian experience, but are rendered invisible or irrational by a framework that universalizes scarcity and individualism. If this paper appears to retrieve something from tradition, it is only because modern categories have made us forget what was never lost.

The point, then, is not to return to the past. It is to recognize that we never left it. These traditions did not vanish. They were devalued, distorted, and rendered illegible. But they remain, often functioning beneath the radar of the state and the university. They are not alternative data. They are alternative theories.

CONCLUSION: DECOLONIZING THE ECONOMIC IMAGINATION

The figure of homo economicus—rational, calculative, driven by self-interest—has long appeared to us as a natural starting point for the disciplines of economics and politics. But as we have argued throughout this chapter, this figure is not a neutral description of human nature. It is a culturally specific myth—myth not as falsehood, but as a guiding narrative that organizes thought and action. Scarcity, similarly, is not simply a material fact but a way of imagining the human condition—an imagination that emerged from particular theological and historical developments in Europe and became secularized into modern economic thought. By tracing these roots—particularly within Protestant Christian anthropology—we have shown how the concept of economic man originated in a theological vision of human depravity and salvation, later transposed into the language of productivity, utility, and rational choice. Through colonial expansion, this narrative was imposed on societies whose realities it could not adequately describe. India, perhaps more than any other place, became the stage for this social engineering: its institutions, its categories, even its anthropology were rewritten to conform to a Western template.

Yet, even after formal decolonization, the cognitive structure remained. Indian policymakers, social scientists, and economists continued to think from within categories they did not produce, diagnosing their own society through a borrowed lens that was often unable to make sense of what it saw. The result was not merely policy failure. It was cognitive dissonance—a persistent sense of misfit between theory and reality, abstraction and practice, prescription and experience. But this chapter does not end with a lament. For if scarcity and economic man are myths, then they can be reimagined. If they are products of a particular culture, then they need not be the universal grammar of economic life. And if India has inherited its categories from elsewhere, then it can also unlearn them, or better yet, replace them with concepts born of its own traditions. To do this is not to romanticize the past or to reject everything Western. It is to recognize that our social sciences are not universal sciences. They are the theories of one culture extended over the world. The question is not whether we use Western categories or Indian ones. It is whether the categories we use allow us to understand our world—or merely to misdescribe it.

This is the promise of experiential knowledge. Indian society, through centuries of lived practice, has preserved forms of understanding that do not appear as theories, but which organize economic, political, and social life. These include the ethics of trade in business communities; the cooperative norms of water sharing in agrarian villages; the systems of mutual aid embedded in caste associations; the ecological wisdom of traditional farming; and the integrative role of religious institutions. These are not "cultural practices" to be studied as data. They are alternative conceptual orders. To think from these orders is to do something new. It is to construct an anthropology that does not begin with lack, but with relational sufficiency; to develop economic models that incorporate dharma as a regulative principle, not merely an ethical add-on; to treat cooperation, not competition, as the default mode of human organization; and to model political life not around the solitary individual, but around the embedded person situated in networks of duty, trust, and role.

Such work cannot be done within the silo of any one discipline. It requires Sanskritists, anthropologists, political theorists, and economists working together—not to "apply" Indian culture to Western theories, but to generate new theories from within India's civilizational knowledge systems. This is not a hybridization. It is conceptual innovation. It is called the movement from being consumers of theory to producers of theory.

For Indian policymakers, this also implies a shift in posture. Instead of viewing communities as passive recipients of development, they must be seen as repositories of knowledge. Policies must be informed not merely by empirical data, but by how people experience their world. Success must be measured not only by GDP or efficiency, but by cultural continuity, social cohesion, and normative stability. Policy, then, becomes not an act of intervention but of translation—of aligning institutional forms with local intelligibilities. Globally, too, this shift has implications. The West is increasingly struggling under the weight of its own myth—growth without limit, rationality without responsibility, autonomy without community. Climate breakdown, inequality, and cultural alienation are not failures of policy. They are failures of imagination. India, by reimagining its own economic life from its traditions, may contribute to the world not by offering solutions within the same paradigm, but by articulating a different paradigm altogether.

The alternative is not to replace economic man with another caricature. It is to develop the figure of economic humanity—a being who is not defined by scarcity and desire, but by responsibility, meaning, and mutuality. In Indian terms, this may be nārāya a: the person as a node in a larger order of life, fulfilling duties, sustaining relationships, and navigating material needs without losing sight of ethical ends. The call, then, is for conceptual decolonization—not the rejection of Western ideas, but the freedom to think otherwise. To recognize that we are not fated to live in the categories we inherited. That we may think from where we are, in the languages we have, and in the concepts we understand. And that in doing so, we may discover not only a clearer understanding of ourselves, but also offer something new to the world.

In this sense, rethinking scarcity is not merely a critique. It is a gesture of hope. The myth of economic man, like all myths, once revealed as a story, loses its power to constrain. What we do next is up to us. Do we repeat it, revise it, or replace it? The answer will shape not only the future of economics, but the story we tell about what it means to be human.

REFERENCES

Adams, M. S., & Mittiga, R. (2020). Material scarcity and scalar justice. *Philosophical Studies, 178*(7), 2237–2256. DOI: 10.1007/s11098-020-01539-3

Agamben, G. (2011). *The Kingdom and the Glory: For a Theological Genealogy of Economy and Government* (Chiesa, L., & Mandarini, M., Trans.). Stanford University Press.

Badjatya, K. (2024). The Concept of Puru Rtha from the Present Perspective: An Observation. *Journal of Social Sciences and Humanities*. Advance online publication. DOI: 10.53469/jssh.2024.06(08).20

Bhanot, D., & Verma, S. (2020). Lived experiences of the Indian stigmatized group in reference to socio-political empowerment: A phenomenological approach. *The Qualitative Report*. Advance online publication. DOI: 10.46743/2160-3715/2020.4143

Bhinekawati, R. (2021). Comparing the concept of scarcity: Conventional vs. Islamic economics. Journal of Applied Business and Economics. https://doi.org/DOI: 10.33423/jabe.v23i3.4352

Boland, T., & Griffin, R. (2021). Archaic Anthropology: The Presence of the Past in the Present. The Reformation of Welfare. https://doi.org/.DOI: 10.46692/9781529211344.002

Bratoeva, M. (2024). *The Song of Desire (Kāma): If you meet Kāma, don't kill him*. Filosofiya-Philosophy., DOI: 10.53656/phil2024-01-04

Braun, E. (2021). The institutional preconditions of homo economicus. *Journal of Economic Methodology*, *28*, 231–246. DOI: 10.1080/1350178X.2021.1898659

Budini, S. (2024). The humanistic foundation to sustainability. *Humanistic Management Journal*. Advance online publication. DOI: 10.1007/s41463-024-00172-0

Chaudhuri, B. (2022). Programmed welfare: An ethnographic account of algorithmic practices in the public distribution system in India. *New Media & Society, 24*(5), 887–902. DOI: 10.1177/14614448221079034

Darity, W. (2022). Alternatives to the scarcity principle. *The Journal of Economic Education, 53*(4), 340–347. DOI: 10.1080/00220485.2022.2111387

Dash, P. (2023). Purusarthas: The Value Paradigms of Human Life (The Bhagavat Gita Perspective). Knowledgeable Research: A Multidisciplinary Journal. https://doi.org/.DOI: 10.57067/kr.v1i12.112

Deshpande, A. (2017). Stigma or red tape? Roadblocks in the use of affirmative action. In The Empire of Disgust. https://doi.org/DOI: 10.1093/oso/9780199487837.003.0002

Devi, S. (2020). HARMONY IN SOCIETY THROUGH PURU ĀRTHAS..

di Somma, E. (2022). Trust, faith, and social imaginary. In Relational Anthropology for Contemporary Economics. https://doi.org/DOI: 10.1007/978-3-030-84690-9_9

Erasmo, V. (2022). *Amartya Sen's earlier conception of economic agents.* Erasmus Journal for Philosophy and Economics., DOI: 10.23941/ejpe.v15i1.596

Gangopadhyay, K., Jacob, R. T., & Jayanth, R. S. S. (2020). How effective is theory-based learning of ethics in India? *IIM Kozhikode Society & Management Review, 9*, 55–61. DOI: 10.1177/2277975219889778

Ghosh, S. (2022). Time, scarcity, and abundance. *Frontiers in Research Metrics and Analytics, 7*. Advance online publication. DOI: 10.3389/frma.2022.974706 PMID: 36118014

Gibson-Graham, J. K. (2006). *A postcapitalist politics.* University of Minnesota Press.

Giraud, G. (2023). Economics as Religion and Christianity as oikonomia: Giorgio Agamben and the Homo Sacer. *Religions*. Advance online publication. DOI: 10.3390/rel14121490

Grafov, D. (2022). Informal relations in Indian society. Journal of the Institute of Oriental Studies RAS. https://doi.org/DOI: 10.31696/2618-7302-2022-3-098-111

Gull, I., & Khan, B. A. (2023). *The financial accounting and management of the Dharmarth Trust (1846–1947 A.D.): An insight into the religious affairs of the Dogra State*. International Journal for Multidisciplinary Research., DOI: 10.36948/ijfmr.2023.v05i05.6331

Isomae, J. (2022). Anthropology of Religion. In Weyel, B. (Eds.), *i>International Handbook of Practical Theology</i>*. De Gruyter., DOI: 10.1515/9783110618150-046

Jeffrey, C. (2010). *Timepass: Youth, Class, and the Politics of Waiting in India*. Stanford University Press.

Keerthiraj, M. A., & Vang-Phu, T. (2025). India's BRICS Engagement: A Strategic Lever in South Asia and the Indian Ocean. In A. Gedikli, S. Erdogan, & H. Çalışkan Terzioğlu (Eds.), Changing the Global Political Economy: BRICS Countries and Alternative Relations Strategies (pp. 189-214). IGI Global Scientific Publishing. https://doi.org/DOI: 10.4018/979-8-3693-7393-4.ch006

Klamer, A. (2023). An essay on the need to redefine economics. Journal of Philosophical Economics. https://doi.org/DOI: 10.46298/jpe.10887

Konnova, N. (2020). Economics of values and philosophy of economics. *Humanitarium, 23*, 27–37. DOI: 10.15421/172022

Love, T. (2022). Scarcity. In Stepmother. https://doi.org/DOI: 10.2307/j.ctv1s5nxzd.9

Lushch-Purii, U. (2021). *From homo economicus to homo eudaimonicus*. Anthropological Measurements of Philosophical Research., DOI: 10.15802/ampr.v0i19.235992

Mäki, U. (2021). Homo economicus under multiple pressures. In Philosophy of Economics. https://doi.org/DOI: 10.1007/978-981-15-9395-6_18

Malthus, T. R. (1993). *An Essay on the Principle of Population* (2nd ed.). Oxford University Press. (Original work published 1798)

Martini, N., Sudarma, M., Purwanti, L., & Adib, N. (2025). The Concepts of Performance Measurement based on the Purposes of the Hindu Religion. Finance. *Theory into Practice*. Advance online publication. DOI: 10.26794/2587-5671-2025-29-1-195-203

Minch, D. (2021). Pastoral Criticism, Structural Collaboration: The Role of Ecclesial Power Structures in Modernization and Economic Individualization. *Horizons*, *48*, 367–403. DOI: 10.1017/hor.2021.53

Mishra, D. (2022). Economic Strategy in the Kautilīya Arthaśāstra. .

Misra, A. & Keerthiraj. (2025). Integrating Sustainability in India's Tourism Sector: An Uphill Battle. In S. Poddar, B. Paul, & M. Luperi (Eds.), Sustainable Business Ecosystems and Social Perspectives (pp. 359-386). IGI Global Scientific Publishing. https://doi.org/DOI: 10.4018/979-8-3693-8437-4.ch016

Mondal, S., & Choudry, A. (2024). Dharma in Sri Aurobindo's The Renaissance in India and other essays on Indian culture. Journal of Dharma Studies. https://doi.org/DOI: 10.1007/s42240-024-00176-x

Nagaraj, N., & Prakash, A. (2021). Digital biometric authentication and citizens' right to food: Neglect of the 'local' in India's Aadhaar-enabled Public Distribution System. *Proceedings of the 14th International Conference on Theory and Practice of Electronic Governance*. https://doi.org/DOI: 10.1145/3494193.3494239

Nigam, A., & Chandra, S. (2022). Digital accessibility and information mining of Dharmaśāstric knowledge traditions

Pallesen, T., & Pedersen, K. (2023). Model of Human Fallibility: Traveling Behavioral Assumptions in Public Governance. *Perspectives on Public Management and Governance*. Advance online publication. DOI: 10.1093/ppmgov/gvad001

Pallesen, T., & Pedersen, K. (2023). Model of Human Fallibility: Traveling Behavioral Assumptions in Public Governance. *Perspectives on Public Management and Governance*. Advance online publication. DOI: 10.1093/ppmgov/gvad001

Pires, G. (2024). ONTOLOGICAL ROOTS OF HOMO ECONOMICUS. Interfaces Científicas - Humanas e Sociais. https://doi.org/.DOI: 10.17564/2316-3801.2024v12n2p441-454

Radhakrishnan, S. (1922). The Hindu Dharma. The International Journal of Ethics, 33(1), 1–22. https://doi.org/DOI: 10.1086/INTEJETHI.33.1.2377174

Rela, N. L. (2021). Adam Smith's homo oeconomicus. Manuscrito. https://doi.org/DOI: 10.1590/0100-6045.2021.v44n3.nr

Ribeiro, R. J. (2022). Scarcity as an alibi: On the false ethical discussions about the war on COVID-19. *Philosophies*, *7*(6), 125. DOI: 10.3390/philosophies7060125

Ricardo, D. (1817). *Principles of Political Economy and Taxation*. Dover Publications.

Robbins, J. (2020). Theology and the Anthropology of Christian Life. . https://doi.org/.DOI: 10.1093/oso/9780198845041.001.0001

Roy, A. (2020). Consuming Bollywood. *The Journal of Religion and Film*. Advance online publication. DOI: 10.3726/978-1-4539-1231-7

Sen, A. (2005). *The argumentative Indian: Writings on Indian history, culture and identity*. Farrar, Straus and Giroux.

Shah, G. (2023). Caste, Community, and Crisis Response in India's COVID-19 Lockdown. *Economic and Political Weekly*, *58*(2), 35–42.

Shah, P. (2025). The codependence of Orientalism and the social sciences. *History of the Human Sciences*. Advance online publication. DOI: 10.1177/09526951241306299

Smith, A. (1776). *The Wealth of Nations* (Cannan, E., Ed.). Bantam Classics.

Sun, H., & Teichert, T. (2022). Scarcity in today's consumer markets: Scoping the research landscape by author keywords. Management Review Quarterly, 1–28. https://doi.org/DOI: 10.1007/s11301-022-00295-4

Sunandan, K. N. (2022). Caste, knowledge, and power. https://doi.org/DOI: 10.1017/9781009273138

Swamy, D., Nagarajan, K., & Babu, N. (2021). Yogic Principles of Artha and Dāna with Reference to Individual and Corporate Social Responsibility. *International Journal of Yoga, 14*, 248–255. DOI: 10.4103/ijoy.ijoy_106_21 PMID: 35017868

Thompson, S. P. (2022). *False doctrine, false god, false economy*. The Kenarchy Journal., DOI: 10.62950/vxkla45

Tsing, A. L. (2015). *The mushroom at the end of the world: On the possibility of life in capitalist ruins*. Princeton University Press.

Tuniz, C., & Vipraio, P. T. (2020). Homo oeconomicus. In From Apes to Cyborgs. https://doi.org/DOI: 10.1007/978-3-030-36522-6_11

Upadhyay, S., Sanwal, K., & Goswami, P. (2024). The Concept of Liberation (Moksha) in Indian Philosophy: An Analysis. *African Journal of Biomedical Research*. Advance online publication. DOI: 10.53555/ajbr.v27i4s.6093

von Mises, L. (1949). *Human Action: A Treatise on Economics* (4th rev. ed.). Liberty Fund.

Weber, M. (1905). *The Protestant Ethic and the Spirit of Capitalism* (Kalberg, S., Trans.). Roxbury Publishing Company.

Yashodha. (2019). Trust and kinship: Experimental evidence from rural India. Journal of the Economic Science Association, 5(2), 223–237.

ENDNOTES

1 Not law, religion, or ethics, but the situational obligation that sustains relational order in Indian traditions.

2 The pursuit of material prosperity, not for individual accumulation, but as a means of upholding one's dharma in the world.

3 Desire—not as mere sensual craving, but as a legitimate and aesthetic dimension of human fulfillment within dharmic bounds

4 Liberation, not from the world but from the ignorance that binds Desire to things that do not satisfy.

5 One’s specific obligation arising from their position in a network of relationships—contextual, not universal.

6 A state of contentment grounded in fulfilling one's duties, rather than accumulating possessions.

7 An attitude of friendship and goodwill that shapes ethical conduct toward others.

8 A classificatory framework of social function and responsibility, not reducible to modern notions of caste.

9 Faith or reverence, not as blind belief, but as a trust in the order and meaning of the world one inhabits

Chapter 2

Money as a Cultural Artifact: An Economic Anthropology Analysis of Its Social and Environmental Impacts

Silvio Andrae
https://orcid.org/0000-0002-8586-7812
Independent Researcher, Germany

ABSTRACT

This theoretical study examines money as a cultural artifact in the context of planetary boundaries and social inequality. Starting from the assumption that money is more than a neutral medium of exchange, the article analyzes its semiotic, material, and social dimensions. It integrates perspectives from economic anthropology, systems theory, and network theory with ecological economics, proposing six theses that shed light on the tension between abstraction, infrastructure, power, and meaning in modern monetary systems. Methodologically, the study combines an interdisciplinary literature and concept analysis with the design of a theoretically sound research program. It argues that the current monetary system in the Anthropocene has both ecologically destabilizing and socially selective effects. The outlook discusses the potential of alternative monetary architectures—such as indexed, earmarked, or multicentric

DOI: 10.4018/979-8-3373-1260-6.ch002

currencies—to reintegrate economic, social, and ecological goal systems. The study aims to contribute to a transformative monetary theory in the context of global upheaval.

1. INTRODUCTION

In recent decades, economic and anthropological research has shown a growing interest in the cultural dimension of money. This shift in perspective—away from the idea of money as a neutral medium of exchange and toward an analysis of money as a socially embedded, symbolically charged, and materially effective artifact—is not only an expression of theoretical diversification, but also an epistemological necessity. It should be noted that classical positions, such as Karl Polanyi's substance-oriented approach or Stephen Gudeman's theory of 'populated economies,' as well as network-theoretical perspectives of actor-network theory, show that money is a historically grown, culturally framed, and technically-institutionally structured medium that stabilizes central social patterns of order (Maurer, 2006; Hornborg, 2024b).

Parallel to this theoretical movement, a new awareness of the problem has emerged. Global crisis dynamics—such as growing wealth inequality, climate-related resource conflicts, and the exclusion of large sections of the population from the financial system—make it clear that money reproduces not only economic but also social and ecological orders. Worldwide, two billion people are excluded from basic financial services. It is not due to technical barriers, but instead to normative and administrative mechanisms of exclusion. Empirical asymmetries of this kind are often not questioned, not least because money is taken for granted. It is precisely this taken-for-grantedness—its everyday omnipresence and apparent neutrality—that obscures the symbolic, political, and ecological mechanisms of monetary systems.

The historically deep-rooted origin of this problematic decoupling lies in the idea of general-purpose money, i.e., a form of money that is universally applicable and in which all values can be compared on a numerical scale. According to Polanyi (2001 [1944]), this principle enables heterogeneous goods, social relationships, and ecological processes to be subjected to a monetary logic. As a result, social ties are marginalized and environmental costs are externalized (Polanyi, 2001 [1944]). Money should be regarded as an autonomous carrier of value whose social construction becomes invisible due to its functional ubiquity. This phenomenon can be described as commodity fetishism according to Marx, as metaphysical abstraction according to Simmel, or as a semiotic void effect according to Hornborg.

At the same time, recent developments—from cryptocurrencies to digital central bank currencies to complementary currencies—show that money is neither static nor natural, but should be viewed as a malleable socio-technical arrangement. As Graeber (2001) emphasizes, there is no such thing as 'true money.' Monetary orders are therefore historical processes of negotiation about value, meaning, and legitimacy. This paper examines the potential that arises from the malleability of money and shows that this potential extends to both social participation and ecological sustainability.

Against this background, this study pursues a twofold objective: On the one hand, it develops an interdisciplinary theoretical framework that understands money as a semiotic, formally structured, and materially effective medium. Second, on this basis, central theses are formulated that contribute to a systematic critique of current monetary systems and outline a conceptual research program for a multicentric economy designed to reflect and promote social and ecological sustainability.

The investigation focuses on the following key analytical questions:

- How does money as a cultural artifact structure social orders and ecological metabolic regimes?
- What contributions do anthropological, systems theory, semiotic, and network theory perspectives make to the reconstruction of monetary power and meaning structures?
- How can the fetish character of money—understood as semiotic autonomy and material effectiveness—be grasped in a theoretically consistent way?

The structure of this article follows a theoretical-argumentative order. Section 2 systematizes four central perspectives: the economic anthropological, systems theory, semiotic, and network theory approaches.

The implications of these perspectives for understanding money are then elaborated. In Section 3, seven theses on the function of money in late modern societies are formulated. The aspects discussed include the semiotic void, social inequality, and ecological externalities. In Section 4, an interdisciplinary research program is developed, linking conceptual modeling and empirical approaches. Section 5 explores the theoretical tensions and the potential of alternative forms of money in the context of a 'multicentric economy.' Section 6 summarizes the central findings and outlines future research possibilities.

This work thus contributes to the theoretical integration of heterogeneous discourses on money and develops a heuristic framework for analyzing its symbolic, technical, and ecological dimensions. This work explicitly links monetary theory, critical semiotics, and political ecology. This connection aims to explain money as a malleable infrastructure for sustainable transformation.

2. THEORETICAL FRAMEWORK

2.1 Basic Principles of Economic Anthropology

The tradition of economic anthropology does not view economic activity as an isolated, rationally calculated activity but rather as something deeply embedded in social, symbolic, and material structures. In his work, 'The Great Transformation,' Karl Polanyi (2001) distinguishes between three fundamental 'forms of integration' of economic organization—reciprocity, redistribution, and the market—and argues that even in market-oriented societies, economic exchange remains permeated by moral obligations and political institutions (see Gemici, 2008). In pre-modern, substantive economies, economic activity was an integral part of social, religious, and political orders. Exchange relationships did not primarily follow market mechanisms but were based on principles such as gift-giving, obligation, or communal distribution.

Building on Polanyi, Richard Bohannan and Bill Maurer developed the concept of general-purpose money and special-purpose money. While the latter circulates only in clearly defined social or ritual contexts—such as bride price shells, ritual beads, or community vouchers—only general-purpose money allows for the universal comparability of all goods and services on a uniform numerical scale. This abstraction marks a central step in the emergence of market-driven economies in which efficiency, interchangeability, and accumulation dominate over other social or cosmological systems of order (Maurer, 2006). The establishment of general-purpose money can thus be understood as a key event in the 'great transformation' in the course of which the economic system detached itself from its social embeddedness as a seemingly autonomous subsystem.

Stephen Gudeman shifts the focus away from market mechanisms and toward cultural values. For him, economic activity in households ('the house') and local communities is characterized by participatory production and care processes whose value is not reflected in prices. Gudeman's insight that mainstream economics fails to recognize that concepts such as 'rationality' or 'efficiency' are historically contingent ideologies (Gudeman, 1986) is a significant revelation. In pre-modern agrarian economies, prosperity was instead the result of natural cycles, social bonds, and the communal significance of goods. The modern fixation on profit and accumulation ignores these contexts. For Gudeman, this is the reason why the economy remains structurally incapable of integrating ecological and social consequences into its calculations:

Since money functions as an abstract, seemingly neutral carrier of value, environmental destruction and social inequality are systematically externalized (see also Hornborg, 2024a; Maurer, 2006). Alf Hornborg expands this economic, anthropological approach with a semiotic and ecological perspective. He describes money as an 'empty sign' that is neither indexical nor iconic nor purely symbolic but can take on any meaning. This semiotic status is unique and explains the fetish character of money. The socially assigned value appears as an inherent property, which leads to the decoupling of economic practices from real social and material conditions. Ecologically, this results in a 'thermodynamic deficit': universal commensuration through general-purpose money accelerates resource consumption and entropy, degrades natural processes into mere input-output relationships, and renders environmental costs invisible within the monetary cycle (Hornborg, 2024a).

Viviana Zelizer, on the other hand, employs micro-sociological case studies—such as life insurance, household finances, and children's piggy banks—to demonstrate that even with highly fungible money, social boundaries ('earmarking') persist. People structure their budgets according to moral codes (e.g., rent, alms, leisure), creating multiple social meanings within a single currency—a phenomenon Zelizer refers to as 'multiple monies' (Zelizer, 2017).

Marshall Sahlins distinguishes between three types of reciprocity—generalized, balanced, and negative—and makes it clear that acts of exchange are not only economic transactions but also performatively create social closeness or distance. The gift economy is thus not understood as a primitive precursor to the market but as an independent order with its specific logic (Sahlins, 1972).

David Graeber (2011) delivers a compelling critique of the barter myth prevalent in classical economics, which posits that money originated from the exchange of goods. Instead, his global historical analysis shows that debt and credit relationships chronologically preceded the use of coinage. The barter-based origin of money is thus an ideologically motivated fiction that naturalizes market logic. This deconstruction of economic history is a fascinating engagement for the reader. Central to this is the distinction between commodity and credit theories of money. The former see money as a universal commodity with high exchangeability and ownership characteristics—an understanding that implicitly refers to real value logic. Although property is understood as a social institution, it remains relationally decoupled from concrete interactions. The credit theory, on the other hand—as in Armstrong & Siddiqui (2019), for example—understands money as a social relationship: as a claim and promise of payment between concrete actors. From this perspective, money appears not as a mere possession but as a dynamic network of intertemporal obligations.

Current anthropological studies on digital payment systems such as M-Pesa, Alipay, and Revolut reveal that money is undergoing new forms of social (re)embedding in the platform economy. These systems, through algorithmic scoring, KYC regimes, and social control mechanisms, are not just creating new infrastructures for transactions, but also reinforcing exclusions based on data-driven criteria. This information about the latest developments in economic anthropology will keep the reader informed and engaged.

In summary, anthropological theories of money share a common concern: to reflect on the moral, symbolic, and ecological conditions of economic activity and to expose the supposed neutrality of money as a cultural construct. They thus open an analytical window onto the blind spots of mainstream economics, where power, meaning, and relationships with nature are systematically ignored. This perspective serves as the normative and theoretical foundation for the subsequent sections, which delve into the intricate interplay between money fetishism, social inequality, and ecological degradation.

2.2 Philosophy of Money

Since Georg Simmel, the philosophy of money has attempted to reveal the logical, moral, and affective consequences of an exchange system based on money. In the following, (1) Simmel's basic ideas are reconstructed, (2) deconstructive extensions by Jacques Derrida are elaborated, and (3) recent updates in the context of the platform economy, 'assetization' (Birch & Muniesa, 2020) and digital money are outlined.

Georg Simmel's analysis of money as a dependent variable, a significant contribution within the neoclassical tradition, provides a solid foundation for understanding the socializing function of the economy. He views the economy as a field of specialized interactions, which must be examined in terms of their socializing function. These interactions take concrete form in the exchange of valuable things—a process that money systematically optimizes. Values do not arise from the production of goods but from the social interest in their exchange. Simmel, therefore, understands money not merely as a medium of exchange but as a social-ontological form that detaches individuals from their former personal ties and transfers them into anonymous market relationships.

In his 'Philosophy of Money,' Simmel describes money as an autonomous form of social interaction that suspends traditional status and dependency relationships. By abstracting the qualities of goods to a uniform numerical scale, money levels all differences and thus allows for previously unattainable comparability. This creates new opportunities for individual development, but at the same time, it brings with it alienation: social relationships are reduced to price relations, and value appears as an inherent property of the monetary object itself—a classic case of fetishization (Maurer, 2006; McNeill, 2020).

Simmel's dictum that 'all money is only an instruction to society' is famous—a bill of exchange in which the name of the payee is not filled in. According to this view, banknotes embody a collective certificate of trust in society as a whole (Dodd, 2015). The monetization of time in the form of wages, interest, and returns makes time itself tradable, resulting in an unprecedented rationalization of human activities. This trust in the monetary system is what keeps it functioning, and without it, monetary transactions—and, by extension, society as a whole—would collapse.

Trust in the recyclability of money is increasingly replacing interpersonal trust; without this belief, monetary transactions—and, by extension, society as a whole—would collapse. Jacques Derrida expands Simmel's perspective with a deconstructive approach to the money sign as a medium of permanent shifts in meaning.

In Mal d'Archive (1994), he describes the archive as a paradoxical place: it is both a repository of the past and a source of new meanings. Applied to money, this means that every monetary unit—whether a banknote or a digital accounting entry—refers to an endless chain of debt and credit relationships that can never be fully traced back to their origin.

As in the archive, money also leaves 'traces': every transaction leaves behind a string of characters whose meaning can only be established through subsequent transactions. This process creates a permanent field of tension between expectation and memory—similar to the 'archive fever' that drives both a return to the origin and new deviations.

In 'Donner le temps I: La fausse monnaie' (1991), Derrida deconstructs the boundary between real and fake money using Baudelaire's story 'La fausse monnaie.' His thesis: As long as an object functions as money, the distinction between authenticity and counterfeiting is not objective but rather an effect of social attribution. This deconstruction challenges the traditional understanding of money's authenticity.

The value of a monetary sign is, therefore, never fixed but is constantly (re)produced through repeated acts of social interpretation. Money is simultaneously a gift, a debt, and a promise—and thus marks an aporia that cannot be resolved definitively. Derrida makes it clear that value, like meaning, is always relational and processual.

Just as words only unfold their meaning in the web of other words, monetary value also arises in the interplay between actors, discourses, and material infrastructures. There is no original, guaranteed reference—any attempt to fix the 'true' value of money leads to endless semantic leafing through a dictionary.

Bitcoin functions as a practical deconstruction of the idea that money is a natural given. The creation of a new monetary system with its own rules and protocols for controlling inflation and preventing double-spending exposes the existing monetary order as a contingent construct. Every cryptocurrency brings its value model with it, indicating that economic variables such as inflation or distribution are not inevitable but rather the result of political and technical decisions. It follows that money has no fixed basis. Its value is always the result of circulating forces—from human desire to regulatory structures to geophysical conditions such as the scarcity of strategic raw materials. Value is not absolute but relational—it lives in circulation.

Money is not 'outside the text'—it is written and can be rewritten. The central question is to what extent technological innovations such as cryptographically secured distributed ledger systems open up new perspectives on the computing and clearing properties of money. This aspect is often neglected in classical economics. Maurer (2017) bases his analysis on the theoretical work of alternative monetary theorists, such as Geoffrey Ingham (2004) and Randall Wray (2025), who, in contrast to the mainstream perspective, understand money not primarily as a medium of exchange but as a symbolically and institutionally embedded unit of account, known as the ‘money of account.’ While Viviana Zelizer focused on the social diversity and moral marking of monetary practices, Ingham—following the chartalist tradition—emphasizes the constitutive role of state tax sovereignty and institutional credit architectures for the validity of book money. Even within plural social contexts, according to Ingham, accounts are ultimately settled in the dominant unit of account—typically in the currency of a sovereign state. Against this backdrop, Maurer poses the critical question of whether and to what extent technological developments, such as Bitcoin, as well as private stablecoins and new platform-based payment services, can disrupt existing relationships between the state, the financial system, and monetary power. The study examines the potential of these new monetary technology arrangements to supplant the monopoly of state-issued currencies, offering a tantalizing glimpse into a future where established accounting systems are revolutionized.

Cagli and Dimpfl (2025) investigate the relationship between Bitcoin and other cryptocurrencies, as well as monetary policy uncertainty. Due to its structural independence from central banks and monetary policy control mechanisms, Bitcoin is often interpreted as a potential hedge against macroeconomic instability and monetary uncertainty. The authors' findings support this interpretation, showing that the returns and volatilities of leading cryptocurrencies are largely unaffected by monetary policy uncertainty. This suggests that cryptocurrencies continue to occupy a structurally independent position outside the monetary policy logic of the fiat system—even as they become increasingly embedded in institutional and technological infrastructures.

In recent debates, Simmel's analysis of money has been updated and expanded in light of digital transformation processes. The platform economy, the assetization of previously non-monetary resources, and the technological mediation of trust offer new perspectives on the role of money in the 21st century. Digital platforms such as TikTok, YouTube, and Instagram are creating new types of economies in which monetary valuation is reflected in real time. This development lends Simmel's thesis of the 'depersonalization' of monetary transactions a new, algorithmically mediated quality (Zander, 2025). Social relationships are now being replaced by automated feedback loops in the form of quantified rewards—which is accelerating the economization of the social sphere. Understanding these changes is crucial in the rapidly evolving financial landscape.

At the same time, processes of so-called assetization show how data, reputation values, and even CO_2 certificates are being transformed into tradable asset rights. Birch and Muniesa (2020) make it clear that this involves a fundamental shift from exchange to rent logic: the goal is no longer the circulation of value but the extraction of long-term income claims. As a result, money is increasingly losing its traditional role as a medium of circulation in favor of a function as an infrastructure of capitalized rights designed for permanence and controlled scarcity. In this logic, the value of an asset is determined less by its utility or exchangeability than by its ability to generate future income streams. This dynamic is particularly evident in the financialization of knowledge, nature, and infrastructure.

Despite this radical deregulation and standardization, a persistent social coding of money use is evident. Viviana Zelizer (2017) has demonstrated, through the concept of 'special monies,' that even highly fungible means of payment remain structured by moral and cultural boundaries in everyday life. For example, budgets are divided into clearly distinguishable segments through earmarking—such as rent, donations, and pocket money—or digital financial service providers offer functions like 'pockets' or spending targets that align with traditional household practices. Even in the age of digital payments, money remains a morally differentiated medium that retains its social significance while transforming it.

Finally, a central element of contemporary monetary theory is the technological externalization of trust. While Simmel regarded trust as the social foundation of monetary transactions, based on the willingness to accept a banknote as a collective promise, this trust is increasingly shifting to technical systems in the digital economy. Stablecoins, digital wallets, smart contracts, and central bank digital currencies (CBDCs) are based on algorithmic protocols, automated verification mechanisms, and so-called oracles, which act as intermediary truth authorities. Philosophers of technology, such as Coeckelbergh (2015), analyze this development as a shift from interpersonal to infrastructural trust: money becomes an information technology architecture that not only maps social relations but actively shapes them.

These technological transformations also raise ecological questions. In connection with Hornborg's (2024a) concept of the 'thermodynamic deficit,' it becomes clear that the increasing abstraction and virtualization of money are transforming material and energetic processes without adequately reflecting their ecological price. The philosophy of money must, therefore, be supplemented by a planetary-ecological perspective that metabolically rethinks not only the relationship between sign and value but also between value and the environment.

Simmel reveals how money transforms society into an anonymous, calculative exchange order; Derrida exposes that this order is based on an endless shift of signs. Current debates on platform economy, assetization, and digital money show that both dimensions—alienation and instability—are escalating in the present. The following sections explore Simmel's dialectic and Derrida's aporias to analyze how current monetary innovations (CBDCs, tokenized assets,, and algorithmic stablecoins) not only reflect social inequality and ecological externalities but also technically reinforce them—and what paths of reform might follow.

2.3 Sociological and Systems Theory Perspectives

Talcott Parsons (1978) already assigned money to the 'A-System' (adaptation) of his AGIL scheme and interpreted it as a generalized medium of trust—a fiduciary device that makes economic activity coordinable. Niklas Luhmann (1984) radicalized this idea by conceiving money as a symbolic, generalized medium of communication that constitutes an independent economic system within society through payment transactions. The underlying binary code 'payment/non-payment' reduces complexity and allows economic communication to be largely decoupled from concrete content. It is replaced by the mediation of abstract exchange values; material or emotional ties remain hidden (Baxter, 2013; Baraldi et al., 2021).

In a market economy, access to resources is regulated by money transfers, whereby the material scarcity of resources is reflected in a scarcity of money itself. In this sense, money not only has an informational function (value standard), but also an operational function of transferring access rights to social resources (means of payment).

Luhmann identifies money not as a commodity, but as stabilized communication routines—an ensemble of behavioral conventions. Its function unfolds precisely through its contrast to the world of goods: money is a medium that belongs to the operational infrastructure of market-based exchange processes. According to Luhmann, social systems do not differ in terms of resources or preferences, but in terms of their communication logics. The meaning of money is exhausted in its reference to a system that enables and structures its use (Luhmann, 1988).

Legal relationships structured by contracts are quantified in monetary units and settled through monetary payments. Money circulates only as long as actors trust in its reusability—in future follow-up communication. Monetary payments extinguish debt relationships, which transforms the economic system into a formal order whose rationality is based on the value standard of money itself. This order is compatible with a liberal property constitution and at the same time shapes the legal infrastructure of the market.

Money is thus not a disruptive factor, but the constituent mechanism of market economy coherence. The rule that resources can only be acquired through monetary payment standardizes economic behavior and creates incentives to earn money. Personal relationships of trust tend to be supplanted by monetary constraints. At the same time, the principle of uniform allocation via prices creates a sense of fairness, as allocations are transparent and, in principle, accessible to all—regardless of status or origin.

However, money does not completely replace the social power of direct resource distribution—it transforms it. While violent conflicts over resources dominated in pre-modern societies, conflicts in monetary societies often manifest themselves as acquisitive crime. Similarly, the illusion of objective distribution through prices can conceal or even exacerbate social inequalities. In monetary societies, inequality manifests itself as a difference between those who can pay and those who cannot.

However, this microeconomic asymmetry in favor of the money owner does not mean that money remains stable at the macroeconomic level. The scarcity of resources is transferred to the scarcity of money—but not on a one-to-one basis. The money supply is independent of the real quantity of goods with, which leads to a paradoxical situation: The scarcity of all goods relative to money can increase if, for example, money is hoarded. Payment itself thus increases the degree of scarcity of resources—a phenomenon that Luhmann describes as the 'scarcity paradox.' This paradox implicitly contradicts his assumption that the monetary system calms the distribution conflict.

This is because when rising prices undermine the purchasing power of nominal monetary claims, the distribution conflict intensifies. The economic background to this imbalance lies in the stop-flow problem: while goods are produced on an ongoing basis, money is often held as an asset. Even marginal changes in the propensity to hold money can significantly influence the demand for goods—a structural risk of monetary systems.

Confidence in the stability of the value of money is therefore a systemically critical factor. This is because monetary contracts are designed to avoid uncertainty—which makes actors all the more sensitive to real or expected changes in value. The resulting equilibrium—a holder-holder game—is precarious: all actors know that the value of their holdings also depends on the willingness of others to pay.

Money structures social interactions by formalizing and facilitating communication processes. At the same time, it allows economic transactions to take place entirely as abstract operations. Material reality—resources, environmental conditions, social norms—takes a back seat to abstract price logic. This decoupling promotes efficiency, but can also marginalize other social functions such as justice, sustainability, or solidarity (Maurer, 2006).

For Luhmann, money flows transform uncertainty into calculable risks: whoever pays externalizes uncertainty to third parties. This structure remains stable only as long as there is trust in future follow-up communication. This is where Jens Beckert's (2016) concept of fictional expectations comes in: capital movements are based on expectations of the future, which are condensed into ratings, prices, or business plans. While systems theory explains the mechanism, economic sociology provides the semantic raw material.

Today, algorithms, APIs, and high-frequency traders are taking over the central communication functions of money. Knorr Cetina and Bruegger (2002) describe financial markets as 'global microstructures' in which human interaction is replaced by machine signal processing. The binary coding of payment/non-payment is literally translated into machine code—a radical intensification of the systems theory concept of formalization.

Actor-network theory (ANT) shifts the focus from system functions to heterogeneous structures of things, discourses, and technologies. In Latour's (2005) and Callon's (1999) perspective, money is not a neutral medium, but an actant that links people, algorithms, power grids, contracts, and raw materials. It has its own agency within these networks: it mediates, stabilizes, and transforms spaces of action and power relations (Maurer, 2006).

In practice, these interdependencies are often 'black-boxed'—for example, in dashboards, smart contracts, or digital currencies. Take stablecoins, for example: their apparent stability is based on complex chains of price oracles, collateral regimes, and code governance. If one component breaks down, the hybrid agency of such constructs manifests itself in the form of market panics, runs, or regulatory interventions. System theory recognizes that the economy only selectively links itself to environmental systems—primarily via monetary prices.

This results in dematerialization: nature appears only as a cost factor or externality. ANT, on the other hand, makes it clear that material actors—server farms, lithium mines, solar panels—are an integral part of monetary networks. Their physical impact contradicts the abstraction of prices and opens up scope for ecological re-materialization, for example through CO_2-indexed tokens.

As an interim conclusion, it can be said that systems theory explains how money reduces complexity and creates social autonomy. ANT adds to this by explaining the material and infrastructural foundations on which this autonomy is based. Together, they reveal a double paradox:

- **Decoupling**: Money abstracts social and ecological ties into binary operations.
- **Entanglement**: This abstraction itself depends on dense material networks.

These insights form the theoretical hinge for Section 3, which develops the methodological operationalization of these complex couplings—from transaction data to ethnographic analyses in FinTech ecosystems.

2.4 Semiotics and Symbolism of Money

From a semiotic perspective, money also reveals a complex sign structure. In Charles S. Peirce's theory of signs (1977), three basic modes can be distinguished: the icon (pictorial similarity), the index (causal or contextual reference), and the symbol (arbitrary, conventionalized sign) (Table 1). Money typically combines all three dimensions: a banknote is materially an icon, its serial number functions as an index, and its acceptance is based on a symbolic system of social conventions—in particular, institutional backing by central banks. Money is thus poly-semiotic—a hybrid bundle of signs with operational, material, and cultural dimensions.

Table 1. Semiotic dimensions of money

Sign function	Example from the world of finance	Consequence
Icon—similarity	Embossed image on a coin, NFT-JPG	Links value to visual authenticity
Index—causal reference	Serial number, blockchain hash, watermark	Refers to a specific issuance or ownership register
Symbol—convention	'€ ', '$ ', smart contract address	Only works because collective belief and law ensure its meaning

With the transition to fiat money, money finally became an 'empty sign'—a token with no intrinsic substance whose validity is legitimized solely by social attribution (Hornborg, 2024c). Jean Baudrillard (1983) describes this dematerialized monetary regime as a third-order simulacrum: a sign that no longer refers to a reality outside itself but circulates in a hyperreality in which reference, substance, and origin have become obsolete. In this reading, the classic fetish character of money (Marx) takes on new sharpness: The money sign masks the social, ecological, and technical conditions of its production—such as the energy-intensive infrastructure of digital payment systems—and appears as an autonomous force that obscures social relations and renders their contingency invisible (Hornborg, 2024a; McNeill, 2020).

Money is not only an economic instrument but also a symbol with normative embeddedness. Its validity is based on institutional trust—for example, in states, central banks, and the rule of law. Elements such as central bank guarantees, deposit insurance, and KYC requirements constitute a complex trust infrastructure. This trust is not just a component, but the very foundation of the monetary system. At the same time, everyday practice defies the universal fungibility of money: social markers—such as wedding money, donations, or tips—are used to ‘label’ certain funds (Bandelj et al., 2017). In this context, Zelizer (2017) and Morduch (2017) refer to 'earmarked monies,' which indicates that multiple forms of money with distinct social functions can coexist within the same currency. Such practices limit the standardizing effect of money and preserve moments of reciprocity and moral order—even if the universalizing logic of the capitalist monetary economy is increasingly displacing these.

New digital forms of money make the semiotic structures of money particularly visible. Non-fungible tokens (NFTs) operationalize Peirce's triad directly in code:

- **Icon**: the visible JPEG or digital object image,
- **Index**: the unique hash value on the blockchain,
- **Symbol**: the token ID that encodes a tradable property right.

However, these ‘ownership relationships’ are not material rights but rather traces of metadata whose validity depends on social consensus within the platform economy. Meme coins, such as Dogecoin or PEPE, also operate primarily on a symbolic level: their market value is not derived from technical utility but from viral imagery, collective insider jokes, and dynamic community narratives. Here, internet culture and financial speculation merge into an accelerated cycle of iconic posts, indexed tweets, and symbolically charged price jumps.

Payments are not mere transactions but illocutionary acts in the sense of speech act theory (Austin, 1962; Searle & Vanderveken, 1985). The statement ‘I hereby pay’ fulfills a social function—but only on condition that a collective infrastructure (account, ledger, clearing system) recognizes this statement as valid. Money thus functions as an institutionalized speech act, a dynamic force that performs its role effectively within a structured system of expectations.

The semiotic logic of money abstracts different values onto a numerical scale. As a result, material differences—such as between fossil and renewable electricity—disappear behind the homogenizing price tag. Hornborg (2024c) describes this as the ‘thermodynamic deficit’ of the money sign, which allows for the externalization of material energy and resource flows because it does not reflect physical limits within the monetary symbol system. The semiotization of the world thus promotes an illusion of unlimited substitutability—with serious ecological consequences.

The semiotic perspective reveals that money is not a neutral accounting mechanism but a complex structure of signs and meanings. It creates trust through performative acts, legitimizes social hierarchies, and, at the same time, conceals the material and ecological foundations of its circulation. Polanyi, Gudeman, and Hornborg make it clear that modern monetary systems are based on historical and cultural preconditions. Simmel emphasizes their psychological and metaphysical dimensions, while Luhmann and systems theory reveal their abstract functional logic . Actor-network theory, in turn, exposes the infrastructural support layer of monetary orders.

Together, these perspectives raise a central question: How could a sign created by humans—money—become one of the most potent forces in global economic, social, and environmental processes? By combining Peirce's sign model, Baudrillard's concept of hyperreality, Zelizer's notion of earmarked monies, and Hornborg's analysis of the fetish character, it becomes clear that money is not merely a medium of exchange but a driving force behind planetary flows of matter and power. Any reform of the monetary system must, therefore, also consider a reform of its symbolic and semiotic logic.

3. THESES AND RESEARCH PROGRAM

Grounded in an interdisciplinary theoretical framework that integrates economic anthropological, systems theory, semiotic, and philosophical perspectives, this article formulates central theses that conceptualize the monetary system as a cultural, social, and ecologically practical artifact. The aim is not to present empirical findings, but rather to provide a structured set of theoretical hypotheses that will form the basis for future research. These theses characterize the monetary system not as a neutral medium of exchange, but as a dynamic infrastructure that enables symbolic power, social structuring, and ecological externalization.

Thesis 1: It posits that money should be regarded as a social-symbolic artifact, grounded in cultural attributions of meaning and lacking ontological stability.

In most standard economic models, money is viewed as a neutral medium that serves as a universal means of exchange, a unit of account, and a store of value. However, this view neglects the symbolic character of money as an artifact produced and reproduced through cultural practices, institutions, and discourses. From an anthropological perspective, money is not an objective carrier of value, but a 'social sign' (Maurer, 2006; Hornborg, 2024a) whose validity is based on collective recognition, historically grown norms, and symbolic orders. It has no inherent value substance, but refers to a dynamic process of cultural constitution of meaning.

The value of money is therefore not given, but is continuously reinterpreted, negotiated, and stabilized in specific cultural contexts. This symbolic fluidity manifests itself in the diversity of money-related rituals (e.g., wedding gifts, tips, pocket money), in the linguistic coding of budget items (cf. Zelizer 2017), and in the narratives used by central banks, advertising agencies, and financial platforms to legitimize trust in certain forms of money. Digital innovations such as stablecoins, meme coins, and NFTs also illustrate the instability of the money sign and its dependence on discursively mediated social consensus. Money is, therefore, not only an economic quantity, but above all a cultural construct. It is a medium of symbolic communication whose authority always remains fragile.

Research question: How do monetary value attributions arise, circulate, and stabilize within different cultural contexts—and through which discursive, ritual, and institutional mechanisms is money symbolically legitimized or questioned?

This research question aims to examine money not only as a functional entity, but also as an expression of collective processes of meaning. The study focuses on the dynamics of symbolic value production, which manifests itself between state monetary policy, media frames of interpretation, and everyday practices.

Possible methodological approach:

An adequate approach to the empirical investigation of this thesis consists of discourse analysis studies of money-related narratives in various social fields:

- For example, in the context of central bank communication, press releases, speeches, and monetary policy reports (e.g., from the ECB or the Fed) can be analyzed to identify the semantic strategies used to generate trust, which manifest themselves in terms such as 'stability,' 'anchor,' and 'robust.'
- Financial media and advertising measures can be analyzed for narrative patterns, metaphors, and emotionalization. To this end, headlines, campaigns, and financial products are examined for the use of specific keywords such as 'haven,' 'investment for generations,' and 'digital freedom.'
- Within the framework of cultural-sociological media analyses, case studies on meme coins, financial influencers, and money practices in social networks can be conducted to reconstruct the viral dynamics of symbolic money attributions.

A complementary analysis of household practices, earmarking, and symbolic budgeting (cf. Zelizer 2017) can shed light on how money also functions as a morally coded medium in everyday life—beyond its formal universality.

> **Thesis 2:** The modern monetary system is characterized by a double paradox. On the one hand, it abstracts social relationships (decoupling), while on the other hand, it is based on dense material and technical networks (interdependence).

A central characteristic of modern money is its ability to abstract. It reduces diverse social, cultural, and material relationships to numerical values, thereby enabling the seemingly neutral exchange of heterogeneous goods, services, and labor. This abstraction forms the basis for the efficiency, calculability, and global mobility of capital. It decouples economic transactions from their original social and ecological contexts. In this context, money manifests itself as an immaterial symbol transmitted through numbers, accounts, and algorithms.

This symbolic decoupling is nevertheless attributable to highly complex material and technical infrastructures, including digital platforms, server farms, global power grids, high-speed satellite communications, and cryptography standards, which are essential for real-time settlement, scalability, and security guarantees in modern payment flows. Stablecoins, algorithmic currencies, and CBDCs require not only code and governance, but also physical energy, computing power, and reliable oracles for price references. This development illustrates that the more abstractly the financial system operates, the more deeply it is integrated into technomaterial networks.

This paradox of decoupling and interdependence is not just a theoretical dilemma, but also shapes real power relations. Access to and control over monetary infrastructure are key factors that determine participation in transactions, capital accumulation, and participation in financial markets. The impression of a dematerialized monetary order thus masks profound asymmetries in terms of technology, energy, and information (Maurer, 2015).

> **Research question**: Which material infrastructures—from digital platforms to energy consumption to data flows—enable the performative abstraction of monetary transactions, and how do they affect power relations, ecological costs, and social participation?

The question focuses on the tension between the cultural semiotization of money and its material prerequisites. The aim is to illustrate the techno-ecological flip side of monetary systems and critically deconstruct the supposed virtuality of money.

Possible methodological approach:

A suitable methodological approach to this question lies in plurilocal infrastructure analyses combined with ethnographic approaches to platform economies:

- Infrastructure research can analyze the physical, digital, and regulatory conditions that enable modern payment architectures (e.g., VISA, Alipay, Ethereum). This paper focuses in particular on the role of server farms, cloud providers, payment gateways, and power consumption.
- Platform analyses focus on investigating algorithmic design principles, governance structures, and API architectures that standardize and monetize transactions.
- In the context of digital ethnography, field research can be conducted in areas such as payment and fintech ecosystems to analyze user practices, performance, and exclusions. For this purpose, the use of mobile money in Kenya, the use of stablecoins in Argentina, and NFT communities are being investigated, for example.

Additionally, it is possible to integrate ecological impact analyses (e.g., the carbon footprint of mining processes or data centers) to quantify the material and energy costs associated with monetary abstraction.

> **Thesis 3:** The universal fungibility of money leads to the externalization of ecological and social costs. Money as an 'empty sign' allows the commensuration of non-commensurable values.

A central characteristic of modern monetary systems is their universal fungibility. Money can be exchanged for a variety of goods, labor, land, emission rights, or biodiversity conservation services. This property can be traced back to the semiotic structure of money as an 'empty sign' (Hornborg, 2024a). Money has no intrinsic meaning, but instead conveys socially negotiable value attributions. Commensuration, i.e., comparative evaluation, enables the analysis of even radically heterogeneous entities along a uniform measure, the price.

However, this semiotic flexibility has serious consequences: it transforms non-commensurable values—such as cultural identities, social cohesion, or ecological integrity—into seemingly measurable and exchangeable quantities. The cultural and ecological conditions of production and consumption are systematically devalued or pushed out of view. As part of this process, costs that are not immediately visible in the price are externalized. Environmental destruction, social exploitation, health impacts, and cultural erosion are often overlooked in economic calculations, despite their tangible effects.

The ability of money to measure is therefore not just a technical property, but a political and ecological mechanism that defines which economic phenomena become visible and which disappear in the shadows of the markets. The decoupling of price and real resource use or social damage is not a malfunction, but an integral part of money-based valuation systems.

> **Research question**: How does monetary abstraction—understood as commensuration via the 'empty sign' of money—contribute to the invisibility of ecological and social externalities, and how does it shape global patterns of value creation and inequality?

This study examines the extent to which price manifests itself as an instrument of epistemic violence. It examines the impact of monetary devaluation or disregard for the fundamental values of ecological and social reproduction on perception, opportunities for action, and political control.

Possible methodological approach:

Several methodological approaches can be usefully combined to analyze these dynamics:

- Modeling ecologically unequal exchange relationships is of essential importance. Building on work by Hornborg, Dorninger et al. (2021) and Moran et al. (2013), input-output models can be used to visualize resource, energy, and emission flows between the center and the periphery. Examples include the material footprint and embodied emissions.
- Qualitative studies on pricing processes in ESG markets can be conducted. Interviews, policy analyses, and discourse analyses can be used to examine how social and ecological criteria are operationalized, reduced, or selectively ignored in 'sustainable' financial products.

- Semiotic analyses target different market logics. Case studies (e.g., CO_2 certificates, biodiversity credits) can be used to reconstruct how complex environmental goods are translated into monetary units—and what meanings are lost or deliberately excluded in the process.

This perspective aims at a critical analysis of pricing and valuation mechanisms as social selection processes that generate, legitimize, and reinforce structurally determined externalities.

> **Thesis 4:** Digitalization is transforming trust in the monetary system from interpersonal expectation to technical verification.

Trust is the fundamental prerequisite for any monetary order. In classical literature on the monetary system, trust is defined as a combination of state authority, social convention, and the stability of interpersonal expectations. Central banks, banking systems, and legal promises of payment functioned as institutional guarantors of monetary reliability, supplemented by cultural practices of creditworthiness as described in locally embedded economies (Gudeman, 2001) or in symbolic-generalized media (Luhmann, 1988).

With the digitalization of money, however, trust is shifting from these personalized and institutionalized forms to technical architectures. Trust is increasingly being transferred to code, algorithms, and cryptographic protocols. Interpersonal assessments are being replaced by automated validation mechanisms, such as smart contracts, oracles, or KYC (Know Your Customer) systems, which are designed to enforce compliance, identity, and transaction security without relying on human discretion. In the current transformation, trust is no longer generated within social interaction, but rather verified by technical processes.

The concept of 'trust by design' (Werbach, 2018) is transforming not only the way monetary systems work, but also our understanding of economic interaction. Relationship management, contingency tolerance, and mutual interpretation are replaced by binary, executive trust in the sense of 'code is law.' This results in new power constellations, which are rooted, for example, in the control power of platform operators or the opacity of algorithmic decisions.

> **Research question**: What new trust architectures (e.g., oracles, smart contracts, digital identity systems) are emerging in the context of digital currencies, and how are they changing the relationship between technical infrastructure, social interaction, and institutional authority in the monetary system?

This study examines the extent to which technical infrastructures are transforming monetary social relations. The question it raises concerns the changing relationship between trust, control, and power in the digital age, particularly about access to money, its regulation, and the social significance of transactions.

Possible methodological approach:

- Comparative analysis of algorithmic governance models in digital currencies, such as stablecoins (e.g., Ethereum, USDC) and government-initiated central bank digital currencies (CBDCs), can contrast design principles (transparency, intervention capacity, control structure) and examine them in terms of their trust logics.
- Technical ethnographies and policy analyses of digital identity protocols, such as the European Digital Identity Wallet or the Chinese social credit system, can help understand how trust is technically implemented and, at the same time, politically standardized.
- The focus of socio-technical mapping studies of decentralized financial systems (DeFi) can be on reconstructing the processes by which new trust networks emerge. Examples include oracles, DAO governance, and automated audits. Additionally, the actors in these networks who exert a significant influence on network dynamics are identified.

This perspective enables a differentiated understanding of digital trust regimes, their social selection mechanisms, and the implications for inclusion, control, and democratic design of digital forms of money.

> **Thesis 5:** Money reproduces social inequality not only through ownership relations, but also through symbolic structures—e.g., through earmarking, moral markings, and semantic coding.

Social inequality in the monetary system manifests itself not only in the unequal distribution of wealth or income, but also in the symbolic structuring of monetary practice. Money is never completely fungible, but is earmarked for specific purposes, morally connoted, and culturally coded in everyday contexts. This insight has been emphasized in particular by economic sociology (cf. Zelizer, 1997) and feminist household research (cf. Nelson, 1995).

This 'semantization of money' manifests itself, for example, in the attribution of specific meanings to certain cash flows (e.g., child support, alms, political donations) in comparison to wages or market transactions. Government budgeting also operates with normative coding, such as the separation of 'social spending' and 'investment.' This separation reflects political priorities and moral patterns of interpretation.

In the processes described, money assumes the role of a medium of social differentiation. It functions not only as a medium of exchange, but also as a carrier of normative distinctions. This study examines how the use and valuation of money are structured and influenced by various factors. It is argued that the earmarking of financial resources, for example, for school supplies for children, as well as the moral labeling of money, for example, through its classification as 'dirty money,' and symbolic inscriptions, such as the gender concept in consumer spending, contribute to the reproduction of existing power and inequality relations.

> **Research question**: How do households, companies, and states structure their cash flows along moral, political, and cultural patterns of order, and to what extent do these semantic codings contribute to the perpetuation of social inequality?

The research question aims to reveal everyday monetary practices and institutional coding as vehicles of social difference. The question it raises concerns the role of symbolic practices—not just economic logic—in shaping, legitimizing, or concealing monetary inequality.

Possible methodological approach:

Qualitative interpretative methods are particularly suitable for analyzing this dimension.

- Micro studies on household budgeting are empirical investigations that aim to explore the categorization, prioritization, and moral evaluation of different sources of income and expenditures by families (see Zelizer, 1994; Bandelj et al., 2020).
- Various empirical studies, utilizing interviews and focus groups, can analyze the meanings attributed to different forms of money and transactions. To this end, households, financial advisors, and social services are surveyed.
- Discourse analyses of budget debates and fiscal policy allow us to analyze the 'austerity measures,' 'performance-based fairness,' 'investment boosters,' and 'rescue packages' presented in political narratives.
- Comparative studies on donation practices, microfinance, or gender budgets provide a deeper understanding of the extent to which normative coding influences monetary scope for action.

Such an approach enables the revelation of symbolic power structures in the use of money, demonstrating that social inequality is reproduced not only through economic resources but also through their cultural patterns of order.

> **Thesis 6:** The semantic and symbolic logic of money can be reformed through new forms of indexation (e.g., CO_2), limited earmarking, or alternative value systems.

Money cannot, therefore, be regarded as a natural medium, but rather as a culturally malleable sign system. Its semantic openness—its function as an 'empty sign' in Hornborg's sense (2024a)—is not only a source of social and ecological decoupling, but also a starting point for transformative reforms. If values are encoded through money, it is possible to renegotiate, recode, and index these values. It can be achieved, for example, by adhering to ecological limits, social inclusion goals, or guidelines that prioritize public welfare.

A future-proof understanding of money would therefore not abolish fungibility, but selectively limit it by introducing new forms of indexation (e.g., CO2-based value anchors), earmarking (e.g., for food, education, or mobility), and complementary currencies (e.g., time banks, regional currencies, or digital commons tokens). Central banks could also link the issuance of CBDCs to new semantic orders, for example, through environmental stability rules, the exclusion of ecologically destructive uses, or the digital 'programming' of money spending.

This implies a post-fossil and public welfare-oriented understanding of money that no longer aims at universal capital accumulation but at planetary regeneration and social participation. However, this requires not only technical but also symbolic and semiotic innovations. This paper examines the need for a new narrative, context, and the legitimacy of money.

> **Research question**: How could post-fossil, regenerative, or public welfare-oriented monetary systems be designed—technically, institutionally, and symbolically—and what social, ecological, and economic effects could be expected?

The research question focuses on the future forms of money, combining an analysis of semantic possibilities with concrete institutional and technological design approaches.

Possible methodological approach:

A research focus that addresses such questions requires the application of methods that are scenario-based, simulation-supported, and normatively informed.

- As part of scenario development for alternative monetary systems, future workshops or deliberation labs with experts and citizens are held to discuss possible monetary configurations in the Capitalocene.
- Agent-based modeling (ABM) can be used to simulate earmarking, indexation, or dual currencies in various macroeconomic contexts of post-growth-oriented monetary systems.
- Simulation-based impact analyses focus on the effect of CO2-indexed digital currencies on consumer behavior, emissions avoidance, and social participation.
- Design ethnographies and living labs serve the participatory evaluation and testing of new forms of money in real, sociocultural contexts (communities, cooperatives, pilot projects).

The analytical techniques presented here have the potential to substantiate the feasibility of alternative forms of money empirically and to analyze their semantic effectiveness as a form of cultural innovation.

The six theses presented in this text form the basis for an expanded, non-reductionist research program on the role of money in the Anthropocene. The analysis of money in the context of the Anthropocene opens up an expanded problem horizon in which ecological, technological, and symbolic dynamics are intertwined. The term 'Anthropocene' refers to a new geological era in which humans—more precisely, certain human social formations—have become the dominant influence on planetary processes. From this perspective, monetary systems are not only seen as technical means of coordinating economic activities, but as central drivers of global socio-ecological change (Haberl et al., 2011). This study examines the extent to which the objects under investigation contribute to the allocation of goods and services. It also discusses the extent to which they influence the modulation of material flows, energy consumption, and land use on an industrial scale.

In scientific discussions, the term 'Capitalocene' (cf. Moore, 2016; Horváth & Lovász, 2024) is therefore increasingly being introduced as a counter-concept to the Anthropocene. The Anthropocene refers to humanity as a whole as the cause of ecological crises. In contrast, the Capitalocene emphasizes the historically specific role of capitalist production and financial logic in the overexploitation of natural resources. In this interpretation, it is not 'humanity itself' but the accumulation regime, motivated by market principles, that is seen as the decisive factor in entering planetary crisis zones. The term Capitalocene thus refers directly to the role of money as an abstract control medium that externalizes nature and renders social costs invisible (cf. Hornborg, 2024a; Malm & Hornborg, 2014).

The universal compensatory power of money, inherent in its ability to translate incommensurable values such as biodiversity, care, or cultural heritage into a numerical scale, should not be understood as a mere technique, but as an expression of a specific symbolic order. This allows decision-making logics to be objectified and thus removed from political and ethical discourse. The Anthropocene thus manifests itself not only as a geophysical phenomenon, but also as a semiotic dispositive structure in which money acts as a central medium. It links externalization, growth, and the fiction of stability in a seemingly neutral sign (Luhmann, 1988; Baudrillard, 1983).

The aim is to understand money not only as an economic instrument of power, but also as a cultural, ecological, and technologically mediated one. The proposed studies combine systemic modeling, semiotic analysis, and socio-ecological research. The strengthening of a new research direction aims to transcend existing dualisms, such as the oppositions between market and morality, exchange and gift, or state and individual.

The theoretical contribution of this article lies in the integration of previously separate perspectives—from Polanyi to Luhmann, from Derrida to Hornborg—and in the formulation of a research framework that responds to the planetary challenges of the 21st century: ecological limits, digital disruptions, and social fragmentation. In this sense, money as a cultural artifact is not only an object of analysis but also functions as a lever for transformation.

4. RESEARCH PROJECT

4.1 Goals and Guiding Questions

By the theses developed in Section 3, the research project focuses on the systematic analysis of the cultural, social, and ecological mechanisms of modern monetary systems. The investigation focuses on the question of what effect money has as a social-symbolic medium, technical infrastructure ensemble, and ecological catalyst. The focus is on the material basis and semantic structure of money circulation, its role in reproducing social inequality, and its effects within the context of planetary boundaries.

This study is uniquely positioned at the intersection of various disciplines, taking a context-sensitive, interdisciplinary approach that integrates economic, anthropological, semiotic, ecological, and sociotechnical perspectives. The central questions of the research project are:

- How does the logic of general-purpose money (GPM) influence the structure, control, and efficiency of local resource economies—especially in the Global South, where ecological pressures and institutional dependencies are particularly high?
- To what extent do digital forms of money—such as stablecoins, central bank digital currencies (CBDCs), or tokenized payment systems—promote or hinder social inclusion, distributive justice, and sustainable allocation?
- What role do culturally coded money practices, such as earmarked money (Zelizer, 2017), play in resisting or reproducing global money logics?
- How can the semiotic structure of money (Peirce, Baudrillard) be operationalized to make processes of externalization, symbolic violence, or asymmetric value allocation visible and analyzable?
- What governance strategies can be derived from a pluralistic theory of money, which acknowledges the diverse roles and functions of money in society and the economy, and reconciles social, economic, and ecological objectives?

The answers to these questions aim not only to deepen our understanding of current monetary orders but also to identify actionable ways in which a resilient, fair, and ecologically sustainable monetary architecture can be designed, offering hope for a more equitable future.

4.2 Conceptual Model

The proposed conceptual model is based on four complementary levels of analysis: the economic level, the social level, the semiotic level, and the ecological level. These levels are examined in their mutual interrelationships (Table 2).

Table 2. Integrative framework model

Dimension	Key question	Exemplary concepts
Semiotic-symbolic	What is the meaning structure of money?	Sign model Earmarking
Infrastructural	What material conditions enable money?	Token systems Server APIs
Socio-institutional	How is money socially standardized and legally codified?	Property Trust Compliance
Ecological-metabolic	What resource flows does money mediate?	Thermodynamic deficit Externalities

Source: own representation.

This model allows for the theoretically sound identification of path dependencies, contradictions, and transformation potentials in current and future monetary regimes. It forms the basis for comparative analyses in different cultural, technological, and ecological contexts.

4.3 Proposals for Research Designs

To provide empirical support for the conceptual theses, a mix of methods is proposed that integrates qualitative, quantitative, and simulation-based approaches:

1. The analysis of local money initiatives (e.g., regional currencies, time banks, or energy coins) in various socioeconomic contexts, using comparative case studies, aims to identify the concrete effects of alternative forms of money on social cohesion, resource management, and political participation.
2. An analysis of key discourses on money is conducted through various forms of communication, including central bank communication, media narratives, and advertising campaigns. This analysis aims to reveal the semantic reproduction of power relations and legitimation strategies.
3. As part of the platform and infrastructure analysis, digital payment systems (e.g., PayPal, Alipay, CBDC prototypes) are examined in terms of technical regulation, energy consumption, access options, and social selection mechanisms.
4. Scenario-based simulation models for alternative monetary architectures (such as indexed CO2 currencies or standard good tokens) are being developed. The aim is to model systemic effects on resource use, social participation, and market stability under various assumptions.

The designs presented here not only serve to analyze existing monetary systems but also aim to identify transformative ways in which these can be reshaped in the interests of ecological, social, and cultural resilience. In Section 5, the findings are used to develop a research agenda for the sustainable redesign of monetary systems, inspiring a vision for a more equitable future.

5. DISCUSSION AND OUTLOOK

The theoretical considerations presented here and the research project outlined suggest that money, as a cultural artifact, has not only an economic dimension but also social, ecological, and infrastructural ones. The anthropological, systems theory, and semiotic perspectives result in an integrative understanding of money as a medium of social order, technical control, and ecological externalization. This transformative potential of our research is a source of hope and inspiration for future developments in the field. From this multi-perspective view, three central lines of discussion emerge that are of significant relevance for future research and political practice.

First, the analysis highlights the structural asymmetry between the logic of general-purpose money and locally embedded practices of reciprocity, care, and ecological responsibility. While the abstraction and universal comparability of money enable efficiency gains, they also lead to a systematic externalization of social and ecological costs. It can be concluded that reforms aimed at a more sustainable monetary order must not be limited to technical parameters such as interest rates or money supply control, but must also reflect symbolic and institutional dimensions of money circulation.

Second, it is necessary to discuss how economic communication can be reorganized so that money no longer functions as an unlimited symbol of universal exchangeability, but is once again linked to normative, social, and ecological contexts. Proposals such as earmarked regional currencies, CO2-indexed tokens, commons-based credit systems, or central platforms with normatively programmed smart contracts point to alternative development paths. A theory-driven, empirically grounded evaluation of such alternatives is a central challenge for future research.

Third, regarding the connection between decoupling (system theory) and interdependence (actor-network theory), the question arises as to how the double paradox of modern monetary systems should be addressed. Money not only functions as a means of abstracting social relations, but is also deeply embedded in technical, legal, and material networks. A forward-looking research program must therefore accomplish two things simultaneously: the re-materialization of the logic of money (e.g., through ecological cost accounting or social indicators, a process of giving material form to the abstract concept of money) and the deconstruction of its symbolic power (e.g., through discursive interventions, artistic practices, or educational policy strategies, a process of breaking down the symbolic power of money into its constituent parts for analysis).

This discussion leads to a normative outlook: The present study deals with the thesis that money, when understood as a cultural artifact, is also a malleable entity. This understanding enables us to recognize that the current monetary order is not a natural law, but rather the outcome of historical decisions, institutional power dynamics, and technological designs. Critical monetary research that takes the symbolic, ecological, and social dimensions seriously can provide impetus for a more just, sustainable, and resilient economic order in the Capitalocene.

Future research agendas should be transdisciplinary, emphasizing the need for collaboration and the urgency of the task at hand. This approach is crucial for building epistemological bridges between the disciplines of anthropology, economics, sociology, media studies, ecology, and technology research. A comprehensive understanding of the complex interrelationships of money requires in-depth analysis that enables one to grasp its full implications and, on this basis, develop appropriate transformation measures.

6. CONCLUSIONS

This study sets out to reconceptualize money as a cultural, social, and ecological artifact on a theoretical basis. The central thesis is that money should not be perceived as a neutral medium of exchange, but rather as a social-symbolic medium with material, semiotic, and political implications. Drawing on economic anthropology, systems theory, and network theory, this study demonstrates that monetary systems are historical constructs that reproduce social power relations and can systematically reinforce ecological externalities.

As Bockelmann (2025) aptly puts it: 'Money may be nothing, but it is not neutral. The whole truth about what money is can be seen in what money does.' Money is not a moral entity—it knows no good or evil. However, it is precisely this supposed neutrality that obscures the fact that money enables both good and destructive actions—and that it is itself part of the structures that produce social inequality and ecological crises.

The analysis of money as a cultural artifact shows that it fulfills a function far beyond economic transactions. Money not only functions as a medium of exchange, but also manifests itself as a social, symbolic, and technological medium for power, meaning, and expectations. From an anthropological perspective, it can be observed that economic practices are embedded in diverse moral and cultural orders that tend to be transformed or suppressed by the introduction of general-purpose money. Polanyi, Gudeman, Hornborg, and Zelizer argue that monetary logics are never purely economic, but always socially and ecologically coded.

From a systems theory perspective, money can be seen as an instrument that translates interactions into a binary communication format, thereby reducing complexity, but also potentially promoting social inequality and ecological blindness. Actor-network theory (ANT) illustrates that this abstraction itself is based on material infrastructures and technical standards that are by no means neutral or stable. From a semiotic perspective, it becomes clear that money operates as a sign that not only conveys meanings, but also shifts, conceals, and creates them. This has far-reaching social and ecological consequences.

The theses developed in Section 3 highlight key areas of tension: money functions as an abstract means of establishing social relationships, but at the same time is stabilized by material infrastructures. It enables universalistic communication, but contributes to the invisibility of ecological and social costs. In addition, it transforms trust through digital technologies and reproduces social inequality across symbolic and functional mechanisms. Finally, it became clear that money can be viewed as a reformable system, with various forms of indexation, earmarking, or participatory design identified as possible approaches.

The research project in Section 4 proposes to translate these theses into a systematic program of transdisciplinary money research. This study uses a combination of qualitative and quantitative methods to analyze the interplay between attributions of meaning, material infrastructures, and ecological effects. Local case studies, platform analyses, and scenario-based simulations are employed to better understand the performative character of monetary orders and the development of alternatives, thereby paving the way for transformative policies.

The transformation of money in the digital age—through CBDCs, stablecoins, NFTs, and other developments—is intensifying these dynamics. At the same time, new opportunities for reforming the monetary system are becoming apparent, manifesting themselves in indexed tokens, participatory budgeting mechanisms, and ecological valuation metrics, among other things. A significant proportion of these developments are motivated by the search for alternatives to the prevailing understanding of money as an impersonal, socially 'corrosive' force. This raises the question of how a future monetary system can be designed that is not only efficient but also fair, sustainable, and culturally legitimate.

This diagnosis implies that no single theory can fully capture the complex power of modern monetary systems (see Bossone, 2025). Instead, an integrative approach is needed that takes into account cultural dimensions of meaning, technological forms of mediation, and ecological materialities in equal measure. Only through an analysis of the structural social inequalities and ecological crises resulting from the current monetary order and transformative policies based on this analysis can these issues be adequately addressed, highlighting the urgency and importance of the topic.

This concept paper forms the theoretical and methodological basis for a transdisciplinary research project. Money is not seen as a given means, but as a malleable medium of social transformation. The aim is to reconstruct the symbolic, infrastructural, and ecological dimensions of monetary orders, examine them comparatively, and translate them into new, responsible design options. The social significance of money, as highlighted by Zelizer, remains of central relevance. Even new forms of money use should not be viewed as mere technical change, but as an expression of cultural shifts in meaning and social negotiation processes (Dodd, 2017). In an era of global transformations, it is therefore not only the understanding of money that is being renegotiated, but also its social function, which is a key aspect of this research.

REFERENCES

Armstrong, P., & Siddiqui, K. (2019). The case for the ontology of money as credit: Money as bearer or basis of 'value'. *Real-world. Economic Review (Kansas City, Mo.), 90*, 98–118.

Austin, J. L. (1962). *How to do things with words*. Clarendon Press.

Bandelj, N., Boston, T., Elyachar, J., Kim, J., McBride, M., & Tufail, Z. (2017). Morals and emotions of money. In Bandelj, N., Wherry, F. F., & Zelizer, V. A. (Eds.), *Money talks: Explaining how money really works* (pp. 39–56). Princeton University Press., DOI: 10.23943/princeton/9780691168685.003.0003

Baraldi, C., Corsi, G., & Esposito, E. (2021). *Unlocking Luhmann: A keyword introduction to systems theory*. Bielefeld University Press. https://library.oapen.org/bitstream/id/87961f81-6012-4c17-837e-f511b974b9d3

Baudrillard, J. (1983). *Simulacra, semiotics*. Semiotext(e).

Baxter, H. (2013). Niklas Luhmann's theory of autopoietic legal systems. *Annual Review of Law and Social Science, 167*, •••. https://scholarship.law.bu.edu/faculty_scholarship/140

Birch, K., & Muniesa, F. (2020). *Assetization: Turning things into assets in technoscientific capitalism*. The MIT Press., DOI: 10.7551/mitpress/12075.001.0001

Bockelmann, E. (2025). *Money: Understanding modern society*. Matthes & Seitz.

Bossone, B. (2025). *Trailblazing visions of money in economic theory. Contributions to Economics*. Springer., DOI: 10.1007/978-3-031-82544-6

Cagli, E. C., & Dimpfl, T. (2025). Have cryptocurrencies arrived in the system of fiat currencies? An appraisal based on monetary policy uncertainty. *Finance Research Letters, 107993*. Advance online publication. DOI: 10.1016/j.frl.2025.107993

Callon, M. (1999). Actor-Network Theory—The market test. *The Sociological Review*, *47*(1, suppl). Advance online publication. DOI: 10.1111/j.1467-954X.1999.tb03488.x

Coeckelbergh, M. (2015). Money as medium and tool: Reading Simmel as a philosopher of technology to understand contemporary financial ICTs and media. *Techné: Research in Philosophy and Technology*, *19*(3), 358–380. DOI: 10.5840/techne2015121039

Derrida, J. (1991). *Given time: I. Counterfeit money*. The University of Chicago Press.

Dodd, N. (2015). Redeeming Simmel's money. *HAU*, *5*(2), 435–441. DOI: 10.14318/hau5.2.030

Dodd, N. (2017). Utopian monies: Complementary currencies, Bitcoin, and the social life of money. In Bandelj, N., Wherry, F. F., & Zelizer, V. A. (Eds.), *Money talks: Explaining how money really works* (pp. 230–248). Princeton University Press., DOI: 10.23943/princeton/9780691168685.003.0015

Dorninger, C., Hornborg, A., Abson, D. J., von Wehrden, H., Schaffartzik, A., & Giljum, S.. (2021). Global patterns of ecologically unequal exchange: Implications for sustainability in the 21st century. *Ecological Economics*, *179*, 106824. DOI: 10.1016/j.ecolecon.2020.106824

Gemici, K. (2008). Karl Polanyi and the antinomies of embeddedness. *Socio-economic Review*, *6*(1), 5–33. DOI: 10.1093/ser/mwl034

Graeber, D. (2001). *Toward an anthropological theory of value: The false coin of our own dreams*. Palgrave.

Graeber, D. (2011). *Debt. The first 5,000 years*. Melville House Publishing.

Gudeman, S. (1986). *Economics as culture: Models and metaphors of livelihood*. Routledge & Kegan Paul.

Gudeman, S. (2001). *The anthropology of economy: Community, market, and culture*. Blackwell.

Haberl, H., Fischer-Kowalski, M., Krausmann, F., Martinez-Alier, J., & Winiwarter, V. (2011). A socio-metabolic transition towards sustainability? Challenges for another Great Transformation. *Sustainable Development, 19*(1), 1–14. DOI: 10.1002/sd.410

Hornborg, A. (2024a). Defetishizing money: Perspectives from economic anthropology. Gudeman Lecture, University of Minnesota, March 20, 2023. *Journal of Ethnographic Theory, 14*(2), 310–319. DOI: 10.1086/731656

Hornborg, A. (2024b). Limiting money: Redesigning the artifact that shapes modern people. *Sustainability Science*. Advance online publication. DOI: 10.1007/s11625-024-01489-3

Hornborg, A. (2024c). *Liquidate: How money is dissolving the world.* Routledge., DOI: 10.4324/9781032702186

Horváth, M., & Lovász, A. (2024). From the Anthropocene to the Capitalocene and beyond. *The Anthropocene Review*. Advance online publication. DOI: 10.1177/20530196241270703

Ingham, G. (2004). *The nature of money*. Cambridge University Press.

Knorr Cetina, K., & Bruegger, U. (2002). Global microstructures: The virtual societies of financial markets. *American Journal of Sociology, 107*(4), 905–950. DOI: 10.1086/341045

Latour, B. (2005). *Reassembling the social: An introduction to Actor-Network-Theory*. Oxford University Press.

Luhmann, N. (1984). Die Wirtschaft der Gesellschaft als autopoietisches System. *Zeitschrift für Soziologie, 11*(4), 366–379.

Luhmann, N. (1988). *Ökologische Kommunikation*. Suhrkamp.

Malm, A., & Hornborg, A. (2014). The geology of mankind? A critique of the Anthropocene narrative. *The Anthropocene Review, 1*(1), 62–69. DOI: 10.1177/2053019613516291

Maurer, B. (2006). The anthropology of money. *Annual Review of Anthropology, 35*, 15–36. DOI: 10.1146/annurev.anthro.35.081705.123127

Maurer, B. (2015). *How would you like to pay? How technology is changing the future of money*. Duke University Press., DOI: 10.1215/9780822375173

Maurer, B. (2017). Blockchains are a diamond's best friend: Zelizer for the Bitcoin moment. In Bandelj, N., Wherry, F. F., & Zelizer, V. A. (Eds.), *Money talks: Explaining how money really works* (pp. 215–229). Princeton University Press., DOI: 10.23943/princeton/9780691168685.003.0014

McNeill, D. (2020). *Fetishism and the theory of value: Reassessing Marx in the 21st century*. Palgrave Macmillan.

Moore, J. W. (2016). *Anthropocene or Capitalocene? Nature, history, and the crisis of capitalism*. PM Press.

Moran, D. D., Lenzen, M., Kanemoto, K., & Geschke, A. (2013). Does ecologically unequal exchange occur? *Ecological Economics*, *89*, 177–186. DOI: 10.1016/j.ecolecon.2013.02.013

Morduch, J. (2017). Economics and the social meaning of money. In Bandelj, N., Wherry, F. F., & Zelizer, V. A. (Eds.), *Money talks: Explaining how money really works* (pp. 25–38). Princeton University Press., DOI: 10.23943/princeton/9780691168685.003.0002

Nelson, J. (1995). Feminism and economics. *The Journal of Economic Perspectives*, *9*(2), 131–148. 110.1257/jep.9.2.131

Parsons, T. (1978). *Action theory and the human condition.*

Polanyi, K. (2001). *[1944]. The Great Transformation: The political and economic origins of our time*. Penguin Modern Classics.

Sahlins, M. (1972). *Stone age economics*. Routledge.

Searle, J. R., & Vanderveken, D. (1985). *Foundations of illocutionary logic*. Cambridge University Press.

Simmel, G. (2004) [1900]. *The philosophy of money*. 3.rd enlarged ed. Routledge.

Werbach, K. (2018). *The Blockchain and the new architecture of trust*. MIT Press.

Wray, L. R. (2025). *Understanding modern money theory: Money and credit in capitalist economies*. Edward Elgar.

Zander, U., Lu, L., & Chimenti, G. (2025). The platform economy and futures of market societies: Salient tensions in ecosystem evolution. *Journal of Business Research, 189*, 115037. DOI: 10.1016/j.jbusres.2024.115037

Zelizer, V. A. (2017). *The social meaning of money: Pin money, paychecks, poor relief, and other currencies*. Princeton University Press. [1] andrae@zedat.fu-berlin.de https://orcid.org/0000-0002-8586-7812

Chapter 3
Capitalism, Socialism, and Communism: Comparative Insights in Modern Economic Anthropology

Surjit Singha
https://orcid.org/0000-0002-5730-8677
Kristu Jayanti University, India

Ranjit Singha
https://orcid.org/0000-0002-3541-8752
Christ University, India

ABSTRACT

This chapter examines capitalism, socialism, and communism from an economic and anthropological perspective, emphasizing that these systems are culturally defined, historically conditioned, and socially lived. It does so through a detailed overview of each system's history, values, and contradictions, taking advantage of ethnographic case studies from around the world to compare the extremes of labour, resource distribution, and cultural impact. The chapter also explores mixed or hybrid economic systems, digital economies, and emerging alternatives for sustainability and equity. By applying classical theories with present-day issues, the

DOI: 10.4018/979-8-3373-1260-6.ch003

chapter emphasizes the significance of anthropological perspectives to explain the effects of economic systems on human conduct, social ties, and future values.

INTRODUCTION

Economic systems—the systems of capitalism, socialism, and communism—are not just theoretical or policy constructs; they are woven into the day-to-day culture of societies. As a discipline within economic anthropology, these systems are analyzed as production and exchange mechanisms and as cultural institutions that influence and are influenced by human behaviours, systems of beliefs, power relations, and historical contingencies. Each system represents a distinct configuration in what is valued as owned, labour, and distribution and is supported by local cultural realities.

The four essential factors defining capitalism are private ownership, profit motive, competitive markets, and capital accumulation (Talan, 2020; Trüeb et al., 2023). It is based on materialist use and prestige and frequently causes social and economic differences. This capitalist culture brings about the value of material wealth and consumption, which can generate a culture of honour and suck up (Trüeb et al., 2023). This structure has been decried as promoting social inequality, wage slavery, and environmental degradation (Talan, 2020).

Capitalism tends to build up a society in which a top-down hierarchical structure, in which wealth accumulation is a goal in itself, in most cases at the expense of those doing the work, is not uncommon (Uhl, 2016). Socialism refers to public or direct worker ownership or workers' self-management of their possessions and the product of their labour. It aims to reduce inequality and improve living conditions (Verdery, 2015).

Anthropologists are exploring how these systems play out in people's daily lives, shape community dynamics and contribute to the overall balance of power globally. Through examination of both macro-structures and micro-level practices, economic anthropology reveals the interconnectedness of the economy with non-economic and sociopolitical dimensions of life. It provides a comparative, cross-culturally informed lens to make sense of the organization, functioning, dynamics, and impacts of competitive markets under capitalism, state planning under socialism, and collective ownership aspirations under communism in actual societies. Few systems are ever pure, and each is a hybrid, a mix of colonial residues, indigenous pride, religious compunctions and geopolitical imperatives.

This chapter presents the anthropological analysis of economic systems, their impacts on daily life, and how they mediate these phenomena in these cultural contexts. It offers a nuanced picture in which capitalism, socialism, or communism are reinvigorated by feeding classical theories with real-life fieldwork as they respond to new challenges like inequality, labour preparedness, or globalization. From this perspective, economic anthropology plays a crucial role in explaining economic outcomes and weaving around them the human stories and the cultural meaning that makes them significant.

THEORETICAL FRAMEWORK: DEBATES IN ECONOMIC ANTHROPOLOGY

Purpose: It establishes the conceptual angle for comparing economic systems via the lens of economic anthropology (but while drawing on primary theoretical debates). It situates the chapter within the larger scholarly conversation.

Economic anthropology provides one of the founding pillars from which debates on culture and society approach the intersections of social life; key debates within economic anthropology have been formative in framing how economic systems are understood as constructs of culture, society, and meaning. The early economic, anthropological theory had been built on two foundational paradigms—formalist and substantivist (Anthroholic, 2023; Polanyi, 1957).

According to formalist theorists, economic behaviour, characterized by rational choice and utility maximization, is universal in all societies. Commonly associated with neoclassical economics, this perspective views economic decision-making as fundamentally individualistic and calculative.

By contrast, substantivists (Karl Polanyi being the most prominent example) argue that economic activities are within social institutions like kinship, religion, and politics. In this light, economic systems do not operate within a vacuum but in the context of a wider cultural and moral order. Reciprocity, redistribution, and householding are the focal modes of exchange in traditional societies (the 'substantive' stance characterizing the opposite standpoint of a market-based exchange).

These distinctions are not merely academic. They deeply influence how we understand capitalism (as disembedded and competitive), socialism (as redistributive and institutional), and communism (as collectivist and moral-economic). This chapter aligns more closely with the substantive view, recognizing economic systems as culturally situated and socially mediated.

Later theoretical developments—especially structuralism and post-structuralism—offered critical tools to analyze how economies are not just material processes but also symbolic and discursive systems. Structuralists like Claude Lévi-Strauss emphasized the deep symbolic logic underpinning social institutions, including economies. Post-structuralists, influenced by Foucault and Derrida, turned attention to how power, ideology, and resistance circulate within and against economic discourses (Carrier, 2005).

Post-structuralism allows us to question taken-for-granted truths about economic "rationality," "efficiency," and "growth." For example, anthropologists have shown how neoliberal capitalism constructs subjects who internalize precarious labor norms as forms of freedom (Bear et al., 2015; Tsing, 2015). In socialist and communist settings, post-structuralist analyses highlight the contradictions between ideological narratives and lived realities (Yurchak, 2006).

The chapter thus builds on substantive and post-structuralist approaches to argue that capitalism, socialism, and communism should not be seen as static or monolithic economic systems but as dynamic, hybridized, and culturally mediated formations. These paradigms help illuminate how state ideologies, grassroots practices, and moral economies intersect in shaping people's everyday lives under different regimes.

Moreover, this framework incorporates recent anthropological interests in moral economy, hybridity, digital economies, and environmental justice. It provides the analytical groundwork for comparing these systems in terms of structure and ideology and through the lens of lived experience, resistance, and cultural continuity.

UNDERSTANDING ECONOMIC SYSTEMS IN ANTHROPOLOGY

Definition and Scope of Economic Systems

Economic systems are organizations that manage resource production, distribution, and consumption. Conventionally, these structures have been classified into capitalism, socialism, and communism (Das, 2025). However, from an anthropological point of view, the concept of an economic system opens onto something much less tree-like or hard-wired. Financial systems are not just limited to market exchanges or the state's policy -they are forms of social organization comprising the customs, morals and values communities establish to deal with the perennial resource distribution problems. This broader concept includes the formal institutions and regulations, informal networks, social relationships, and cultural norms that facilitate exchanges and social practices of goods and services among people and groups.

Anthropological (2023) says that economic systems are deeply ingrained within a society. They are deeply embedded in social structure, belief systems, and power relations, so divorcing them from human action and social organization is impossible. In approaching economies as a cultural phenomenon, anthropologists reveal how ideas about fairness, reciprocity, and debt operate, in which they do not operate as the logic of exchange or only as the logic of the market used by the mainstream economy. This broad approach and focus highlight the diversity of economic life in different societies, challenging the apparent universality of mainstream economic theories.

The Anthropological Lens on Economics

Looking at economic phenomena through an anthropological lens requires a particular type of qualitative, context-sensitive inquiry rather than the quantitative methodology that predominates in mainstream economics. Anthropologists participate in the social settings within which economic action occurs and view this social environment as one in which cultural understandings, past experiences, and interpersonal dynamics influence economic actions (Gauliver, 2023). This ethnographic method allows researchers to record the material features of monetary exchanges and the associated symbolic and emotional elements.

From this standpoint, market practices are considered enmeshed in a broader cultural context in which every transaction carries social connotations. For example, practices of gift exchange, collective work assignments, and pre-modern barter systems demonstrate different logics of circulation that often privilege relational wealth and inclusive social harmony above individual accumulation. Anthropology research has shown that in most societies, economic decisions are determined by relationships, social conventions, morality, religion, and kinship (aspects that economic models largely disregard).

This way, the anthropological lens democratizes economic thought between abstract theory and human experience. As an answer to economists, it lays stress on the fact that the financial is not the architectural assemblage that abides in and of itself, a mere object of mechanics, but is right into the texture and weft of the culture gods, nature spirits, the economic system' were we to translate that last passage into cultural narratives, we should (trans)formulate just that'. This collective focus enhances our understanding of economic behaviour's range and reach. It provides deep insight into how societies mediate the interdependence of people's material requirements and cultural values.

CAPITALISM: CULTURE AND CONSEQUENCES

Historical Development of Capitalism

Capitalism was a relatively new economic system that restructured people's lives globally a few centuries ago. This original flourishing of capitalist exchange developed through mercantile trade and colonial conquest from the fifteenth century on through European powers' inclusion of regions half a world away into a universal economy. The anthropologist Eric Wolf has brilliantly demonstrated how global power relations reconfigured the continents of the world to produce goods for international markets under the auspices of a system of colonialism (Boswell, 1989). European empires built plantations and mines in the Americas, Africa and Asia to remove commodities like sugar, silver and cotton using forced labour (including enslaved people and indentured servants). These colonial operations fed European markets and generated piles of riches to be invested in the industrial development that defined the close relationship between global colonialism and capitalism.

The late 18th and 19th centuries were a critical moment in the development of capitalism due to the Industrial Revolution. Mechanized factories (first in Britain and North America) massively expanded outputs and demanded concentrations of wage workers, which created an urban industrial working class. In this era, capitalism was characterized by the capitalist class (the private leading class of factory and mill owners) hiring wage-earning workers who sold their labour (Encyclopaedia Britannica, 2025).

SOCIALISM: IDEALS AND REALITIES

Evolution of Socialist Economies

A Schumpeterian proviso that would befit the nature of socialism: not only serve as a reminder of, but also a warning against what the self-interests of states can bring when conflated with the wealth of a "Christian banker living in France, but collecting rents all over the world", perturbed the world order. Socialist ideology as an economic and political proposal: Socialism, as a financial and political proposition, is a 19th-century product that emerged as an answer to industrial capitalism's growing inequalities and exploitative labour conditions. Based on the writings of Karl Marx and Friedrich Engels, socialism advocated the state ownership of the means of production, centralized planning, and the redistribution of resources to obtain social justice. When He was drawing up his conceptions of socialism and communism, which he considered a higher stage of development after socialism, he hoped it to be a stage in the long course of the socialist transition from socialism to communism, a view which became a historical process containing different paths in future, such as by "generalizing" and known as "Marxism-Leninism", democratic socialism in Europe but state-dominated socialism in the Soviet Union and China in the meantime (Carrillo, 2023).

From an anthropological perspective, socialism is an ideology and process lived through history, governance, and culture. In the 20th century, we saw socialist systems being tested out in various parts of the globe -- the USSR, Maoist China, Eastern Europe, Cuba, Vietnam and some pockets of Africa. The government and political parties of these socialist countries or nations generally favoured industrialization and collectivized agriculture and had significant state-directed undertakings in housing, health, education, and other social services (Carrillo, 2023; Petras, 2018). In practice, however, these devices resulted in victories and inconsistencies. Although the regime's broadened access to relatively universal services provided some employment security, it also tended to stifle dissent, impose market restrictions, and distort incentives by overcentralizing planning.

Socialist economies also adapted in varying ways to traditional and local traditions. For example, Tanzania's Ujamaa under Julius Nyerere attempted to blend African communal values and socialism with limited success (Yussuf, 2024). Hence, the trajectory of socialism is not monolithic; it is a range of experiments fitted to political compulsions, cultural values and developmental aims.

Anthropological Critiques of Resource Distribution and Collective Ownership

Anthropologists have also scrutinized how collective ownership and resource distribution principles are embodied in socialist and post-socialist states. When converted into a top-down government, the principle of equality was liable to produce bureaucratic structures that divorced local priorities, leading to alternative hierarchies. Such as Katherine Verdery's (2021) findings in her classic ethnographies of Romania, centralized planning in the socialist system created deficits, produced informal economies, and supported patronage networks rather than removing class inequalities (Dunn, 2024).

From an economic and anthropological perspective, one of the most significant drawbacks of socialist models is their lack of rootedness in local systems of exchange and reciprocity. Central planning, which sought to rationalize economic behaviour, tended to ignore the existence of deeply ingrained cultural practices such as kin-based transfer, exchanges in local subsistence markets, or moral economies of reciprocity. James C. Scott (1998), in a classic work on state plans, contended that collectivization schemes imposed by state actors failed to consider the "local knowledge" and environmental knowledge of peasants, leading to resistance, inefficiency, and unintended consequences.

Moreover, collective ownership in many socialist situations worldwide did not always mean democratic control. Instead, the state became the de facto owner, not allowing people meaningful participation in decision-making. Something similar can be said of the Chinese People's Communes or Soviet collective farms: As it turned out, workers and peasants enjoyed little autonomy, even under the cover of worker empowerment. Anthropologists noted that such systems were frequently the cause of moral disenchantment as the gap between socialist dreams and bureaucratic forms became apparent.

However, anthropological research also points to everyday resilience and adaptation. People generated informal economies, engaged in mutual aid and worked their way around systems of the state with ingenuity. Even in many post-socialist settings, people have persisted in some of these survival strategies despite transitioning into market economies, demonstrating that the material culture of socialism often penetrated to a deep level.

Case Studies of Socialist Models

1. Cuba

Cuba is one of the last remaining socialist economies and is frequently cited for its health and welfare orientation despite a deepening economic crisis. Anthropologists observe that Cuba's healthcare and education systems reflect fundamental socialist equity values. At the same time, its dual economy of state and informal sectors highlights how citizens negotiate creatively with state power and scarcity. Tourism and remittances, for example, have generated disparities, undermining the ideological focus on equality (Blue, 2007).

2. The Soviet Union and Post-Soviet Russia

In the Soviet Union, planned economies led to growth in industry and science while suppressing consumer welfare and civic freedom. Anthropological work in post-Soviet Russia demonstrates how the collapse of socialism left people profoundly disoriented. People had to face the loss of security and community following the shock transition to capitalism. However, many carried sentiments of nostalgia for the values of socialism—solidarity and state support (Rivkin-Fish, 2005; Ssorin-Chaikov, 2003).

3. China

This has created a special Chinese model, “socialism with Chinese characteristics.” Following the economic reforms of the late 1970s, the country brought market and financial reform, but the state remains dominant and authoritative. In work on rural de-collectivization and urban economic zones, anthropologists have examined how rural de-collectivization and urban economic zones radically altered people's lives, creating new entrepreneurial opportunities and deepening inequalities (Yan, 2003).

The hybrid forms of state ideology and market behaviour constitute an evolving model.

4. Tanzania – Ujamaa

So-called African socialism, with Julius Nyerere opposed to socialist ideology, was to serve traditional communalism better. More problematic, however, was the extent to which adopting collective villages and implementing egalitarian development in towns and parastatals was resistible and logistically treacherous. Anthropologists have seen that the forced villagization that displaced established kin networks and patterns of agriculture in the Horn of Africa has led to inefficiency and resentment (Hydén, 1980). However, the rhetoric of collective identity and rural honour still has lingering effects in Tanzanian political culture.

COMMUNISM: THEORY AND PRACTICE

Marxist Foundations and Anthropological Views

The idea of communism, as it is in the abstract, is derived from classical Marxist theory. It is a stateless, classless society in which the means of production are owned in common. Communism, as Karl Marx and Friedrich Engels outlined, is the conceptual endpoint of historical materialism—the final stage of social development after capitalism has given way to socialism (Marx & Engels, 1848/1978). However, the revolutionary goal was communism, where there would be no private property for anyone to contemplate, and no exploitation of labour and production would be organized according to human needs rather than profit. Marx was not solely an economist in this sense but a deeply social thinker whose goal was the end of alienation and the birth of genuinely free and equal human relations.

For anthropologists, the utopian idea of communism and its lived instantiation has long been a focus of fascination. From its inception, anthropology's interest in egalitarian states, forager societies included, emphasized that the commodity mode of production had a historical precedent (Woodburn, 1982). Such observations were widely seen as expressions of what has been called "primitive communism," an idea that the founders of socialism were trying to communicate in their descriptions of pre-class societies. This contrast challenged capitalist suppositions of competition and accumulation as natural to the human condition.

However, modern anthropologists have gone beyond ideal types to consider how communist ideology in practice intersects with culture, power, and identity in different settings. Like shorter, Libertarian Communism, as it was modelled in various 20th-century states, existed in forms that differed drastically from Marx's theoretical ideal, such as the Soviet Union, Maoist China and Cambodia under the Khmer Rouge. Anthropologists research the evolution of these systems, the contradictions they involved, and how people lived within them.

Challenges in Implementing Communism

Communism, as it gets past the ideology, has many targets to aim for in its ideological purity notwithstanding. The idea was to produce a classless society. Still, the centralized economic planning and the top-down politics of the typical communist state frequently resulted in the rise of stultifying bureaucracies, repression of dissent, and violations of human rights on a vast scale.

From an anthropological point of view, the key problem is the assumption of applying a universal ideological model to different or changing cultural contexts. In Russia and China, local traditions, rites and kinship relations were repeatedly felt to impede socialist progress and were smashed by force. This top-down process produced cultural disjuncture and, indeed, resistance in some instances (Verdery, 1996; Kipnis, 2008). For example, collectivization in Maoist China, particularly during the Great Leap Forward, destroyed village life and led to one of the deadliest famines in human history.

Another difficulty was the dichotomy between the stated equality and the actual inequality. Privilege for party elites, often labelled with ideological rectitude or technical expertise, came to undermine the promise of classlessness. Anthropologists wrote about the growth of "red bourgeoisie" classes in Eastern Europe and China that, in nominally equal systems, obtained better housing, goods, and education (Humphrey, 1983).

Moreover, in many cases in communist societies, one had to do double duty as a worker and ideological subject. Loyalty to the Party and participation in rituals like public self-criticism or collective labour were frequently mandated as indicators of moral citizenship. Anthropologists, such as Alexei Yurchak (2006), have demonstrated that, over time, they learnt to navigate these demands through what Yurchak termed 'hyper normalization'—performing loyalty in public while privately carving out substantial autonomy. This disconnection between appearance and conviction was a survival tactic in any authoritarian state.

Last but not least, the suppression of markets and coerced collectivism also generated shortages, as well as informal (class) markets (at times also 'āli-dārī/bazaarīs and black markets). Anthropologists looking at life in the USSR and post-Soviet countries observed how people depended on using informal networks, in the form of, among other things, blat (connections, favours), to get basic goods and navigate the system (Ledeneva, 1998). They showed the constraints of ideological control and the ongoing power of social ties, even in controlled economies.

Anthropological Case Studies in Communist Societies

1. Soviet Union and Post-Soviet Transitions

Caroline Humphrey in Buryatia and elsewhere in the Soviet Union found that collectivized farms were bureaucratic and community organizations alike. Workers preserved cultural practices and networks of relatives in even the most regimented state planning and, in post-Soviet transformations, how persons remodelled these structures in the face of market economies (Humphrey, 1991). She and others chronicled communism's double-edged nature that inspired a feeling of collective security and social support yet also bred resentments at inefficiency and coercion.

2. China under Mao and Beyond

In China, the anthropologist Yunxiang Yan wrote about the changing landscape of rural family life under communist rule and after economic reforms. The People's Communes, in the Maoist era, were intended to obliterate such traditional family organizations and collective control of land and labour. Yan (2003) nonetheless discovered that family relationships left their imprint by other means, and the post-1978 reforms brought back various forms of private farming and entrepreneurism. These changes showed how entrenched social norms can persist, even after revolutionary ideological upheaval.

3. Cambodia under the Khmer Rouge

The most egregious example of communist practice coming from a government was in Cambodia under Pol Pot. The Khmer Rouge was looking to create a pure and agrarian communist society, eliminating money, markets, religion and urban life. Anthropologists like Alexander Hinton (2005) have analyzed the genocidal aftermath of this effort, noting how ideological purity turned itself into state terror. The specific Cambodian catastrophe is a vivid example of the perils of totalitarian communism and the deadly consequences of suppressing cultural pluralism and individual autonomy.

4. Cuba's Revolutionary Society

It is more complex and less violent, but Cuba's communism, mediated through Soviet models but informed by local and anti-colonial realities, provides one example. Economic poverty and political censorship aside, Cuba had the highest literacy rates, longest life expectancy, and best public healthcare worldwide. Anthropologists like Fernandes (2006) studied how the Cuban youth and artists appropriated the revolutionary ideology at the same time that they subverted it with music and culture. This demonstrates that resistance, negotiation and creativity can occur even within heavily regulated systems.

Communism remains a potent frame through which to view human dreams of equality, justice, and life together. Anthropologists enrich this understanding by connecting ideological arguments with the lived experiences of people living in communist systems. They demonstrate how government structures are always mediated by local culture, history, and agency. Real-world applications of Marxist ideology still inspire many movements for social reform. Still, anthropological case studies remind us that economic systems can never be implemented equally across the board without consideration of cultural richness and the diversity of human life. With it, anthropology records not only the wishes of communist societies but also their contradictions, providing a finely drawn picture of what life together might require and the struggles it might entail.

SUMMARY COMPARISON OF ECONOMIC SYSTEMS

To address the structural and narrative imbalances across sections, the following vignettes illustrate how individuals live within these systems. These snapshots humanize abstract models and ground them in real, everyday life.

Table 1. Summary comparison of economic sytems

Aspect	Capitalism	Socialism	Communism
Core Values	Individualism, competition, profit	Equality, public welfare, state-led planning	Classlessness, collective ownership
Ownership	Private	Public or cooperative	Collective (ideally stateless)
Labor Structure	Wage labour, gig economy, precarious	State or cooperative labour, job security	Compulsory/assigned labor, ideological alignment
Role of State	Minimal to regulatory (varies by country)	Centralized control over production and redistribution	Total state control; suppression of markets
Economic Equality	High inequality; meritocratic justification	Moderate ideological equality with bureaucratic elite formation	Theoretical equality: elite privilege often develops

continued on following page

Table 1. Continued

Aspect	Capitalism	Socialism	Communism
Cultural Logics	Entrepreneurial success, individual agency	Collective welfare, moral work ethic	Moral citizenship, ideological loyalty
Contradictions	Consumerism vs sustainability; freedom vs inequality	Equality vs bureaucracy; planning vs innovation	Classlessness vs authoritarianism; dissent vs loyalty

Capitalism Vignette

Palm oil plantation workers say their daily routine is "selling body time" in the Indonesian countryside. Li (2014) provides an illustrative case of how capitalist systems intersect with patriarchal obligations and utilize informal mechanisms of resilience to exploit burgeoning proletariats when she describes how families survive through tenuous, low-wage means of support through a combination of kin-based support systems and menial, hazardous wages from maintaining jobs that are inconsistent and pay less than living wages.

Socialism Vignette

For Cuban youth, especially youth in Havana, hip-hop is an outlet of creativity and also an instrument of political dissent. As Fernandes (2006) notes, these artists make use of socialist ideals of health care and education while at the same time opposing censorship by the state, creating what she terms "critical support" of the revolution.

Communism Vignette

Post-Soviet collectivism may now be a dim memory in places such as Buryatia, Russia, but one finds former collective farm workers still maintaining their seasonal rituals around harvest. These practices maintain a sense of belonging to a community and are a means of resisting the atomizing effects of capitalist reform (Humphrey, 1991).

COMPARATIVE ANALYSIS OF ECONOMIC SYSTEMS

Cultural Impacts of Capitalism, Socialism, and Communism

Economic systems are not merely the structures through which resources are allocated but also enfolded in and informing culture. However, anthropologists depict capitalism, socialism, and communism not merely as economies or modes of production; they treat them, more or less explicitly, as cultural hybrids with distinctive values, symbols, moralities and social consequences.

Inspired by market competition, individualism and consumerism, the culture of entrepreneurship, material aspiration, and incessant innovation has flourished under capitalism. It tends to reduce human relationships to the transactional, worrying about efficiency and calculability. Capitalist societies measure success by accumulating wealth and encouraging people to view themselves as economic subjects who control their fates. This mentality can be a crucible for creativity and freedom, but it also fuels estrangement, inequality, and precarity, particularly among the losers in the race. Capitalism has a cultural impact of furthering global consumerism, resulting in the erosion of local traditions that become homogenized through the production and branding of products (Carrier, 2005; Wilk, 2001).

Socialism, which privileges equality, public welfare, and collective control, strives to produce a culture of solidarity and shared responsibility. In most socialist societies, citizens are taught to think about the collective good rather than personal profit. Studies in anthropology, particularly those about the former Soviet Union, Cuba, and Eastern Europe, have examined how socialist values shaped individuals' relationships to work, family, and the state (Verdery, 1996; Rivkin-Fish, 2005). Although socialism frequently championed education, health and employment as universal rights, it also generated bureaucratic cultures and moral compromises when the aspirations did not square with lived experience. Opening up, but even after its collapse, many societies still have cultural nostalgia for the apparent security and dignity of socialist systems.

Communism, that even more monstrous exacerbation of those socialist ideals, dreamed of reviving humanity itself by eliminating private property and class divisions. Mostly in theory, communist experiments (in Maoist China or Cambodia under the Khmer Rouge) attempted to form new cultural norms through mass mobilization, ideological education and social engineering. However, the cultural consequences of those systems were severe, frequently reducing even traditional kinship roles, religious observances, and community governance to a blank slate. Anthropologists who have studied these societies observed the backlash against these transformations and the emergence of new solidarities produced through shared suffering and surveillance (Yurchak, 2006; Hinton, 2005).

All three systems have varying interpretations and implementations of cultural values such as reciprocity, authority, freedom, and morality. Capitalism, we can say, worships the liberty of the individual but commodifies human relationships; socialism celebrates equality but strangles any challenge to it; communism dreams of classlessness but demands near-total control. Economic anthropology demonstrates, therefore, that we cannot fully understand the cultural effects of such systems without taking some account of local histories, values, and social relations.

Hybrid Models and Modern Innovations

Few countries today exist as a "pure" economic system. Instead, we have hybrids that mix capitalism, socialism, and, in some cases, communism with indigenous economic practices and recent innovations to meet the challenges of the modern world.

Some Nordic countries, including Sweden, Norway, and Denmark, embody an amalgamation of capitalist markets and socialist values, which are known in some circles as social democracies. However, they also compete successfully in the private sector, complemented by comprehensive welfare systems, public health systems, and public education. This mix, culturally, leads to both personal freedom and social coherence, achieving high scores on global well-being metrics for these countries.

China is a peculiar hybrid, typically called "socialism with Chinese characteristics." Even as it clung to one-party rule and state ownership of core industries, China pursued market mechanisms, foreign investment and private enterprise. Anthropologists who write about China observe that this hybrid system results in rapid economic reforms, shifting consumption patterns, the dynamism of family, and urbanization with values of hierarchy and collectivism inspired by Confucianism (Yan, 2009).

India offers another scenario where a liberalized capitalist economy operates alongside state subsidies, non-standard labour markets and prevalent caste and kinship-based economic transactions. The same has been true in Latin America, where governments such as those in Bolivia or Venezuela have sought to forge "21st-century socialism", fusing resource nationalism with indigenous political traditions and anti-colonial rhetoric, with mixed success.

The informal economy, widespread in developing and developed countries, is also hybridized. Street vendors, ride-share drivers, home-based workers and many others exist outside of state regulatory frameworks. Still, they are deeply woven into the local cultural infrastructures of trust and reciprocity. Anthropologists demonstrate that these informal systems are not indicators of underdevelopment but responses, albeit often constituting second-best solutions, to the exclusion or the inefficiency of formal economic arrangements (Hart, 1973; De Soto, 2000).

Further, technological change and globalization are transforming economic arrangements in real time. The ascendancy of the platform economy, the proliferation of cryptocurrencies, experiments with universal basic income, and the newfound popularity of cooperatives all offer different perspectives on what the future of economic organization could and perhaps should look like, free of the old silos. For example, digital cooperatives — where users own and manage platforms collectively — try to marry capitalist tools to socialist governance models. Environmental concerns also gave rise to models like degrowth or solidarity economies, in which communities seek to live sustainably and equitably outside the logic of endless growth.

Hybrids are often not planned but are a matter of pragmatics as local cultures evolve in the face of global flows. It is against such divides between market and non-market societies that economic anthropology prompts us to look elsewhere and consider the plurality of financial forms and ways communities navigate between justice, growth, autonomy and sustainability.

Indigenous Economic Models and Environmental Anthropology

While global systems dominate the discourse, local and indigenous economies offer significant alternatives. For instance, in the Andean highlands, reciprocal labour exchange systems like 'ayni' illustrate moral economies where the logic of reciprocity outweighs market transactions (Escobar, 2018). Ayni (spelt also ayni, ayniy) is one of the foundational principles of reciprocity and mutual assistance practised by Indigenous Andean communities, especially among the Quechua and Aymara people of Peru, Bolivia, and Ecuador. Ayni is a system of reciprocal labour exchange grounded in the idea of mutual support and social unity. That means: "Today you, tomorrow me." If a farmer assists a neighbouring farmer in planting crops, the latter reciprocates by helping him to harvest later. Families take turns building houses or helping to irrigate land, with an expectation that they will receive similar help when needed. There's no money involved; the "currency" is trust, obligation, and community honour.

Among the Paniya tribe of Kerala, informal seed exchange networks operate on trust and community obligation rather than on price signals. Informal seed exchange networks among the Paniya tribe of Kerala point to a rich system of social reciprocity and ecological knowledge. Instead of buying seeds from the market, Paniya families depend on intra-community bartering, gifting and seasonal sharing of traditional crop varieties like Njavara rice, horse gram and millets. Such practices are economic but also ritualistic and relational, attaching themselves to festivals, planting rituals, and kinship obligations. Seeds are inherited memory, part of the ancestral cultural legacy —a metaphor that symbolizes food sovereignty and resistance against commercial agriculture's universalizing and homogenizing pressure. This system's logic is now congruent with the concept of a moral economy, in which social and ecological values trump market incentives.

Among the Koch Rajbongshi tribe of Assam and North Bengal, traditional agrarian practices are rooted in cooperative work systems prioritizing community well-being over individual profit. These practices echo principles of mutual aid and time-bound reciprocity. Instead of industrial agriculture, families practice polyculture of an assortment of native crops—(local varieties of rice), native vegetables, and medicinal plants—propagated based on agricultural calendars that are lunar and not written, as is familiar with ecological oral knowledge (also passed down through generations). Village elders (*gaonbura*) make collective environmental decisions on when to clear fields, conserve groves or fish in community ponds, representing a cosmology whereby sacred personified land is to be contemplated. It resists monoculture-based capitalism and sustains a moral ecology that promotes a balance with nature, not commodification. These are examples of what environmental anthropologists describe as cosmopolitical economies, where survival strategies are integrated into ritual and relation ethics.

Environmental anthropology is also a challenge to the orthodoxy of the modern economy. It highlights the importance of traditional ecological knowledge (TEK), which supports sustainable economies. The environment in Amazonian communities is not comparable to a resource but a kin entity that shapes the economy through the ideal of long-term cohabitation rather than short-term exploitation (Escobar, 2018).

These perspectives deepen our understanding of resistance and sustainability by showing how cultural values align with environmental stewardship.

ANTHROPOLOGICAL INSIGHTS INTO MODERN ECONOMIC CHALLENGES

Inequality and Labour Under Different Systems

Throughout our common experience of the contemporary world, there remains an old issue about which we are persistently haunted—the issue of economic inequality, covering the distribution of income and resources, labour rights, and opportunities for social ascent. Those anthropologists concerned with capitalism, socialism, and communism have repeatedly demonstrated the different and contradictory ways each of these societies confronts inequality.

In capitalist societies, such injustice is frequently rationalized based on market logic — those who have contributed or innovated more deserve more. However, ethnographic work repeatedly demonstrates how structural obstacles such as race, class, gender, and colonial history led to unequal access to education, credit and employment (Bear et al., 2015). The proliferation of precarious work in the age of neoliberal capitalism—gig economy work, fixed-term positions, informal employment—has eroded job security and compensation, placing new distinctions within labour markets (Standing, 2011). Anthropologists, such as Tsing (2015), have sought to understand how the value produced by global supply chains entails exploitative labour conditions, if not hostile to workers' well-being.

In socialist economies, the official aspiration may have been to eradicate class divisions. Still, anthropological investigations discovered other forms of stratification between party elites and ordinary workers, say, or between urban and rural populations. In the Soviet Union and Eastern Europe, differential access to housing, consumer goods, and rights was reminiscent of the class distinctions of capitalist societies, only overlaid by the rhetoric of equality (Verdery, 1996). Similarly, as many societies in the degraded socialist bloc have also attempted to turn themselves into market economies, they have, in many cases, succeeded mainly in creating new levels of oligarchic wealth and social division.

Communist governments, especially the authoritarian ones, sought extreme levelling by abolishing private property and standardizing labour specializations. However, reducing the independence of people, coercive collectivization, and the absence of incentives resulted in resistance, waste and informal hierarchies. Anthropologists researching such systems have stressed that "the mere imposition of a solution from above down", in which the community was not involved, means that "injustice is perpetuated and new contradictions and exclusions are produced".

In the end, anthropologists insist that inequality is not just about salaries and net worth; it is a social and moral condition, an affliction that is intrinsic to the human experience and must be confronted and vanquished for our collective welfare. By recounting their lived experiences, they reveal how formal equality can sit alongside informal inequality and what real people do to challenge, adapt, or internalize it.

The Role of Technology and Digital Economies

Technology — and digital technology in particular — has become a transformative force in economic life, changing the way goods are produced, consumed and traded. Anthropologists work with technology as more than just a tool but also as a cultural artefact that rearranges labour, value systems, and modes of human interaction.

Digital platforms (e.g., Uber, Amazon, Fiverr) have given rise to new modes of work and entrepreneurship. However, such a system often masks exploitation as flexibility. Participants in the platform economy usually work without traditional social safety nets, prompting scholars to describe it as "algorithmic precarity" (Grey & Suri, 2019). Anthropological perspectives help us understand how digital workers — from content moderators in the Philippines to AI trainers in Kenya — are deeply implicated in global value chains, even as they remain hidden from the users and corporations they help.

Digital economies also prompt concerns about surveillance, the ownership of data and the monetization of attention. Social media has subscription-based users actively producing, rather than passively consuming, data, erasing the distinctions between play and work. In some communities, digital connection has facilitated informal business, education and activism; in others, it has amplified dependence and domination by powerful tech actors. For example, mobile money services such as M-Pesa in Kenya have transformed local economies but have also introduced new modalities of financial surveillance and inequality.

Moreover, there are still digital divides between rural and urban people, men and women, and the Global North and South. Anthropologists remind us that access to technology is unequal and linked to power, infrastructure, and cultural norms. In response, alternative models such as platform cooperatives and decentralized digital commons are beginning to appear, providing windows on what technology might look like to underwrite better, just economic relations.

Prospects for Sustainable Economic Futures

Against climate change, resource shortage, and possible ecological breakdown, the fault lines in the current regime of economics are visible. Sustainability has been critiqued through anthropological scholarship, for it refocuses attention on modes of knowing -indigenous knowledge systems, moral economies, and alternative livelihoods based on balance, reciprocation, and resilience.

Moreover, even those traditional people routinely run over by capitalist development have managed to sustain themselves from generation to generation over time and have done so in a way that is in balance with the environments from which they derive their living, based on spiritual, community or inter-generational values. On the one side, anthropologists have demonstrated that these worldviews challenge the forms of capitalist extractives and the exponentially growing reasoning of modern economies (Escobar, 2018). The concept of Buen Vivir ('living well') in Andean and Amazonian societies, for example, is premised on equilibrium with nature and the community, not on accumulation.

Urban anthropology has also considered how grassroots mobilizations worldwide, including the eco-village and degrowth movements, advocate post-capitalist futures. These are better things like coop housing, circular economies, slow food movements, and local currency to aid in transitioning away from a reliance on global supply chains and start building regional resilience. All of this is small in scale, yet it shows how economic imagination and cultural practice are involved in what it means to envisage something that is not their exploitative system.

In institutions, the recognition of the significance of integrating indicators of society and the environment into economic planning is growing. Thinking like the "Doughnut Economy" (Raworth, 2017) promotes the idea of an economy that operates within ecological limits but also ensures some fundamental human rights. Anthropologists can contribute significantly to examining how these frameworks are adopted, contested, or reconfigured in specific cultural contexts.

Anthropology insists that we think of ecology because we need to conceive sustainability not as an ecological question alone but as a complete reconfiguration of value, work, and well-being. By making prominent human narratives, local knowledge and cultural pluralism, anthropological insights contribute to mapping paths to more sustainable and equitable economic futures.

RECOMMENDATIONS AND SOLUTIONS

Key to the task of responding to the complex and dynamic challenges of contemporary economic systems is that anthropological understandings have a human and culturally informed basis for policy innovation. The most urgent are the publicly embedded economic culture policies. Economic prescriptions disregarding local context, tradition and social relations do not deliver or deliver only in the short term. Anthropological research universally indicates that kinship relations, religious beliefs, customary laws, and moral codes inform economic transactions. Accordingly, those reforms should be decentralized and based on locally rooted knowledge systems, while community engagement should take precedence. It does so by being more policy-relevant, practical, respectful and driven by the affected communities.

This was closely associated with the need to maintain hybrid and plural economies. Many of the more thriving economies of today are hybrids, combining market freedoms with social protections of varying forms, ranging from cooperatively owned enterprises and mutual aid networks to informal markets.

Models that combine —cultural values and realistic experience — such hybrid models are more inclusive, resilient and adaptable to address in-equality, unemployment and marginalization. For example, informal economies in much of the Global South are not archaic. Instead, they are tactical practices and responses to being pushed outside formal economies. We must help understand and validate practices that aid equitable and place-based development.

Another burning problem is the protection of labour in the digital economy. The emergence of gig work, algorithmic management and globalized freelancing have introduced new precarity. On the contrary, income is unpredictable, there are no benefits, and a performance measurement is based on surveillance. This has especially brutal limits in the Global South, where many content moderators, microtaskers, and invisible workers are left out in the cold.

Simultaneously, there is an even higher demand for solid constructions that are technically sound and culturally grounded. For decades, anthropologists have observed how Native and local people oversee natural resources by engaging in reciprocal relations, seasonal rhythms and stewardship considered spiritual. These systems are often more efficient at encouraging sustainable use than market-based conservation. Mainstreaming such ecological ethics into policy measures — through methods like community forest management, culturally sensitive climate action and recognition of land rights — can enhance global environmental governance in ways that do not undermine cultural sovereignty.

When economic anthropology becomes a component of school curricula and general public discourse, we give citizens the tools to question prevailing economic ideologies and stories. It helps communities feel they can ask questions about inequitable systems and find other systems to believe in and struggle with over time. Methods combining participation and education, such as storytelling, local industrial case studies, and dialogue between a community and a project developer/representative, can help demystify economic concepts and enable grassroots activism. In other words, what anthropological approaches encourage us to appreciate is a vision of economies not simply as markets or numbers but as lived social worlds formed by history, culture and power. We owe ourselves to enshrine these policy and practice values to construct more equitable, resilient and human-centred economies.

FUTURE RESEARCH DIRECTIONS

As the world changes more quickly and dynamically than ever, economic anthropology offers dynamic interventions that respond to the world's truths as they are remade and reinvented for the future. The COVID-19 crisis has highlighted the vulnerability of global and local economies. Future research should prioritize understanding the post-pandemic economic realities, including how the crisis redefined labour markets, framed informal economies, and modified household survival strategies across diverse cultural settings. Ethnography offers an essential window into how communities coped with disrupted supply chains, unemployment, and public health care, often through mutual aid, kin networks, and informal markets. Understanding these adaptations reveals the resilience and the policies that could effectively support those marginalized during a disaster.

Work cultures and AI Automation: The effects of artificial intelligence (AI) and automation on labour cultures will be a focal point for research. With human jobs more and more supplanted by machines in both physical and intellectual realms, it is worth examining what this does to our hearts and minds. Anthropologists of the economy are well-positioned to interrogate how the logic of algorithmic management and AI technologies reframe efforts to conceptualize the forms of value, activity, identity, and will that compose the human. As an illustration, gig work and automation in work performance can encroach upon autonomy and generate experiences of alienation and precariousness. The design of labour policies to ensure human dignity in technology by accommodation, dissent or autonomy is best left to how societies interpret and respond to such changes.

As such, the issue of climate-induced economic migration is a critical frontier of research. Climate change is already forcing millions of others from their homes due to rising sea levels, drought, floods, and desertification. What is needed in future anthropological research is studies that look at how these coercive migrations transform economic systems, kinship structures, and survival strategies. Such studies could usefully record not only the travails of climate migrants but also the cultural strategies they employ in remaking their livelihoods and communities. In addition, anthropologists can help formulate policies related to resettlement and adaptation that are appropriate and sustainable to the context and not technocratically delivered responses.

New directions in anthropological study are opened with cryptocurrency and decentralized economies. Blockchain technologies promise to disintermediate finance and transfer and increase transparency. That sets up a kind of inequality between the two, a speculation, a game of exclusion of a different sort but just as insidiously as revenge porn. It is less the technicalities that matter but rather how communities use cryptocurrencies: Are they an instrument of empowerment, a risk instrument, or an instrument of evasion, and which role plays the perspective of economic anthropologists? Concerning things like digital value, trust in algorithmic systems, or the socio-political terrain over which highway infrastructure tends to go, Glimpses and even vast thematic implications of these incipient economic behaviours can be found at ground level, especially in high crypto penetration areas such as Africa, Latin America and Southeast Asia.

Finally, future research should take indigenous and decolonial economies more seriously. These models challenge capitalist reasons, and those working with him have all been grounded in alternative reciprocal, common landholding and ecologically sustainable practices. We need economic anthropologists to look more deeply into resistance mechanisms against extractive development from indigenous peoples, such as the hybridization or entanglement of capitalist economic formations or the assertion of economic sovereignty. This would involve investigating sustainable economic systems based on gift economy, traditional ecological knowledge and spiritual economies informed by inherent interdependence. Decolonial frames also empower anthropologists to challenge the epistemological foundations of conventional economic thinking and offer more plural interpretations of value, wealth and well-being.

The future of economic anthropology may continue this responsiveness to global iterations of change while showing us the stories of the edge-dwellers amongst us. In offering extended longitudinal ethnography and cultural analysis, anthropologists have a role in designing new economic futures that are more just, sustainable and inclusive by better grasping the human mechanisms of economic change.

DISCUSSION

This chapter shows that capitalism, socialism, and communism are not static and monolithic systems but historically and ideologically influenced cultural constructs that are highly flexible and subject to local interpretation. In contrast, the importance of economic anthropology is a realm in which we can examine how humans live, resist and transform these systems daily.

Growing digital economies, an ongoing ecological crisis, and bottom-up innovations indicate a necessity to reconceptualize economic life beyond the traditional polarisations. Anthropological methods that are deep and sensitive to culture can provide crucial diagnostic tools for understanding systemic failures while helping to co-create solutions in partnership with communities. The discipline invites scholars and practitioners to listen attentively, think relationally and keep human dignity at the forefront of economic conversations.

For as economies are perceived not simply as mechanisms of production and exchange but as spaces of meaning, identity and morality, economic anthropology offers more than a mere empirical critique of existing economic practice by bringing a major, if 'critical', humanist dimension into global debates; at a time of distress and transformation, simply put, it seems we need it.

CONCLUSION

In this essay, we have traced the cultural basis, structural conditions, and everyday life of capitalism, socialism, and communism from an economic anthropological standpoint. These systems are not dogmas, immutable, or just financial; they are part and parcel of human histories, periods of ideology and individual practices. Given their cultural variation, anthropologists have demonstrated how economic systems construct social ties, values and moralities and how people, in turn, rework, oppose and transform these in their own enumerative and narrative styles.

Capitalism itself gives birth to innovation, competition, and market growth, but at the same time, it yields inequality, alienation or even precarious labour. The history of socialism, in its pursuit of equality and the common good, was one of centralized control and hidden hierarchies as much as it was of egalitarian ideals. Communism, inspired by the vision of a society without classes, often went wrong and produced repression and moral despair despite its goals oriented to social justice.

The comparative analysis shows that no system works in isolation, and hierarchical mixes and local particularities emerge in the context of history, politics, and culture. Modern-day crafts — be it digital cooperatives or solidarity economies — remind us that we are still obsessed with fashioning production systems that are efficient, equitable, sustainable, and culturally resonant.

The wealth of anthropological knowledge of the cultural human response, both menacing and hopeful, has never been more needed than during such a time of deep human trial as we are now undergoing, from climate change to disruptive technology to inequality. They enable us to challenge assumptions, understand economic behaviour in situ, and envision futures that fully reflect the breadth of human experience and ethical commitment. Drawing economic systems from real people's narratives, pains and hopes, economic anthropology helps us realize that however we choose to move forward, it cannot be merely about numbers or models; it has to be about culture, the community and compassion.

REFERENCES

Anthroholic. (2023). *Formalist and substantivist debate in economic anthropology. Anthroholic*. https://anthroholic.com/formalist-and-substantivist-debate

Bear, L., Ho, K., Tsing, A., & Yanagisako, S. (2015, March 30). *Gens: A feminist manifesto for the study of capitalism*. Society for Cultural Anthropology. https://culanth.org/fieldsights/gens-a-feminist-manifesto-for-the-study-of-capitalism

Blue, S. A. (2007). The Erosion of Cuban Health Care. *Latin American Research Review*, *42*(1), 161–173. DOI: 10.1353/lar.2007.0011

Boswell, T. (1989). Colonial Empires and the Capitalist World-Economy: A Time Series Analysis of Colonisation, 1640-1960. *American Sociological Review*, *54*(2), 180. DOI: 10.2307/2095789

Carrier, J. G. (Ed.). (2005). *A handbook of economic anthropology*. Edward Elgar Publishing., DOI: 10.4337/9781845423469

Carrillo, F. (2023). From Marx to Now: Exploring collective ownership, classlessness, and the evolving state. *Social Science Chronicle*, *2*(1). Advance online publication. DOI: 10.56106/ssc.2023.011

Das, N. (2025). *Economic systems: Capitalism, socialism, Communism*. Ilearnlot. https://www.ilearnlot.com/economic-system-capitalism-socialism-and-communism/59995/

De Soto, H. (2000). *The mystery of capital: Why capitalism triumphs in the West and fails everywhere else*. Basic Books. https://www.hachettebookgroup.com/titles/hernando-de-soto/the-mystery-of-capital/9780465016150/

Dunn, E. C. (2024). Time and space in the work of Katherine Verdery. *Journal of Ethnographic Theory*, *14*(2), 490–493. DOI: 10.1086/731280

Encyclopaedia Britannica. (2025). *Industrial Revolution: Definition, history, dates, summary, & facts*. https://www.britannica.com/event/Industrial-Revolution

Escobar, A. (2018). *Designs for the Pluriverse: Radical Interdependence, Autonomy, and the Making of Worlds*. Duke University Press. https://www.dukeupress.edu/designs-for-the-pluriverse

Fernandes, S. (2006). *Cuba represents! Cuban arts, state power, and the making of new revolutionary cultures*. Duke University Press., DOI: 10.1215/9780822388227

Gauliver, C. (2023). Economic anthropology: From cultural norms to social relations and their complexities. *Anthropology; a Guide to First Degree Courses in UK Universities, 11*(3), 1000317. https://www.longdom.org/open-access-pdfs/economic-anthropology-from-cultural-norms-to-social-relations-and-their-complexities.pdf

Grey, M. L., & Suri, S. (2019). *Ghost Work: How to Stop Silicon Valley from Building a New Global Underclass*. Houghton Mifflin Harcourt. https://www.harpercollins.com/products/ghost-work-mary-l-graysiddharth-suri

Hart, K. (1973). Informal income opportunities and urban employment in Ghana. *The Journal of Modern African Studies, 11*(1), 61–89. DOI: 10.1017/S0022278X00008089

Hinton, A. L. (2005). *Why did they kill? Cambodia in the shadow of genocide*. University of California Press., DOI: 10.1525/9780520937949

Humphrey, C. (1983). *Karl Marx's collective: Economy, society and religion in a Siberian collective farm*. Cambridge University Press., https://www.amazon.com/Karl-Marx-Collective-Cambridge-Anthropology/dp/052127401X

Humphrey, C. (1991). *The unmaking of Soviet life: Everyday economies after socialism*. Cornell University Press. https://lccn.loc.gov/91118707

Hydén, G. (1980). Beyond Ujamaa in Tanzania: Underdevelopment and an uncaptured peasantry. University of California Press.https://books.google.co.in/books/about/Beyond_Ujamaa_in_Tanzania.html?id=VGkqAAAAYAAJ&redir_esc=y

Kipnis, A. B. (2008). Audit cultures: Neoliberal governmentality, socialist legacy, or technologies of governing? *American Ethnologist, 35*(2), 275–289. DOI: 10.1111/j.1548-1425.2008.00034.x

Ledeneva, A. V. (1998). *Russia's economy of favours: Blat, networking and informal exchange*. Cambridge University Press., https://www.cambridge.org/9780521621748

Li, T. M. (2014). *Land's end: Capitalist relations on an indigenous frontier*. Duke University Press. https://www.dukeupress.edu/lands-end

Petras, J. F. (2018). Twentieth-Century socialist revolutions and their class components: Russia, China, Cuba, and Vietnam. In *Springer eBooks* (pp. 85–113). https://doi.org/DOI: 10.1007/978-3-319-92354-3_5

Polanyi, K. (1957). *The great transformation: The political and economic origins of our time* (2nd ed.). Beacon Press., https://inctpped.ie.ufrj.br/spiderweb/pdf_4/Great_Transformation.pdf

Raworth, K. (2017). *Doughnut economics: Seven ways to think like a 21st-century economist*. Chelsea Green Publishing. https://www.kateraworth.com/doughnut/

Rivkin-Fish, M. (2005). *Women's health in post-Soviet Russia: The politics of intervention*. Indiana University Press., https://iupress.org/9780253217677/womens-health-in-post-soviet-russia/

Rivkin-Fish, M. (2005). *Women's health in post-Soviet Russia: The politics of intervention*. Indiana University Press., https://iupress.org/9780253217677/womens-health-in-post-soviet-russia/

Scott, J. C. (1998). *Seeing like a state: How certain schemes to improve the human condition have failed*. Yale University Press. https://archive.org/details/seeinglikestate00jame

Ssorin-Chaikov, N. V. (2003). *The social life of the state in subarctic Siberia*. Stanford University Press., https://www.sup.org/books/asian-studies/social-life-state-subarctic-siberia

Standing, G. (2011). *The precariat: The new dangerous class*. Bloomsbury Academic. https://www.bloomsbury.com/uk/precariat-9781849663512/

Talan, G. (2020). A holistic business model based on South Asian philosophies. In *Contemporary issues in South Asia* (pp. 33–46). Nova Science Publishers, Inc.

Trüeb, R. M., Gadzhigoroeva, A., Kopera, D., Luu, N. C., & Dmitriev, A. (2023). The Problem with Capitalism in the Trichological Sciences. *International Journal of Trichology, 15*(3), 79–84. DOI: 10.4103/ijt.ijt_15_23 PMID: 38179012

Tsing, A. L. (2015). *The mushroom at the end of the world: On the possibility of life in capitalist ruins*. Princeton University Press., DOI: 10.2307/j.ctvc77bcc

Uhl, P. (2016). The alternative community as revolutionary avant-garde. In *The Power of the Powerless: Citizens Against the State in Central and Eastern Europe* (pp. 187–188). Routledge. https://doi.org/DOI: 10.4324/9781315487373-15

Verdery, K. (1996). *What was socialism, and what comes next?* Princeton University Press., https://press.princeton.edu/books/paperback/9780691011325/what-was-socialism-and-what-comes-next

Verdery, K. (2015). Socialist Societies: Anthropological aspects. In *Elsevier eBooks* (pp. 849–853). https://doi.org/DOI: 10.1016/b978-0-08-097086-8.12147-6

Wilk, R. R. (2001). Consuming morality. *Journal of Consumer Culture, 1*(2), 245–260. DOI: 10.1177/146954050100100208

Yan, Y. (2003). *Private life under socialism: Love, intimacy, and family change in a Chinese village, 1949–1999*. Stanford University Press., https://www.sup.org/books/asian-studies/private-life-under-socialism

Yan, Y. (2009). *The individualization of Chinese society*. Berg Publishers. https://www.bloomsbury.com/us/individualization-of-chinese-society-9781847883780/

Yurchak, A. (2006). *Everything was forever, until it was no more: The last Soviet generation*. Princeton University Press., https://press.princeton.edu/books/paperback/9780691121178/everything-was-forever-until-it-was-no-more

Yussuf, D. (2024). *Ujamaa: How Julius Nyerere's socialist philosophy evolved in Tanzania.* TRT Afrika Insight. https://www.trtafrika.com/insight/ujamaa-how-julius-nyereres-socialist-philosophy-evolved-in-tanzania-18220801

KEY TERMS AND DEFINITIONS

Capitalism: An economic system where private individuals or corporations own and control the means of production and operate for profit. Markets determine prices, production, and distribution of goods. It emphasizes competition, innovation, and minimal government interference.

Communism: A classless, stateless economic system in which property is communally owned. Production and distribution are managed on a single board (called a collective), and private ownership is abolished. It strives to eradicate exploitation and seek equality.

Comparative economic systems: A study of the different types of economic systems (capitalism, socialism, mixed). This will be an assessment of their structures, processes and social impacts. The aim is to determine which more successfully achieves economic and social objectives.

Cultural Economy: An Approach that examines how cultural values, beliefs, and practices shape economic behaviour (Cultural Economy). It tried to understand consumption, labour, exchange and production politically, socially, culturally, economically, psychically, and symbolically. This view emphasizes the embeddedness of the economy in society.

Economic Anthropology: A field within anthropology that studies how people in human societies provide themselves with the material things they need to live. It examines traditional and modern economies across cultures. The main topics are exchange, reciprocity, redistribution and market forms.

Globalization: The growing interdependence of the world's economies, cultures and populations. This includes moving goods, services, information, and people across national frontiers. Globalization is the integration of locals to change a specific area's economy and identity.

Socialism: An economic system where the state or community owns and regulates the means of production. It emphasizes social welfare, equal distribution of income, and collective decision-making. It focuses on reducing exploitation and ensuring access to basic needs.

Chapter 4
Islamic Finance and the Anthropology of Money:
Exploring Ethical Alternatives to Interest-Based Systems

Early Ridho Kismawadi
https://orcid.org/0000-0002-9420-5212
IAIN Langsa, Indonesia

Razali Haron
https://orcid.org/0000-0003-0415-4093
International Islamic University, Malaysia

Dede Ruslan
State University of Medan, Indonesia

ABSTRACT

This paper explores the role of Islamic finance in challenging the dominant capitalist economic system by offering an alternative money ontology, which is based on the principles of social justice, wealth redistribution, and solidarity. This study examines how Islamic finance through mechanisms such as the prohibition of usury, qard hasan (interest-free loans), zakat (obligatory charity), and waqf redefines money not as a commodity for personal gain but as a tool for social responsibility and economic equity.

DOI: 10.4018/979-8-3373-1260-6.ch004

In contrast to conventional finance which emphasizes the accumulation of individual wealth, Islamic finance emphasizes transactions related to real assets and productive activities, which aim to foster social welfare and community welfare. Through this analysis, we argue that Islamic finance presents a viable and ethical alternative to interest-based systems, offering a more equitable and sustainable approach to global economic development.

INTRODUCTION

Islamic finance has emerged as an important alternative to conventional interest-based financial systems, based on ethical principles and risk-sharing mechanisms(Ayub and Khan 2021; Chiad and Gherbi 2024; Wahyudi, Lestari, et al. 2025). Previous research has consistently shown that Islamic finance provides a more ethical, transparent, and stable financial model by prohibiting interest (riba) and promoting investments that are aligned with socially responsible and sharia-compliant practices. The anthropological study of money, such as those conducted by scholars such as Karl Polanyi and Bronislaw Malinowski, has explored the social, cultural, and economic role of money in society, providing valuable insights into how financial systems affect social structures (Hart and Ortiz 2014). However, the integration between Islamic finance and the anthropological study of money is still limited, so there is a gap in understanding how this ethical financial model can be positioned as a viable alternative to the dominant interest-based financial system.

Islamic finance has proven to be more resilient to financial crises compared to conventional financial systems, especially during the 2007-2008 global financial crisis (Elmawazini, Khiyar, and Aydilek 2020; Hassan, Rabbani, and Mohd. Ali 2020; Rabbani et al. 2021; Srairi, Bourkhis, and Houcine 2022). This is due to the basic principles of Islamic finance that emphasize risk sharing, the prohibition of excessive speculation, and the avoidance of interest (riba). The system focuses more on transactions backed by real assets and ethical investments, which reduces the impact of market fluctuations caused by speculation-based financial instruments. Provisions in Islamic finance that promote transparency and fairness help create a more stable and sustainable system, as well as provide better protection against global economic uncertainty. Islamic finance, with its risk-sharing mechanisms and prohibition of investment in unethical or dangerous sectors, offers a more resilient model of economic shocks, so it can be a safer solution in the face of the global financial crisis.

Although there is significant academic literature on Islamic finance and the anthropology of money, there is still a lack of academic exploration linking these two fields. In particular, the intersection between Islamic financial ethical alternatives to interest-based systems and the social, cultural, and economic dimensions of money in anthropology is still understudied. This paper aims to fill this gap by exploring how Islamic finance offers ethical financial practices as an alternative to interest-based systems and examining the potential of Islamic finance as a sustainable solution in the global financial landscape.

This paper is unique in its approach to integrating Islamic finance with the anthropology of money, by offering a critical examination of how ethical financial models can function in practice outside of traditional economic systems. In contrast to most studies that focus only on the technical and financial aspects of Islamic finance, this paper explores its cultural and social dimensions, examining how these models challenge or complement conventional ideas about money and finance from an anthropological perspective. This interdisciplinary approach is designed to provide a more holistic understanding of Islamic finance in the context of broader human economic behaviour.

Money is not only an economic tool, but also a social and cultural construct that is firmly embedded in the values and ethics of the people who use it. Examining Islamic finance through the lens of money anthropology, this paper explores how the Islamic financial system provides an ethical alternative to interest-based financial models. This research is based on the belief that Islamic finance can offer solutions to existing inequalities in the global financial system, such as the concentration of wealth and ethical issues surrounding interest-bearing loans. This paper argues that a deeper understanding of the cultural and social foundations of Islamic finance can provide valuable insights to reshape contemporary financial practices.

This research aims to answer the following questions: How does Islamic finance, with its ethical principles and interest prohibition, offer an alternative to conventional interest-based financial systems from an anthropological perspective? In particular, this paper investigates the social, cultural, and economic implications of Islamic finance and its role in creating a more equitable and sustainable financial system.

This study uses a mixed method approach, combining qualitative analysis of Islamic financial principles and case studies of Islamic financial institutions with the theory of money anthropology. Data were collected from the existing literature, as well as an analysis of the application of the Islamic financial model in the real world. This interdisciplinary approach allows for a comprehensive exploration of how Islamic finance operates in a variety of cultural and social contexts, as well as how it challenges or complements the dominant financial system.

The paper finds that Islamic finance, with its ethical approach to finance, offers a viable alternative to traditional interest-based systems by promoting risk sharing, ethical investment, and financial justice. Key findings include the positive impact of Islamic finance in promoting financial inclusion, reducing income inequality, and promoting social responsibility. This study shows that the Islamic financial system has the potential to reduce ethical issues arising from interest-bearing loans, such as exploitation and the creation of wealth imbalances.

An additional finding of the study is the growing global interest in Islamic finance, especially in non-Muslim-majority countries. The study highlights how Islamic finance is not only relevant in Islamic societies but is increasingly being adopted by global financial markets due to its ethical underpinnings and appeal to socially responsible investors. This trend suggests that Islamic finance can play an important role in shaping the future of the global financial system, offering an ethical financial model that transcends cultural and religious boundaries.

To ensure the reliability of the findings, the study combines comparative analysis with conventional financial systems, focusing on their impact on wealth distribution, economic inequality, and ethical considerations. This study uses quantitative and qualitative data to assess the effectiveness of

Islamic finance in various regions and sectors, providing a more comprehensive understanding of its potential as a global financial alternative.

This paper contributes to the field of Islamic finance and the anthropology of money by offering an interdisciplinary examination of how Islamic finance provides an ethical alternative to interest-based financial systems. This paper provides valuable insights into the cultural and social underpinnings of Islamic finance, offering a broader perspective on its role in shaping global financial practices and addressing ethical challenges in contemporary economic systems.

Method

This study uses a mixed-methods approach to explore the intersection between Islamic finance and money anthropology, combining qualitative and quantitative methodologies to provide a comprehensive analysis of ethical finance alternatives to interest-based systems. This dual approach allows for a holistic understanding of how Islamic financial principles, such as zakat, waqf, and risk-sharing mechanisms, reshape the social and cultural role of money, providing insight into its potential to address global economic inequality.

ANTHROPOLOGY AND THE ETHICAL FINANCIAL MODEL

Anthropology examines finance and capitalism by uncovering contradictions, spatial inequality, and increasing inequality, exploitation, and political crises, viewing capitalist social relations as drivers of financialization and securitization that bind societies to systemic risk. Entities are valued through capitalist frameworks, influenced by local and global property dynamics, state interventions, as well as financial claims, which deepen inequality by concentrating wealth on the elite (Fotaki and Prasad 2015; Pagano 2014; Schneider and Soskice 2009; Tolbert, Lyson, and Irwin 1998). Money is seen as integrated in social hierarchies and networks of exchange, carrying diverse meanings that shape the identities and bonds of society. Within this framework, anthropologists explore ethical financial models by challenging destructive narratives about money, where practices such as cash flow optimization or shareholder value prioritization are denounced as immoral because they prioritize profit over community well-being. Academics such as Elizabeth Hirschman highlight the coexistence of traditional cultural elements in the modern economy (Дискурсі and Культурної 2020), while Parry and Bloch argue that money adapts to cultural matrices, not inherently destroys them, as seen in the concept of moral economy in which communities resist the disruptions of capitalism (Ortiz 2019).

Marcel Mauss views the plasticity of money as a tool of social transformation, potentially enabling a fair system through the manipulation of currencies and credit (Ortiz 2019). Leonardo Polo's philosophy places money as a means to human well-being, criticizes the excessive accumulation of wealth and views investment as a "convocation" to create job opportunities, towards a mass-oriented capitalism (Córdova 2020). Alternative currencies and local exchange systems foster trust and fairness, as demonstrated by Viviana Zelizer's work on the emotional and social role of money (Ortiz 2019). Resistance to dominant financial models, such as the "kunizacija" movement in Croatia, reflects efforts for a fairer economic system (Miku and Planck 2014). This approach is essential for ethical finance, offering a holistic lens that links the material and symbolic dimensions of money to national identity and global inequality, providing ethnographic insights into local practices, informing counter-politics by uncovering the impact of capitalism on everyday life, analysing the tensions of resource distribution, and contextualizing local realities in global financial flows to map class transformations and guide economic models which is fair.

Financial anthropology has opened up insights into the complexities of money and capitalism, uncovering the tensions between social hierarchies, inequality, and economic practices that often prioritize profit over the well-being of society. This approach offers a critical lens for exploring ethical financial models that seek to balance the material and symbolic dimensions of money. In this context, Islamic finance emerged as an attractive alternative that challenged the interest-based system, emphasizing the principles of justice, trust, and collective well-being. Islamic finance reconceptualizes money, integrating cultural and moral values to create a more inclusive and equitable economic system.

RECONCEPTUALIZING MONEY THROUGH AN ANTHROPOLOGICAL LENS IN THE CONTEXT OF ISLAMIC FINANCE

Money, in the view of anthropology, is not simply a medium of exchange, a store of value, or a measure of wealth. It is a social and cultural construct that reflects the values, norms, and collective identity of the people who use it. This anthropological approach allows us to see money as more than an economic entity, it is a reflection of the social relations, power, and cultural significance given to it. In the context of Islamic finance, money is interpreted fundamentally differently than the conventional financial system, which often views money as a commodity that can be traded for profit. Islamic finance with its ethical principles, such as the prohibition of riba (interest), maisir (gambling), gharar (uncertainty), and bathil (injustice), as well as mechanisms such as mudarabah and musharakah, represents an alternative view of money that prioritizes justice ('adl), balance (mizan), and social welfare (maslahah) (Ahmed and Aassouli 2022; Benmamoun and Sobh 2024; Jarbou, Irimia-Diéguez, and Prieto-Rodríguez 2024). This reconceptualization not only challenges the paradigm of individualistic capitalism, but also offers insight into how money can be used to reinforce communal and ethical values.

The anthropology of money emphasizes that the function and meaning of money are not universal, but rather shaped by certain cultural and historical contexts. In many traditional societies, money is not only used for economic transactions, but also to strengthen social relationships, signify status, or as part of rituals. For example, in barter systems or the reward economy, "money" often has a symbolic value that goes beyond its practical usefulness. In this context, money becomes a medium that reflects social norms and collective identity.

Islamic finance adopts a similar view, where money is not positioned as the ultimate goal, but as a tool to achieve a greater goal, which is justice and the welfare of society. Shari'a principles such as the prohibition of riba show that money should not "work" on its own to make a profit without real economic activity. In conventional systems, money is often treated as a commodity that can generate interest, a practice that is considered exploitative in Islam because it creates inequality without a productive contribution. In contrast, in Islamic finance, money must be linked to real ventures such as trade, investment, or production that provide benefits to society. This perspective is in line with the anthropological view that money is a product of social interaction, not an entity isolated from cultural values.

Islamic finance is based on a set of ethical principles derived from the Qur'an and Sunnah, which directly shape the way money is understood and used. These principles include: Prohibition of Riba (Interest), Riba is prohibited because it is considered a form of exploitation that enriches one party without any risk or effort that is commensurate. In the conventional system, interest allows money to "flourish" without productive activity, whereas in Islam, profits must come from real work or investments that create added value.

Maisir (Gambling), Maisir refers to unethical speculation, in which profits are made from luck or uncertainty without any real contribution. This reflects the view that money should not be used for activities that do not have a clear economic basis. Gharar (Uncertainty), Gharar prohibits transactions that are ambiguous or non-transparent, which may lead to injustice or conflict. This principle emphasizes that the use of money must be clear, fair, and mutually beneficial. Prohibition of Bathil (Injustice), Bathil includes all forms of transactions that violate sharia or unfairly harm one of the parties. This reinforces Islamic finance's commitment to social justice.

These principles created a view of money that was not oriented to the accumulation of capital alone, but to the creation of collective welfare. Money in Islam should be used for halal (permissible) and beneficial activities, such as investing in projects that support community development. This is in contrast to the conventional system, where money is often directed towards speculative or interest-based instruments that can exacerbate economic inequality.

One of the tangible manifestations of the alternative Islamic financial view of money is profit-sharing mechanisms such as mudarabah and musharakah (Ben Jedidia and Hamza 2024; Umam et al. 2021). In mudarabah, one party provides capital (rabb al-mal) while the other party provides expertise or energy (mudarib). The profits are divided according to the agreement, while the losses are borne by the capital owners. In musharakah, all parties contribute capital and share profits and losses according to the proportion of their contributions. This mechanism reflects the communal values that distinguish Islamic finance from individualistic capitalism. In an interest-based system, lenders demand fixed returns regardless of the outcome of the project, thus unfairly burdening the borrower. On the other hand, mudarabah and musharakah divide the risks and rewards proportionately, which is in line with the principles of justice ('adl) and balance (mizan). From an anthropological perspective, this mechanism strengthens social relations by encouraging collaboration, trust, and solidarity between economic actors. Money, in this case, becomes a tool for building communal bonds, not just for the benefit of individuals.

The conventional financial system, dominated by the paradigm of capitalism, often views money as the ultimate goal of accumulating individual wealth as a priority, sometimes at the expense of the interests of society. In contrast, Islamic finance places money as a means to achieve maslahah (social welfare). The concept of maslahah emphasizes that economic activities, including the use of money, must contribute to the common good. Practices such as zakat (obligatory alms) and sadaqah (voluntary alms) are real examples of how money in Islam is used for the redistribution of wealth and the reduction of inequality. In anthropology, this practice is similar to the reward economic system found in traditional societies, where wealth is diverted to strengthen social cohesion. Thus, money in Islamic finance has not only an economic function, but also a profound social and ethical function.

Through an anthropological lens, money in Islamic finance can be seen as a reflection of the collective identity of Muslims, which prioritizes justice, solidarity, and balance. It challenges the view of individualistic capitalism that often separates money from moral and social values. In the conventional system, money is a tool to increase personal wealth, while in Islam, money is a means to achieve the nobler goals of the welfare of the ummah and social justice. This reconceptualization has far-reaching implications, not only in the context of Islamic finance, but also in the global discussion of how economic systems can be designed to be more inclusive and ethical. By integrating communal values and a ban on exploitative practices, Islamic finance offers a relevant alternative amid criticisms of modern capitalism, such as economic inequality and recurrent financial crises.

Islamic Finance and the Ontology of Money: Challenging Universal Assumptions about Economic Value

Islamic finance, within the framework of sharia principles, offers a radical alternative view of the ontology of money compared to the conventional financial system. In the capitalist world, money is understood as a commodity that can be traded to make a profit through interest or speculation (Basu and Nag 2020; Sun et al. 2019). However, in Islamic finance, money is positioned differently. Money is not considered a commodity that can generate profits through interest (usury), but rather as a medium of exchange that must be linked to real assets and productive activities. This approach, which separates money from speculation and unfair profits, can be further analysed using an anthropological lens to critique universal assumptions about economic value dominated by the capitalist paradigm. In this paper, we will explore how zakat and waqf in Islamic finance create a form of "money" that functions as a tool of social redistribution, not just individual accumulation. Using anthropological theories of value, such as those developed by David Graeber and Marilyn Strathern, we can show how Islamic finance offers an alternative ontology of money that is more aligned with social justice and collective ethics.

In Islamic finance, money is not considered an entity that can generate profits through interest or speculation-based transactions. Instead, money must be connected to real assets and productive activities, which contribute to the well-being of society and the economy as a whole (Abdul Rahman, Dahiru Muhammad, and Mahayudin 2013; Abubakar, Hassan, and Haruna 2019; Choudhury and Hoque 2017; Incekara, Tatoğlu, and Ustaoğlu 2014). The concept of money in Islamic finance emphasizes social justice, wealth redistribution, and the avoidance of exploitation, which is contrary to the logic of capitalist economics that prioritizes the accumulation of individual wealth.

Zakat, which is the obligation for Muslims to give a portion of their wealth to those in need, and waqf (waqf), which refers to assets donated for social or religious purposes, are two highly relevant Islamic financial mechanisms in creating an ontology of money that serves more than just individual accumulation. In both of these practices, money serves as a tool for social redistribution and the development of collective well-being, rather than as a means to enrich a particular individual or group. Zakat requires Muslims who have wealth beyond a certain threshold to donate a portion of their wealth to those in need. This creates a network of social solidarity, where money not only revolves among individuals with financial power, but also flows to improve the well-being of society as a whole. Thus, zakat challenges the logic of capitalism, where money is often seen as an instrument to magnify individual accumulation, without regard to social inequality.

Meanwhile, waqf refers to the act of donating assets for purposes that benefit the community, such as the construction of schools, hospitals, or other social facilities. Waqf shows that money, or rather an asset, is not only for personal or commercial gain, but can also be used to create sustainable social benefits. Waqf creates a more equitable and sustainable social structure, where such assets are managed for the public benefit and not traded for individual benefit. Waqf reflects an ontology of money that prioritizes social value, resilience, and community empowerment, not just the development of personal wealth.

David Graeber, in his famous work Debt: The First 5,000 Years, argues that debt and money in many cultures have a social and moral dimension, not just a financial dimension. Graeber argues that money was not originally intended to create financial gain, but rather as a means of creating social relationships and regulating social obligations. In this context, money in Islamic finance, as reflected in zakat and waqf, can be seen as a social media that binds individuals in a network of solidarity and collective responsibility.

Marilyn Strathern, in her analysis of values in society, highlights that the concept of value in many cultures focuses not only on personal gain, but also includes social values and interpersonal relationships. In Islamic finance, the principle of reciprocity that underlies zakat and waqf shows that economic value cannot be understood only in terms of individual accumulation or material gain, but also in strengthening social relationships, collective well-being, and social justice. It challenges the concept of economic value centered on the dominant individual ownership in the capitalist paradigm.

In many societies that practice Islamic finance, money is seen as a medium of exchange that should be used for the common good, not as a commodity that can be exploited for individual benefit alone. Sharia principles in Islamic finance, such as avoiding usury and social responsibility, create a system that emphasizes the fair distribution and redistribution of wealth. Zakat and waqf create a social structure that not only focuses on wealth accumulation but also on the redistribution of wealth to minimize social inequality. This system not only promotes social justice, but also promotes economic resilience based on collective values, not on individual interests.

Islamic finance offers a very different alternative to the dominant capitalist financial system, where money is often seen as an instrument for accumulating personal gain. In Islamic finance, money serves as a social medium that binds individuals in a network of solidarity, and aims to create social justice as well as collective sustainability. The ontology of money in Islamic finance reflects not only financial value but also social, ethical, and sustainability value.

Islamic Finance as a Challenge to the Hegemony of the Interest-Based System

Islamic finance, which is rooted in sharia principles, emerged as a significant challenge to the hegemony of the interest-based financial system that dominates the global economy (Mahmoud et al. 2025; Martikainen and Brekke 2022; Morshed, Othman, and Al-Amarneh 2024). In the anthropology of money, the financial system is not just an economic mechanism, but a reflection of cultural values and the power structure of society. The interest-based system, which is the backbone of conventional finance, allows the accumulation of wealth without commensurate productive activity. In this model, capital owners earn a fixed profit through interest, regardless of the success or failure of the financed project. This creates an imbalance, where the risk is entirely borne by the borrower, while the lender is guaranteed a return with no real contribution to the real economy.

From an anthropological point of view, these systems perpetuate wealth inequality and exploitation because they allow the concentration of capital in the hands of a few, often at the expense of disadvantaged groups. For example, in many postcolonial societies, the interest-based system inherited from Western colonizers has reinforced an unjust power structure, where access to capital is limited to certain elites. This creates a cycle of poverty and dependence, where local communities find it difficult to develop economically. In this context, Islamic finance emerged as an alternative that not only challenged the dominance of the interest-based system, but also as a way to reclaim economic autonomy rooted in local values.

Islamic finance prohibits usury and emphasizes transactions backed by real assets, such as trade, investment, or productive ventures. One of its core principles is risk-sharing, which is reflected in mechanisms such as mudarabah (profit-sharing) and musharakah (partnership). In mudarabah, the capital owner and the business manager share the profits according to the agreement, while the losses are borne by the capital owners. In musharakah, all parties contribute capital and share risks and rewards proportionally. This model ensures that profits are derived from real economic activity and that risks are distributed fairly, in line with the principles of social justice in Islam.

From an anthropological perspective, risk-sharing reflects communal values that prioritize solidarity and justice, in contrast to the individualism often associated with interest-based capitalism. In many cultures, including Muslim societies, economic relations are inseparable from social relations; Financial transactions are expected to strengthen community bonds, not break them. Therefore, Islamic finance can be seen as an attempt to align economic practices with broader cultural and ethical norms, offering an alternative that challenges conventional paradigms.

Sukuk, or sharia bonds, are financial instruments that represent ownership of a specific real asset or business, rather than simply a promise to pay interest (Almustafa 2025; Wahyudi, Lestari, et al. 2025; Zaheer and van Wijnbergen 2025). Sukuk investors share the profits and losses of the financed projects, in line with the principle of risk-sharing. Malaysia, as one of the largest Islamic financial centers, has successfully used sukuk to finance infrastructure projects, such as toll roads and airports. Sukuk holders receive returns based on project income instead of fixed interest, ensuring investments are linked to real economic activity and encouraging transparency. From an anthropological perspective, the adoption of sukuk in Malaysia reflects the desire to align economic development with the dominant Islamic values in society. It also points to efforts to create a more inclusive financial system, where risks and rewards are shared fairly, rather than concentrated on capital owners.

Takaful is an insurance system that is in accordance with Islamic law, based on the principle of mutual help (ta'awun) and risk-sharing, not risk transfer as in conventional insurance. In takaful, participants contribute to the collective fund that is used to pay for legitimate claims. If there is a surplus after the payment of the claim, the funds can be returned to the participant or donated to charitable purposes, reflecting the value of justice and social welfare. Takaful also ensures that the investment of funds is carried out in a halal sector, avoiding activities such as gambling or alcohol production. Takaful has become an important part of the Islamic finance industry in many countries. In Malaysia, for example, takaful is growing rapidly as an alternative to conventional insurance, supported by a strong Islamic financial infrastructure. Companies such as Takaful Malaysia provide products such as family takaful (life protection) and general takaful (asset protection), which allow people to manage risk without violating sharia principles.

Outside the Muslim world, such as in the UK, takaful is becoming known through providers such as Salaam Takaful, which offers products to the Muslim and non-Muslim communities interested in ethically-based financial solutions. From an anthropological perspective, the adoption of takaful reflects strong communal values in Islamic finance. In Malaysia, people see takaful as a way to meet practical needs while affirming their religious and cultural identity. Meanwhile, in the UK, takaful's appeal to non-Muslims suggests that principles such as transparency and solidarity can transcend religious boundaries, resonating with universal values of social justice. However, challenges such as low financial literacy in some countries (e.g. Indonesia) suggest that local interpretations of takaful vary from symbols of religious observance to practical solutions that are sometimes misunderstood as expensive products. Globally, takaful shows how Islamic finance can adapt to the needs of modern society while maintaining its ethical core.

Waqf is a form of endowment in Islam, in which assets in the form of land, buildings, or cash funds are permanently dedicated to charitable or social purposes (Ishak et al. 2025; Jafar, Ibrahim, and Malik 2025; Mohamed and Akande 2025; Wahyudi, Tubarat, et al. 2025). Waqf's principal assets remain intact, while the revenue generated is used to support projects such as education, health, or infrastructure. Waqf reflects Islamic financial principles that emphasize collective well-being and wealth redistribution, aiming to reduce social inequality and promote justice. Waqf has a long history in Muslim society, but it is now undergoing innovation for modern relevance. In Turkey, cash waqf allows individuals to donate money that is then invested, with the proceeds used to finance schools or hospitals. In Singapore, institutions such as Warees Investments manage waqf assets such as commercial properties to generate income that supports vulnerable communities, including non-Muslims. In Malaysia, the concept of share waqf allows companies or individuals to donate shares, with the dividends used for social projects such as educational scholarships.

Anthropologically, waqf shows how Islamic finance integrates economic and social values. In Singapore, waqf is adapted in a multicultural and secular context, becoming a tool to strengthen social cohesion among different ethnic and religious groups. In Turkey, waqf is seen as a way to preserve Islamic heritage while meeting contemporary needs. Meanwhile, in Malaysia, innovations such as stock waqf reflect efforts to align tradition with modern capital markets, attracting wider participation from the public. The global interpretation of waqf demonstrates its versatility as an instrument that not only serves the Muslim community, but also contributes to inclusive social development, making it relevant to the world's diverse society. Islamic finance offers an attractive alternative and is often more focused on the values of social justice, transparency, and risk-sharing. Although challenges in its implementation still exist, especially related to product suitability with risk-sharing principles and higher transaction costs, Islamic finance remains a relevant and flexible option. This is evident from the adoption of Islamic finance not only in Muslim-majority countries but also in countries with minority Muslim populations, where it is seen as an ethical choice in accordance with universal principles. Islamic finance, with its flexibility, can expand further to meet the needs of diverse cultures around the world.

Islamic Finance and Sustainability: Solutions to Global Inequality

The principle of gharar (uncertainty or excessive speculation) is also an integral part of Islamic finance. Gharar in the context of Islamic finance refers to transactions that contain high uncertainty or speculation that is detrimental to one of the parties. It involves non-transparent, opaque, or unpredictable trading or investments, which often leads to losses for one party and exacerbates inequality. In the Islamic financial system, transactions must be based on sufficient clarity, transparency, and certainty so that both parties can fully understand the conditions and expected outcomes. This prevents harmful speculative practices, which are often found in conventional financial instruments such as derivatives and options, leading to financial instability and economic inequality. Islamic finance prioritizes integrity and fairness in every transaction, ensuring that risks and profits are shared equally, and that no party is forced to bear an unfair burden.

Islamic finance also places a strong emphasis on socially responsible and sustainable investment. This principle is reflected in the prohibition of investment in sectors deemed morally or environmentally destructive, such as gambling, alcohol and tobacco, which directly create a negative impact on social well-being and environmental sustainability. Instead, Islamic finance encourages investment in projects that provide positive social and environmental benefits, such as green infrastructure development, renewable energy, and poverty alleviation. Thus, Islamic finance offers a more ethical and sustainable alternative to investment, aiming to create a positive impact for the wider community, not just for financiers. This makes it relevant for individuals, companies, and countries that are increasingly looking for ways to integrate sustainability principles in their investment decisions. In the context of global inequality, Islamic finance serves as a tool to address the problems of poverty, inequality in the distribution of wealth, and environmental damage by encouraging investments that lead to inclusive and environmentally friendly social development.

However, despite offering a wide range of advantages, Islamic finance faces several challenges in its implementation. One of the biggest challenges is the higher transaction fees compared to the conventional financial system. This happens because the process of ensuring that transactions are compliant with sharia principles often requires more oversight and administrative procedures. For example, Islamic financial institutions may have to engage third parties to ensure that their investment products comply with sharia law, which can increase operational costs. In addition, in many countries, Islamic finance operates within a legal framework that was originally designed for the conventional interest-based financial system. This often creates a mismatch between sharia principles and practices in the conventional financial system, hindering the development and application of Islamic finance more broadly.

Despite these challenges, Islamic finance still has great potential to serve as an alternative solution to inequality and sustainability issues. In many countries, especially in Muslim-majority countries, the Islamic financial system has become an integral part of daily life, providing an opportunity to create a more inclusive and equitable economic system. In countries with minority Muslim populations, such as Europe or North America, Islamic finance is often accepted as a fairer ethical choice, prioritizing transparency and social sustainability, and offering a more inclusive approach to global issues such as economic inequality and environmental damage.

Many studies have explored ethical alternatives to interest-based systems, which are often thought to exacerbate social and economic inequalities. The interest system leads to the diversion of resources from the poorer group to the wealthier group, creating inequality in the distribution of wealth. From the perspective of economic anthropology, it is not only a matter of the flow of money, but also how social and political forces are influenced by the distribution of resources in the existing economic system. Islamic finance offers a fairer alternative by prioritizing risk-sharing rather than imposing fixed interest payments.

Islamic finance also leads to socially responsible investments, which prioritize social and environmental sustainability. In the context of economic anthropology, socially responsible investing can be seen as a way to create a more inclusive and sustainable economic system, which prioritizes collective well-being over individual interests. This is particularly relevant to the concept of green finance and impact investing, which aims to support projects that have a positive impact on society and the environment.

However, Islamic finance has its own uniqueness in this approach, because in addition to prioritizing social and environmental impacts, it also emphasizes ethical and religious values. For example, in investments that do not damage morals, Islamic finance ensures that funds are allocated only to projects that provide sustainable social and environmental benefits, such as renewable energy, poverty alleviation, or education. In this regard, Islamic finance not only prioritizes financial gains, but also ensures that the investment creates a positive social impact, in line with the principles of social justice and sustainability that are important in economic anthropology.

Islamic finance can be compared to other ethical finance movements, such as green finance and impact investing, which also aim to create a more sustainable and equitable financial system. Green finance emphasizes more on projects that focus on environmental sustainability, while impact investing focuses on achieving positive social or environmental impacts. Islamic finance, although it has similarities with these two movements, has a more structured and value-based approach, which integrates the principles of religious ethics in every financial transaction. Islamic finance ensures that every investment decision is not only financially profitable, but also has a positive social and environmental impact, which creates a fairer and more sustainable economic system.

Islamic finance can also offer a framework for achieving the Sustainable Development Goals (SDGs) adopted by the UN, focusing attention on social justice, poverty alleviation, and climate change. By emphasizing the principles of risk-sharing, social justice, and investments that support sustainability, Islamic finance can help reduce global inequality and promote sustainability in the global financial system.

Islamic Finance in a Postcolonial Context Negotiating Economic Identity and Power

The approach of economic anthropology offers an in-depth perspective for analysing Islamic finance, given that economics is not only a matter of financial transactions, but also of the relationship of power, culture, and identity in society. In this context, Islamic finance can be seen as a renegotiation of economic power that was previously dominated by Western colonial and capitalist powers. Islamic finance, with its principles that prioritize ethical values, transparency, and fair risk-sharing, acts as a form of cultural and economic resistance that responds to the inequality and inequality left behind by colonialism.

During the colonial period, countries with significant Muslim populations were forced to adopt an interest-based financial system dominated by the Western banking system. This practice not only changed the way people transacted financially, but also had an impact on broader social and cultural structures. The interest system is often seen as a tool of exploitation that exacerbates economic inequality, widens the gap between rich and poor, and exacerbates social inequality. Riba applied in the conventional financial system, where the debtor has to pay fixed interest even in difficult economic circumstances, gives an unfair advantage to lenders and creates a system that is highly susceptible to financial instability.

Islamic finance, with its prohibition on usury and excessive speculation, offers a fairer and more transparent alternative to this financial system. Islamic finance not only aims to provide a practical alternative in financial transactions, but also serves as a resistance to the Western economic hegemony imposed during the colonial era. In many ways, the application of sharia principles in economics can be seen as an attempt to regain control over economic resources that were previously concentrated in the Western financial system. Thus, Islamic finance prioritizes local values that are more equitable and appropriate to the cultural context of Muslim society, while reducing dependence on the international financial system driven by the principles of global capitalism.

Islamic finance does not just offer alternative financial solutions; It is also a process of economic identity building rooted in local social and cultural values. In many countries with colonial histories, such as Malaysia and Nigeria, the Islamic financial system has evolved as a symbol of the revival of an economic identity that seeks to return economic power to local communities, reducing dependence on Western financial institutions. Islamic finance leverages principles that are deeply associated with Muslim societies, such as social justice, profit and risk sharing, and helping others.

For example, in Malaysia, the development of Islamic banks has become a symbol of the revival of an economy focused on local values. Islamic finance in this country is not only driven by financial interests, but also plays a role in building a more inclusive and sustainable social structure. Islamic banks in Malaysia not only cater to Muslims, but also attract non-Muslim customers with the ethical principles offered. Malaysia's success in integrating Islamic finance into the national financial system has given a strong signal that Islamic finance is a practical solution that is not only relevant for the Muslim community, but also for anyone who wants a fairer and more sustainable financial system.

In Nigeria, although the majority of the population is non-Muslim, the development of Islamic banks and Islamic financial products is increasingly widespread as an alternative option that prioritizes social ethics and sustainability. Here, Islamic finance is seen as a tool to liberate society from the injustices of the interest-based financial system, which often exacerbates economic inequality. In Nigeria, many people see Islamic finance as part of an effort to build a more self-reliant economic identity linked to fair local values, while reducing the negative impact of economic globalization.

In Malaysia, Islamic banks function not only as an alternative to banking, but also as a symbol of the revival of an economic identity rooted in Islamic principles. Malaysia has successfully integrated Islamic finance into the national financial system by developing sharia products that appeal to Muslims and non-Muslims alike, as well as introducing a more transparent and equitable banking system. Islamic finance in Malaysia is a prime example of how countries with a majority Muslim population can use sharia-based finance to strengthen local economic identities and respond to the challenges of globalization that often bring injustice and social inequality.

Meanwhile, in Nigeria, despite being a country with a minority Muslim population, Islamic finance, especially in the form of Islamic banks, is increasingly being looked at as an alternative solution in the face of economic inequality triggered by the conventional interest-based banking system. Islamic banks in Nigeria offer fairer and more transparent products, which support sustainability and social diversity, while responding to the major challenges faced by developing countries in the face of economic globalization.

Islamic finance in postcolonial countries was not only a tool for negotiating economic identity, but also in response to the pressures of globalization that had adverse effects on the local economy. With increasing global interconnection, many countries are facing pressure to adopt financial systems driven by Western capitalism. Islamic finance offers a middle ground, which is to respect local values based on social justice and religious ethics, while avoiding the financial exploitation that is often presented by the interest system in conventional finance. Islamic finance provides space for countries with colonial histories to restructure their economic systems, in a more equitable and sustainable way.

Islamic finance in the postcolonial context not only serves as an alternative tool in financial transactions, but also as an instrument for negotiating cultural identity and economic power in countries with colonial histories. With a ban on usury, gharar, and a focus on socially responsible investments, Islamic finance offers a fairer and more sustainable solution, allowing countries to reclaim their economic autonomy. Case studies in Malaysia and Nigeria show how Islamic finance is not only relevant to Muslims, but also provides solutions for the wider community in building a self-reliant, fair, and sustainable local economic identity. Islamic finance offers a very potential approach to confronting the challenges of globalization, which often imposes an unfair interest-based financial system, and provides an avenue for postcolonial countries to reformulate their economic power in a more equitable manner.

Islamic Finance and the Gift Economy: Tracing Reciprocal Practices in the Financial System

One of the interesting dimensions of Islamic finance is its ability to adopt practices that reflect the logic of reciprocity and social solidarity, two very profound principles in the gift economy, as initiated by Marcel Mauss in his work The Gift (1925). In Mauss's view, the gift economy is not a commercial transaction in which goods or services are provided with the aim of obtaining personal gain. Instead, he emphasizes on the social value and relationships built through reciprocity and the social obligations inherent in giving.

Islamic financial principles, such as qard hasan (interest-free loans) and zakat (obligatory alms), have similar characteristics to the gift economy, which aims to strengthen social ties and redistribute wealth within society (Aderemi and Ishak 2023; Hasan, Hassan, and Rashid 2021; Sadr 2014). In contrast to economic systems that focus on individual profit, Islamic financial mechanisms are often designed to create social solidarity and reduce socio-economic disparities. In this article, we will explore how these principles function in the context of the larger global economy and how they challenge the logic of capitalist markets that prioritize personal profit and competition.

The theory of reward economics developed by Marcel Mauss focuses on how the giving of goods or services in a community function not only as an economic transaction, but also as a form of social relations that bind individuals or groups within a larger network of obligations. In The Gift, Mauss explains that in many traditional societies, gifts are not simply gifts without expectation of reciprocity, but often involve strong social reciprocity. This gift-giving creates a relationship of obligation between the giver and the recipient, where the recipient is expected to give back a gift or similar service in the future, although not always in the same form.

In Islamic finance, this concept is seen in practices such as qard hasan and zakat, which aim not only to provide direct economic benefits, but also to strengthen social bonds and ensure the redistribution of wealth in society. For example, in qard hasan, an individual gives a loan to another party without interest, in the hope that the borrower will return it without any additional financial burden. This creates a relationship of solidarity between the lender and the recipient, where both support each other on an equal footing.

Qard hasan (interest-free loans) is a prime example of Islamic finance that reflects the reciprocal logic found in the gift economy. In qard hasan, the lender does not receive interest or financial gain from the loan, but provides assistance solely to support the recipient in meeting their needs. In this case, the principle of qard hasan challenges the conventional interest-based banking system, which requires the borrower to pay more than the amount borrowed. In an interest-based system, personal gain from lending is at the heart of the transaction, while in qard hasan, what is more important is the strengthening of social bonds and support for the common well-being.

In the context of the gift economy, lending in the form of qard hasan emphasizes the value of social solidarity and collective responsibility. Lenders who offer funds to others hope that they will repay the loan in a fair way, not only as a financial obligation, but also as part of mutual support in the community. Thus, qard hasan builds closer social relationships than just financial relationships driven by personal gain.

The principle of zakat, which is one of the five pillars of Islam, also reflects the logic of the economics of gifts in a broader context. Zakat is an obligation for Muslims to give a portion of their wealth to the needy, with the aim of redistributing wealth and reducing socio-economic inequality in society. Zakat is not only considered a religious obligation, but also a form of social responsibility to help those who are less fortunate, thus creating a sense of solidarity in the community.

Like the gift economy, zakat serves to strengthen social ties between individuals in society. Although zakat aims to help underprivileged individuals, it also serves as a way to strengthen social relations between rich and poor, and build a sense of community within society. Zakat challenges the logic of the capitalist market, which often prioritizes the accumulation of wealth by individuals and ignores the social inequality that occurs. In this context, zakat serves as a wealth redistribution mechanism that not only reduces socio-economic disparities, but also supports the values of solidarity and collective well-being that are the cornerstones of Islamic finance.

Islamic finance, with principles such as qard hasan and zakat, challenges the logic of the capitalist market that prioritizes individual profit and wealth accumulation without regard to its social impact. In capitalist markets, transactions are driven by the desire for personal gain, often without regard to the inequality that arises or the social impact that is left behind. In contrast, Islamic finance focuses on fair risk sharing, social solidarity, and shared well-being. Qard hasan, with the principle of interest-free lending, and zakat, with the principle of wealth redistribution, both aim to create a mutually supportive community, which places more emphasis on social justice than personal gain.

For example, when compared to the interest system in conventional banking, Islamic finance with qard hasan does not concentrate profits on lenders. Rather, profits come from building fair social relations and helping collective well-being, with no party being harmed. Zakat, as a mechanism of wealth redistribution, focuses on ensuring that wealth is distributed in a way that reduces social inequality, thus challenging capitalist structures that often ignore the welfare of the wider society.

Islamic financial practices, such as qard hasan and zakat, can also be analyzed in different cultural contexts to understand how they function in different societies. In countries with Muslim-majority populations, such as Malaysia and Indonesia, qard hasan and zakat are often accepted as part of broader socio-economic policies. In these countries, Islamic financial principles are accepted as a tool to strengthen social welfare and reduce social inequality.

However, in countries with minority Muslim populations, such as Europe or the United States, acceptance of these practices can be different. Although qard hasan and zakat may not be religiously obligatory, many individuals are attracted to Islamic financial principles because they reflect the values of social solidarity and collective responsibility that are relevant to modern socio-economic challenges. This shows that Islamic finance, although rooted in the context of Islamic culture, offers an ethical alternative that is acceptable in various cultures and financial systems around the world.

DESIGNING A FAIRER FINANCIAL SYSTEM

Designing a fairer financial system requires an approach that integrates Islamic financial principles with the mechanisms that exist in today's global financial system. The conventional financial system, which is often dominated by interest-based practices (usury), has been shown to exacerbate economic inequality and social inequality. These systems focus on individual profits, ignore broader social and economic impacts, and often lead to the concentration of wealth in a handful of individuals or institutions. Islamic finance, with its principles that emphasize social justice, wealth redistribution, and social solidarity, offers a more equitable and sustainable alternative. By integrating these principles, we can design a more inclusive and equitable financial system.

One of the first steps to create a fairer financial system is to abolish riba (interest) as a key element in financial transactions. In Islamic finance, usury is prohibited because it is considered a form of exploitation, in which the lender makes a profit without sharing the risk, while the borrower is burdened with the obligation to pay more than what is borrowed. In the Islamic banking system, transactions are more focused on sharing risks and benefits, as seen in the products of mudharabah (profit-sharing partnerships) and musharakah (risk-sharing partnerships). This creates a fairer balance in the financial relationship, where profits and losses are shared proportionally between both parties. This approach aims to build mutually supportive financial relationships and reduce inequality between the rich and the poor.

Furthermore, the application of the principle of risk sharing can also help in creating a fairer financial system. In the Islamic financial system, both the lender and the borrower share the profits and losses based on mutual agreement. This principle not only ensures a fairer division in transactions, but also creates a more equal partnership between the financier and the recipient. This is very different from the conventional banking system which often benefits the party who has the capital through interest, while the weaker party is only responsible for the debt that must be paid with interest. Islamic finance avoids such exploitation by prioritizing social justice, where all parties involved in the transaction have a shared responsibility for both risks and benefits.

In addition, it is important to introduce cooperation between Islamic banks and conventional financial institutions to expand access to fairer financial products. This collaboration will allow the two systems to share knowledge, resources, and products that accommodate the needs of different groups. Established conventional financial institutions can integrate sharia-compliant products such as sukuk (sharia bonds) and murabaha (buying and selling with an agreed profit margin), which are more transparent and fairer in terms of profit sharing. Thus, this cooperation can introduce more socially inclusive products, which promote economic growth without harming the weaker parties. Governments can also help create a regulatory framework that allows Islamic banks and conventional banks to operate side by side and complement each other, to provide consumers with wider choice in choosing financial products that are in line with ethical and social principles.

The importance of financial literacy based on cultural values must also be a priority in designing a fairer financial system. Financial literacy education that teaches Islamic financial principles should be introduced at the school and community levels. This literacy aims to build awareness of the importance of risk sharing, responsible investment, and wealth redistribution as core values in a fairer financial system. This education will help individuals to understand that money is not only a tool for personal accumulation, but also a tool for creating collective well-being. Through a better understanding of sharia-based finance, people can more easily move away from the conventional banking system driven by personal profit, towards a more inclusive and equitable system.

The implementation of wealth redistribution mechanisms, such as zakat and waqf (waqf), can accelerate the achievement of social justice goals (Kato 2022; Pericoli 2025). Zakat as an obligation for Muslims to give part of their wealth to those in need, serves as a tool to reduce poverty and improve social conditions directly. The government can facilitate the implementation of zakat in the tax system to ensure that the contributions of Muslims are used for social benefits and wealth redistribution. Waqf, which refers to assets donated to social or religious purposes, such as education and health, can also be a very important source of funding for long-term social projects. The implementation of policies that support the transparent and accountable management of waqf funds will ensure that these assets are used to build social infrastructure that benefits the wider community.

Designing a fairer financial system requires integrating Islamic financial principles that prioritize social justice, wealth redistribution, and social solidarity into the global financial system. Collaboration between Islamic banks and conventional financial institutions, increasing financial literacy based on cultural values, and the implementation of wealth redistribution mechanisms such as zakat and waqf can strengthen this system. Policies that support ethically-based finance will help ensure that money is used not only for the accumulation of individual wealth, but also to create social well-being and alleviate socio-economic inequality. With these steps, we can realize a more inclusive, sustainable, and equitable financial system for all levels of society.

CONCLUSION

In relation to the Anthropology of Money, Islamic finance offers an alternative ontology of money that challenges the concept of money in today's dominating global capitalist system. The anthropology of money, as posited by thinkers such as David Graeber and Marilyn Strathern, views money not only as a free-flowing medium of exchange or commodity in the market, but as a social entity that regulates social relations and collective obligations. In Islamic finance, money is not treated as a commodity that can be traded for personal gain, but rather as a medium of exchange linked to real activities and productive assets, which further supports the principles of reciprocity and social solidarity. Islamic finance affirms that the value of money must be connected to a greater purpose than simply the accumulation of individual wealth.

Islamic financial principles, such as the prohibition of usury, qard hasan (interest-free loans), zakat, and waqf (waqf), created a money system that focused more on the redistribution of wealth and social responsibility. Money in Islamic finance serves as a tool to support collective well-being and the redistribution of resources, not to add to personal wealth or market speculation. In this case, Islamic finance is closely related to the anthropological theory of money which considers money as a binding medium of social relations, and a reciprocal relationship that affirms social obligations between givers and receivers.

Through practices such as zakat, money is not only seen as a means of exchange that generates profits, but as a means to create social balance by reducing poverty and social inequality. Waqf also plays a similar role, where donated assets aim to create long-term benefits for society, such as education and health. Both of these instruments position money as a medium of solidarity that connects individuals with society, which is in line with Graeber's view that money has a social and moral dimension, not just an economic one.

The Islamic financial system, with its underlying ethical principles, offers a fairer and more sustainable solution to a global financial system that is often dominated by a capitalist logic that prioritizes personal gain and the accumulation of individual wealth. By integrating the principles of reciprocity and social justice, Islamic finance provides a more sustainable ontology of money, which aims to improve the social structure and redistribution of wealth within society. This makes it a more ethical and inclusive alternative, not only in the context of Muslim-majority countries, but also in a broader global context, where Islamic finance can be used to create a more equitable and sustainable economic system for all walks of life.

Islamic finance, in relation to the anthropology of money, not only offers an alternative to interest-based financial systems, but also digs deeper into how the value of money can be used to build social solidarity and support economic justice. Islamic finance challenges the dominant assumptions in Western economic theory about the value of money, and replaces it with a more ethical framework that places collective welfare and wealth redistribution at the centre of the economy.

REFERENCES

Дискурсі, Г. У., & Культурної, З. (2020)... *ГЛОБАЛЬНИЙ КАПІТАЛІЗМ VS ТРАДИЦІЙНА КУЛЬТУРА*, *39*(100), 248–258.

Abdul Rahman, R., Dahiru Muhammad, A., & Mahayudin, I. (2013). Applicability of the Islamic Micro-Investment Model (IMIM) in Islamic Bank in Malaysia. *World Applied Sciences Journal*, *24*(5), 609–616. DOI: 10.5829/idosi.wasj.2013.24.05.13213

Abubakar, M., Hassan, M. K., & Haruna, M. A. 2019. "Cryptocurrency Tide and Islamic Finance Development: Any Issue?" Pp. 189–200 in *International Finance Review*. Vol. 20.

Aderemi, A. M. R., & Ishak, M. S. I. (2023). Qard Hasan as a Feasible Islamic Financial Instrument for Crowdfunding: Its Potential and Possible Application for Financing Micro-Enterprises in Malaysia. *Qualitative Research in Financial Markets*, *15*(1), 58–76. DOI: 10.1108/QRFM-08-2021-0145

Ahmed, H., & Aassouli, D. (2022). Entrepreneurial Finance, Agency Problems and Islamic Ethics: Complementarities and Constraints. *Venture Capital*, *24*(1), 25–46. DOI: 10.1080/13691066.2022.2067017

Almustafa, E. (2025). Islamic Financing Mechanisms for Renewable Energy Projects: Mapping Research Trends and Future Directions. *International Journal of Energy Economics and Policy*, *15*(3), 453–470. DOI: 10.32479/ijeep.18866

Ayub, M., & Khan, M. F. (2021). Evolving monetary economics in Islamic perspective. *Journal of Islamic Monetary Economics and Finance*, *7*(2), 317–340. DOI: 10.21098/jimf.v7i2.1372

Basu, M., & Nag, R. N. (2020). Open Economy Macroeconomics of Commodity Price Fluctuation, Sectoral Inter-Linkage and Employment. *Journal of Economic Studies (Glasgow, Scotland)*, *47*(6), 1467–1494. DOI: 10.1108/JES-11-2018-0399

Ben Jedidia, K., & Hamza, H. (2024). Does PLS in Islamic Banking Limit Excessive Money Creation? *Journal of Islamic Accounting and Business Research, 15*(3), 422–442. DOI: 10.1108/JIABR-02-2022-0047

Benmamoun, M., & Sobh, R. (2024). An Islamic Perspective on AI Ethics: A Case Study of Wahed Invest Robo Advisory. *Journal of Business Ethics Education, 21*, 231–244. DOI: 10.5840/jbee20242114

Chiad, F., & Gherbi, A. (2024). The role of Islamic banks in promoting economic growth and financial stability: Evidence from Saudi Arabia. *Investment Management and Financial Innovations, 21*(3), 357–369. DOI: 10.21511/imfi.21(3).2024.29

Choudhury, M. A., & Hoque, M. N. (2017). The Future of Monetary Reform and the Real Economy: A Problem of Trade versus Interest. *ACRN Journal of Finance and Risk Perspectives, 6*(4), 37–52.

Córdova, G. C. (2020). Notes on the Anthropological Approach to Money and Investment According to Leonardo Polo. *Studia Poliana, 22*(22), 119–131. DOI: 10.15581/013.22.119-131

Elmawazini, K., Khiyar, K. A., & Aydilek, A. (2020). Types of Banking Institutions and Economic Growth. *International Journal of Islamic and Middle Eastern Finance and Management, 13*(4), 553–578. DOI: 10.1108/IMEFM-09-2018-0304

Fotaki, M., & Prasad, A. (2015). Questioning Neoliberal Capitalism and Economic Inequality in Business Schools. *Academy of Management Learning & Education, 14*(4), 556–575. DOI: 10.5465/amle.2014.0182

Hart, K., & Ortiz, H. (2014). The Anthropology of Money and Finance: Between Ethnography and World History. *Annual Review of Anthropology, 43*(1), 465–482. DOI: 10.1146/annurev-anthro-102313-025814

Hasan, R., M. K. Hassan, and M. Rashid. 2021. "Qard Hasan (Interest-Free Loan) as a Tool for Sustainable Development-Global Evidence." Pp. 307–30 in *Islamic Finance and Sustainable Development: A Sustainable Economic Framework for Muslim and Non-Muslim Countries.*

Hassan, M. K., Rabbani, M. R., & Mohd. Ali, M. A. (2020). Challenges for the Islamic Finance and Banking in Post COVID Era and the Role of Fintech. *Journal of Economic Cooperation and Development, 41*(3), 93–116.

Incekara, A., F. Y. Tatoğlu, and M. Ustaoğlu. 2014. "Modeling Islamic Finance and Inclusive Growth for Emerging Markets: Evidence and Roadmap of Turkey and Malaysia." Pp. 74–95 in *Islamic Finance Alternatives for Emerging Economies: Empirical Evidence from Turkey.*

Ishak, A. H., Amira Mohamad, S. N., Ab Manan, S. K., Yahaya, M. H., Wan Daud, W. N., & Sharif, D. (2025). The Critical Success Factors of Waqf Land Development for Sustainable Agriculture. *Social Sciences & Humanities Open, 11.* Advance online publication. DOI: 10.1016/j.ssaho.2024.101244

Jafar, A., H. Ibrahim, and R. Malik. 2025. "Waqf: From Classical Charitable System to Modern Financial Tool." *International Journal of Ethics and Systems*. doi: .DOI: 10.1108/IJOES-10-2024-0354

Jarbou, S. I., Irimia-Diéguez, A., & Prieto-Rodríguez, M. (2024). Financial Performance of Islamic and Conventional Banks in MENA Region: A GLS Approach. *Journal of Islamic Accounting and Business Research.* Advance online publication. DOI: 10.1108/JIABR-11-2023-0380

Kato, T. 2022. "Islamic and Capitalist Economies: Comparison Using Econophysics Models of Wealth Exchange and Redistribution." *PLoS ONE* 17(9 September). doi: .DOI: 10.1371/journal.pone.0275113

Mahmoud, M. A., Umar, U. H., Danlami, M. R., & Ado, M. B. (2025). An Analysis of Islamic Financing Access in Nigeria: Perspectives of MSME Owners. *International Journal of Islamic and Middle Eastern Finance and Management, 18*(1), 49–67. DOI: 10.1108/IMEFM-02-2024-0072

Martikainen, T., & Brekke, T. (2022). The Rejection of Interest-Based Loans among Muslim Entrepreneurs and Professionals in Finland. *Journal of Muslims in Europe, 6*(2), 1–17. DOI: 10.1163/22117954-bja10074

Miku, Marek, and Max Planck. 2014. "Uvođenje Eura i Nacionalna Valuta u Hrvatskoj." 195–210.

Mohamed, A., & Akande, A. E. (2025). *Waqf-Led Buildings and Green Infrastructure Role in Environmental Sustainability: Understanding Critical Gaps in Current Research Landscape*. Management and Sustainability., DOI: 10.1108/MSAR-09-2024-0152

Morshed, A., Othman, M. D., & Al-Amarneh, A. (2024). Investigating the applicability of the expected credit loss model to Islamic sukuk: Law aspects. *Corporate Law and Governance Review*, *6*(3), 81–89. DOI: 10.22495/clgrv6i3p9

Ortiz, H. (2019). The Political Anthropology of Finance and the Anthropology of Money. *Sociologia & Antropologia*, *9*(3), 773–795. DOI: 10.1590/2238-38752019v933

Pagano, U. (2014). The Crisis of Intellectual Monopoly Capitalism. *Cambridge Journal of Economics*, *38*(6), 1409–1429. DOI: 10.1093/cje/beu025

Pericoli, A. (2025). Islamic Instruments for Refugee Financing: The IsDB and UNHCR Collaborative Approach. *Global Policy*, *16*(S1), 46–56. DOI: 10.1111/1758-5899.13476

Rabbani, M. R., Bashar, A., Nawaz, N., Karim, S., Ali, M. A. M., Rahiman, H. U., & Alam, M. S. (2021). Exploring the Role of Islamic Fintech in Combating the Aftershocks of Covid-19: The Open Social Innovation of the Islamic Financial System. *Journal of Open Innovation*, *7*(2). Advance online publication. DOI: 10.3390/joitmc7020136

Sadr, S. K. (2014). Qar asan financing in Islamic banks. *ISRA International Journal of Islamic Finance*, *6*(2), 7–20. DOI: 10.12816/0019261

Schneider, B. R., & Soskice, D. (2009). Inequality in Developed Countries and Latin America: Coordinated, Liberal and Hierarchical Systems. *Economy and Society*, *38*(1), 17–52. DOI: 10.1080/03085140802560496

Srairi, S., Bourkhis, K., & Houcine, A. (2022). Does Bank Governance Affect Risk and Efficiency? Evidence from Islamic Banks in GCC Countries. *International Journal of Islamic and Middle Eastern Finance and Management*, *15*(3), 644–663. DOI: 10.1108/IMEFM-05-2020-0206

Sun, Z., Wang, Y., Zhou, X., & Yang, L. (2019). The Roundabout from Interest Rates to Commodity Prices in China: The Role of Money Flow. *Resources Policy*, *61*, 627–642. DOI: 10.1016/j.resourpol.2018.10.011

Tolbert, C. M., Lyson, T. A., & Irwin, M. D. (1998). Local Capitalism, Civic Engagement, and Socioeconomic Well-Being. *Social Forces*, *77*(2), 401–428. DOI: 10.2307/3005533

Umam, K., Ismail, A. G., Tohirin, A., & Sriyana, J. (2021). Islamic endogenous money: Evidence from the Islamic banking system in Indonesia and Malaysia. *Journal of Islamic Monetary Economics and Finance*, *7*(3), 545–560. DOI: 10.21098/jimf.v7i3.1351

Wahyudi, H., Lestari, W. R., Said, U. B., Leny, S. M., & Awaluddin, I. (2025). Dynamics of Growth and Stability in the Islamic Financial Services Industry on ECA, GCC, MENA, SSA, and EAP. *International Journal of Economics and Financial Issues*, *15*(3), 448–456. DOI: 10.32479/ijefi.19200

Wahyudi, H., Tubarat, C. P. T., Rodliyah, N., Kusnadi, A., & Leny, S. M. (2025). The Nexus of Crowdfunding and E-Wakaf to Islamic Fintech in Indonesia in the Era of Industrial Revolution 5.0. *Journal of Ecohumanism*, *4*(1), 208–219. DOI: 10.62754/joe.v4i1.4657

Zaheer, S., & van Wijnbergen, S. (2025). Sukuk Defaults: On Distress Resolution in Islamic Finance. *Qualitative Research in Financial Markets*, *17*(2), 292–311. DOI: 10.1108/QRFM-08-2023-0203

Chapter 5
Bridging the Divide:
An Anthropological Analysis of Development, Economic Inequality, and the Systemic Marginalization of the Koch Rajbongshi Tribe

Surjit Singha
https://orcid.org/0000-0002-5730-8677
Kristu Jayanti University, India

ABSTRACT

This chapter provides the framework for critically examining development and economic inequality as cultural marginalization across the globe and in grassroots experiences. Taking the Koch Rajbongshi tribe as a case of systematic oversight, it analyzes the exclusion of indigenous communities by dominant growth paradigms. Using ethnographic accounts, policy reports and theoretical contributions, including (but not limited to) recent work by Sen, Piketty and Fraser, this chapter contends that development needs to articulate social justice, cultural identity and historical recognition alongside its existing GDP-influenced neo-economic character. It compares effective models of literacy-led equity, like those of Kerala and

DOI: 10.4018/979-8-3373-1260-6.ch005

Mizoram, with ongoing exclusion because of bureaucratic inertia. Primary insight and real-time development make the case for a recognition and redistribution-based people-centred development model much stronger.

INTRODUCTION

The Economic Gap is among the most critical and persistent global challenges. It sets out the global and regional human condition, the poor and rich, the unequal, the perpetrators and victims, and the excluded. Historically, development projects have been touted as an instrument of poverty alleviation and economic development, but in practice, they often generate unequal effects that favour specific constituencies while marginalizing others. Economic anthropology offers a critical lens on these complications by uncovering how financial systems are culturally and historically patterned and structurally sustained. This anthropological lens enables us to look past aggregate inequality statistics and consider the lived experiences of those affected by development policies and economic reconfiguration. This report by UNDESA (2023) explores the economic and social implications of the ageing of the human population, providing recommendations to create equitable, inclusive societies for people of all ages.

In most cases, development is followed by a tag of modernization, infrastructure development, and lifestyle development. However, anthropological research has consistently argued that development interventions, mainly if top-down or created without the participation of the local community, will only exacerbate social hierarchies. Such interventions can be directed toward the urban elite, foreign corporations, or the politically privileged at the expense of rural inhabitants who possess indigenous knowledge systems or communal access to resources (Ferguson, 1994; Scott, 1998). So, development is a double-edged sword – sure, it might create wealth and progress in the positive realms, but it is also reproducing or exacerbating inequalities in the negative ones.

Since the distant past, anthropologists have been concerned about "how wealth, power, and resources are distributed in society" (Lavenda & Schultz, 2015, p. 27). Subfields and Related Disciplines Building on

Marxist critiques of capitalism (Marx, 1990), structuralist analyses of institutional power (Polanyi, 2001), and culturalist explanations of values and belief systems (Geertz, 1973), economic anthropology explores the process of producing and reproducing inequality over time. These approaches stress that economic inequality is not a natural or inevitable feature of human societies but results from historical patterns, policy choices, cultural practices, and institutional formations.

In addition, the cultural aspects of inequality are foundational to how the economy functions. For example, beliefs about male-female roles, kinship duties to work a particular plot of land, land ownership, and labour relations may determine who will control access to resources and exclusion. Caste, class, and ethnic-based intersectional inequalities add complexity to the development scene. Programs can reinforce rather than transform hierarchies when cultural meaning is ignored or flattened out in development programming (Crenshaw, 1989). In this respect, anthropology reminds us of the vital importance of local communities, the experiences and aspirations, the worldviews and perceptions of the world of ordinary people with whom we are researching.

In a critique of development theory and its separation from the anthropological lived reality of economic inequality, this chapter seeks to provide greater theoretical comprehensiveness to empirical case studies. It will examine how the development has taken place historically (Escobar, 2012), how globalization transformed local economies (Tsing, 2005) and how often the policy frameworks are inadequate to address structural impediments (Stiglitz, 2012). Critically, the chapter will also showcase alternatives: participation practices that privilege local voices, policies that draw on indigenous knowledge systems, and innovations in policy not just to reduce poverty but to transform a world in which poverty emerges in the first instance.

In doing so, the chapter adds to a burgeoning literature that demands development to be conceived not simply in terms of economic growth or infrastructure development but as a socially inclusive, culturally respectful and structurally transforming process. Thus, by problematizing economic inequality in light of economic anthropology, equitable development is not just a normative goal but a moral imperative that demands that we confront the underlying logic of power, culture, and history.

BACKGROUND

Economic fairness has long been a worldwide issue and has regained increasing attention in recent decades because it profoundly affects social welfare, political stability and sustainable development (UNDP, 2024). Although economic growth is often considered to lead to better living standards, it has not always resulted in fair outcomes for all elements of society. Such development programs have accelerated existing inequalities as elites in urban areas are favoured, structural imbalances are exacerbated, and weaker segments of society have been marginalized (Stiglitz, 2012; Scott, 1998).

Economic anthropology provides a crucial conceptual resource for making sense of these complexities because it focuses on how economic practices are nested in cultural norms, historical patterns, and institutions of society (Polanyi, 2001; Geertz, 1973). It aims to go beyond standard economic measures to see how people encounter and interpret inequality daily. From this perspective, economic systems are not only the production and distribution procedures but are constructed by power relations, belief systems, and cultural values (Tsing, 2005).

The worldwide circulation of development projects—particularly in postcolonial and Global South settings—has revealed a contradiction between the fantasy of modernization and the practice of exclusion (Ferguson, 1994; Escobar, 2012). More recently, such cycles have also been marked by mega infrastructure projects, structural adjustment programmes, and the promotion of market-led policies that have sometimes destroyed traditional livelihoods, community displacements, and local knowledge systems (Frank, 1967). Moreover, these patterns indicate clearly that "poverty" is an outcome not only of economic surplus falling short but also of a historically imposed and culturally enforced architecture.

Additionally, the increasing emphasis on inclusive and sustainable development advocated by global frameworks such as the UN Sustainable Development Goals (SDGs) demands a more critical look at how development is conceptualized and implemented (UNDP, 2024). In this perspective, attention should be directed to the fundamental structural and cultural causes of inequality rather than the formulaic imposition of models that do not account for local differences (Sen, 1999; Sharma & Gupta, 2006).

This chapter is inspired by the conviction that addressing economic inequality must be based on interdisciplinary perspectives and human-focused practices. Situated within a broader sociocultural and historical framework, it highlights how inequalities are produced, reproduced and contested and suggests alternative development paths underpinned by justice, inclusion and dignity for all.

Theoretical Framework

This chapter utilizes three key theoretical traditions in economic anthropology to understand the development-ambiguous relationship:

Marxist Perspective

Based on the teachings of Karl Marx, this trend focuses on class struggle and work exploitation in the capitalist world. It sees economic inequality as part and parcel of capitalism, where the few own the means of production, and the many are dispossessed. Development has commonly been criticized as an instrument of capitalist accumulation, thus reproducing and exacerbating social and economic inequalities (Marx, 1867/1990; Marx & Engels, 1848/2004).

Structuralist Approach

The structural view emphasizes institutional arrangements (governing elites, international organizations, and legal frameworks) in determining economic relationships. It demonstrates how structural disparities are integrated into the policies and governance, perpetuating unequal access to resources, opportunities, and power. This approach helps us understand why development strategies are frequently elitist and exclude people experiencing poverty (Prebisch, 1950; Furtado, 2022).

Culturalist Perspective

The second culturalist perspective focuses on cultural beliefs, values, and practices regarding economic behaviours and perceptions of inequality. It examines how norms of culture around gender, caste, ethnicity, or meritocracy shape what, who gets what, and why. It also captures how local epistemologies or cosmologies can be marginalized or utilized in development (Geertz, 1973; Tsing, 2005).

CONCEPTUAL FRAMEWORK

The theoretical lens for this chapter is intended to investigate how development dynamics come together with sociocultural and structural mechanisms to undergird or contest economic inequality. At the heart of this approach is the recognition that development, traditionally seen as synonymous with social and economic change led by policy and external investment, can either perpetuate or address inequality depending on the extent to which it is inclusive and culturally relevant (Escobar, 2012; Sen, 1999).

The significance of power and structure is crucial, as institutional, political, and economic arrangements play a significant role in who benefits from development efforts and who remains disenfranchised (Scott, 1998; Ferguson, 1994). Just as crucial is local ways of knowing; that is to say, knowing based on people's experience at a close range, layered with all the cultural and ecological complexities (Tsing, 2005; Geertz, 1973). These institutions are frequently ignored in top-down development approaches; however, their importance for sustainability and equity cannot be overstated (Sharma & Gupta, 2006).

The social dimensions of inequality involve the norms, values and beliefs that make inequality acceptable or unacceptable in societies (Crenshaw, 1989; Polanyi, 2001). Ultimately, participation and inclusion are key elements for making development effective, as this creates local ownership and ties interventions to community needs (Furtado, 2022; Prebisch, 1950). By connecting the macro levels of governance and policy to the micro- and individual-level experiences of living, this framework offers a complete anthropological view of a complex system to analyze and respond to development and economic inequity.

THE ICE MODEL: INEQUALITY–CULTURE–EQUITY FRAMEWORK FOR CONTEXTUAL DEVELOPMENT

Purpose of the ICE Model

The ICE Model offers an integrated lens to examine inequality, cultural influence, and equity-oriented development in a localized context. It is specifically designed for research or chapters analyzing the mismatch between development ideals and real-world practices, particularly in postcolonial, Indigenous, or marginalized communities.

Table 1. Model Components

Component	Description	Theoretical Anchors
I: Inequality Realities	Examines the structural and systemic roots of economic, political, and social inequality. Focuses on elite capture, historical marginalization, digital divide, and urban-rural differentials.	Amartya Sen (Sen, 1999), Thomas Piketty (Piketty, 2014), James Ferguson (Ferguson, 2006)
C: Cultural Continuums	Recognizes that indigenous traditions, belief systems, and social organization shape how communities perceive and engage with development. Validates non-Western or vernacular knowledge systems.	Arturo Escobar (Escobar, 2018), Claude Lévi-Strauss (Lévi-Strauss, 1962), Linda Tuhiwai Smith (Smith, 2021)
E: Equity-Centered Development	Advocates policies that move beyond equality and towards equity by considering intersectionality, localized participation, and redistribution tailored to cultural contexts.	SDG Goals (United Nations, 2015), UNDP Inclusive Development Index (UNDP, 2016), Fraser's Theory of Redistribution & Recognition (Fraser, 2008)

Visual Representation

[Inequality Realities]
↓
[Cultural Continuums]
↓
[Equity-Centered Development]
↓
[Sustainable & Just Outcomes]

Applications

- **Policy Analysis**: Evaluate whether existing development policies are culturally sensitive and structurally aware.
- **Community-Centred Research**: Engages Indigenous and local actors in identifying context-specific inequalities.
- **Development Planning**: A checklist or framework to avoid top-down, one-size-fits-all interventions.

UNDERSTANDING ECONOMIC INEQUALITY

Definitions: Economic inequality, Personal income distribution , Wealth distribution, Employment distribution, Wealth inequality. This gap expresses itself in different ways, such as inequality in income, assets, education, health, and political participation (UNDP, 2024; Sen, 1999). Indeed, inequality proves not to be simply an economic problem but rather an entrenched social-cultural process that shapes both people's agency and capacity to achieve their well-being, perpetuates hierarchies and patterns of domination that constrain the possible avenues for inclusive growth (Stiglitz, 2012; Polanyi, 2001). It works at different scales—at the level of households, social groups, and across regions or nations—leading to both the analysis of vertical inequality (between individuals) and horizontal inequality (between culturally defined groups, such as ethnicities, castes, or genders) (Crenshaw, 1989; Tsing, 2005).

Theoretical traditions in anthropology are beneficial regarding these dynamics. The Marxist viewpoint sees inequality as a result of capitalism in which workers' labour is exploited, and the means of production are owned and controlled by an elite few, creating structural inequalities (Marx, 1867/1990; Marx & Engels, 1848/2004). Structuralist methodologies, as inspired by scholars such as Prebisch and Furtado, prioritize how politically, legally, and economically structured institutions institutionalize and perpetuate inequality as embodied in the system of governance, policy, and global power disparities (Furtado, 2022; Prebisch, 1950). Culturalist approaches that are based on the work of anthropologists like Geertz and Tsing emphasize how ideologies about meritocracy, gender roles, and caste are internalized to reproduce inequality by legitimizing social stratification and exclusion (Geertz, 1973; Tsing, 2005). These approaches highlight the complexity of inequality and provide a strong base for critiquing and framing development policies and programs to promote equity and justice.

HISTORICAL TRAJECTORIES OF ECONOMIC DISPARITIES

Economic inequality has its roots in historical processes such as colonization, enslavement, land dispossession and an economy based on extraction. These events produced durable economic institutions that benefited certain groups at the expense of others, commonly along racial, ethnic, and geographic lines (Frank, 1967; Rodney, 1982). In many postcolonial settings, development was often based on Western models emphasizing industrialization and economic growth rather than distribution and equity (Escobar, 2012; Ferguson, 1994). Consequently, several countries inherited and continue to maintain arrangements that discriminated against and excluded and were complicit in centralizing power in the hands of urban dwellers (Stiglitz, 2012; Polanyi, 2001).

The trends toward globalization in the latter part of the 20th century also served to redefine economic differences. As globalization expanded new markets and technical opportunities, it also enhanced the extent to which local economies faced exposure to international fluctuation and made transnational corporations more powerful (Tsing, 2005; Scott, 1998). Trade liberalization, liberalization, and structural adjustment—often imposed by international financial institutions—led to cuts in public expenditure and large-scale privatization, affecting people with low incomes most and exacerbating inequality (Sen, 1999; UNDP, 2024).

It is essential to appreciate these historical trajectories to realize that the contemporary economic disparities are not accidental or natural but have been made and inherited, as much through policy actions as systemic processes (Furtado, 2022; Prebisch, 1950). The historical lens enables development practitioners to challenge current frameworks and devise interventions that tackle underlying causes, not merely symptoms, of problems.

DEVELOPMENT AND INEQUALITY: A COMPLEX RELATIONSHIP

'Development', perceived as synonymous with progress, modernization and a higher standard of living, has been tirelessly advanced as an antidote to poverty and underdevelopment. However, from an anthropological perspective, development has downsides (Ferguson, 1994; Escobar, 2012). Some thrive amid growing infrastructure, healthcare, education and employment opportunities, while marginalization, dispossession, and exclusion exist for others. This paradox becomes apparent, particularly when development is oriented around top-down, technocratic 'solutions' oblivious to local sociocultural realities and power relations (Scott, 1998; Sharma & Gupta, 2006).

For example, megadevelopment projects—such as dams, highways or urban reconstruction projects—have frequently forced resettlement of local and indigenous communities without adequate compensation or consideration for their resettlement and reestablishment (Cernea, 2000; Tsing, 2005). Equally, the imposition of market-led systems often voids subsistence economies and traditional livelihoods, undermining cultural autonomy and reinforcing dependency (Polanyi, 2001; Stiglitz, 2012). When development enters the state, it favours dominant classes, urban elites and multinational corporations, undermining the already frustrating level of equality. Hence, development can empower communities and perpetuate inequalities when it is not participatory, inclusive, and culturally sensitive (Sen, 1999; UNDP, 2024).

Case Studies

Success story: Kerala in India is an example in the right direction regarding development with distributive justice. Through public health, education and land reforms, Kerala has achieved high levels of literacy, low levels of infant mortality and relatively low levels of income inequality. Much of the success has been due to an emphasis on grassroots political mobilization, active civil society and a focus on human development instead of economic growth.

Similar to Kerala's model of development with distributive justice, the state of Mizoram recently became the first Indian state to achieve full functional literacy, marking a significant milestone in India's inclusive education journey. This success was enabled through the ULLAS – Nav Bharat Saaksharta Karyakram, a volunteer-driven adult education initiative under the Ministry of Education. The programme targeted adults above 15 years old who had not completed school, focusing on five key areas: foundational literacy and numeracy, critical life skills, basic education, vocational skills, and continuing education.

In 2023, a door-to-door survey identified 3,026 non-literate individuals across the state, and 1,692 of them were actively engaged in learning. With the help of 292 volunteer teachers, including students, educators, and local coordinators, Mizoram's literacy rate rose to 98.2%, surpassing the Government of India's benchmark of 95% for full literacy. The achievement reflects Mizoram's strong cultural values, community participation, and alignment with the NEP 2020 vision for a literate and empowered India (Ministry of Education, 2025).

The Koch Rajbongshi Tribe of Assam: A Struggle for Recognition and Equity

If states like Kerala and Mizoram shine like bright beacons in terms of inclusive development in terms of literacy and empowerment by activating bottom-up actions, in sharp contrast is the story of the Koch Rajbongshi tribe of Assam. It is a story not of an absence of possibility but of bureaucratic stagnation, red tape, and a perpetual disregard for constitutional rights.

Based on both ethnographic review and primary interviews conducted with local community members and cultural practitioners in Kokrajhar, Bongaigaon, Chirang, Baksa, Dhubri, Goalpara, Barpeta, Nalbari, Udalguri, Darrang and Kamrup, it is evident that Koch Rajbongshis have a long heritage of tribal ancestry, separate languages, and traditional practices in common with other Scheduled Tribes (ST) in the area. For decades, their demand for ST recognition under the Indian Constitution has been brushed aside, resulting in an active silence, delay and political ambivalence.

Community members said that despite this history of contribution to Assam's cultural and political heritage, the community members are categorized as Other Backward Class (OBC) community in Assam and the Scheduled Caste (SC) community in West Bengal. As one elderly person from the Gossaigaon area put it, "We are tribals by culture but not by certificate.' The identity has been mired in documents. Such "caste trap" is blocking the access for the community to the complete range of tribal affirmative action in education, public employment and legislative assembly.

In subsequent statements, community leaders alleged that many fact-finding commissions and verification surveys have been instituted in the past. Still, each was either not concluded or mired in bureaucratic red tape. Despite such communities with a similar socio-economic profile getting included in the ST list, the Koch Rajbongshis continue to suffer from a policy-level exclusion, which seems deliberately engineered to keep them disempowered.

The consequences are dire: lack of access to education, limited access to employment, and being erased from tribal policymaking. The distinct nature of development anthropology is essential, in contrast to more state-led initiatives like the ULLAS–New India Literacy Programme—which empowered learners even in the most inaccessible corners of Mizoram through a mighty force of volunteerism and cultural unity—the Koch Rajbongshis are kept out of the development framework by a reluctant ethnopolitics and bureaucratic semantic ambiguity.

There is no escape from the conclusion that this case illustrates one of the significant failures of the promise of inclusive development that India has made for some decades concerning its people. From what we can tell from personal testimonies, Scheduled Tribe (ST) denial is not merely a question of law or administration — it is an experience of being-temporarily-elsewhere, a feeling that is resonating in student dreams, job fantasies and the lives of tribal elders. Under this framework, the geographical or capacity constraints never obfuscate development, but the political will and a lack of recognition (Singha & Singha, 2023; Konwar & Das, 2012).

Failure – Narmada Valley Project, India. On the other hand, the Narmada dam project in India is a well-known and well-documented example of an equity failure in development. The project was intended to supply electricity and irrigation, but displaced hundreds of thousands of tribal and rural people without proper rehabilitation. Despite legal challenges and international appeals, many of the affected people became homeless, landless, and without livelihoods, demonstrating how a megaproject can so easily widen social and economic gaps when human rights and local participation are disrespected.

Mixed results – African structural adjustment programmes (SAPS): Systems were introduced in several African countries in the 1980s and 1990s, following the direction of the IMF and the World Bank, to foster growth by promoting liberalization and privatization. Some economies stabilized, but the Programs also "triggered considerable downsizing in education, healthcare and public employment—much of it affecting poor people—and increased social unrest".

To avoid such unintended consequences, the preceding case studies stress the need for context-sensitive approaches and integrated planning to prevent further inequality.

THE ROLE OF GLOBALIZATION IN SHAPING ECONOMIC INEQUALITY

Globalization, the rapidly growing integration of economies, societies, and cultures, has been particularly critical for development and inequality. It has opened new markets, technology, and knowledge networks, which have sparked economic growth and innovation in countries such as China and Vietnam. It has also helped fuel an expanding gap within and between countries. Widening global trade and investment gains tend to concentrate among skilled labour, urbanized places or capital-rich countries. In contrast, unskilled workers in rural locations or developing countries suffer from job losses, stagnation of wages, and economic subordination (Milanović, 2018).

Jobs were outsourced, industries were deregulated, and the leverage moved from the workers and local communities to multinationals. Furthermore, globalization advances a model of development that may be characterized as one-size-fits-all and neoliberal--one which favours market efficiency, privatization, and minimal state intervention while ignoring structural inequalities and local diversities (Harvey, 2005). In most cases, local customs and industry have become outdated, which is a crushing economic and cultural blow (Tsing, 2005).

The increasing challenges to global development are both external to and within the single sovereign countries, and the interrelations between the multiple trends are pretty complex, which depends on how the development process and the globalized one are conceived, adopted and managed and which can work in such a way to alleviate or to increase economic inequality. The capacity to negotiate such terrain and challenge more equitable and inclusive development models is inherently rooted in a complex, anthropologically informed understanding. The digital economy's rapid expansion has increased income inequalities, particularly for rural and indigenous communities without access to technology or digital literacy (OECD, 2021). The report by OECD (2023) examines the evolving landscape of international aid, highlighting the need for fundamental development cooperation changes amidst global crises and shifting geopolitical dynamics. These include support for locally led transformations, reforming financial systems, and rebalancing power in development relations.

Singha (2024) highlighted that promoting empathy and compassion contributes to shaping inclusive social spaces and equitable growth. However, compassion is not just an ethical quality but a motivation to act and stop others from suffering. At a grassroots level, when embedded in community-level interventions or school systems, compassion solidifies the social fabric through increased understanding of each other and a sharing of pain and suffering. Mindfulness-based interventions (MBIs) in formal spaces such as schools and workplaces have been shown to cultivate the (thinking) skills (such as emotional resilience and communication) upon which inclusive development agendas can be constructed.

CULTURAL DIMENSIONS OF INEQUALITY

Local knowledge systems based on indigenous traditions, oral histories, community practices and ecological wisdom support local communities in relating to the environment, regulating resources and defining social relationships (Gadgil et al., 1993; Odora Hoppers, 2009). Yet many development projects either ignore or undermine these systems, favouring universal, occidental templates (Santos 2007; Visvanathan 1997). This marginalization produces an epistemic injustice and unequal access to knowledge and voice from marginalized communities in decision-making (Santos, 2007).

Indigenous agricultural practices (e.g. those embodied in Kandyan home-gardens, wherein diversity and functional complementarity have been established and sustained using traditional, low-input farmer practices) tend to be overlooked or eclipsed by science and policy priorities that tend to favour high-input, industrialized farming systems, however contextually ill-adapted or less sustainable (Halladay & Gilmour, 1995). In health care, biomedical model-based approaches can obscure the importance of traditional healers' practices and disengage communities from their care systems (Redvers & Blondin, 2020). Fricker (2007) shows how indicators such as HDI, GDI, and GDP can marginalize local knowledge and priorities by privileging measurable, quantitative data over qualitative cultural well-being.

Bring back the dignity to local knowledge. It is a matter of conservation and development-based, sustainable, and inclusive development (Odora Hoppers, 2009; UNDP, 2024). Acknowledging the validity of Indigenous epistemologies undermines universalistic discourses of expertise and development. It opens up spaces for the co-production of solutions more authentically rooted in the needs and realities of communities (Santos, 2007).

INTERSECTIONALITY: GENDER, ETHNICITY, AND CLASS

Intersectionality, coined by Crenshaw, provides a conceptual framework to analyze how different identities (of gender, race, caste, religion, and social class) intersect and combine to create new forms of disadvantage (Crenshaw, 1989). In South Asia, "Dalit women bear a triple burden of caste, class, and gender", resulting in restricted access to education, health, jobs, and a high risk of violence and discrimination (Sabharwal & Sonalkar, 2015). Indigenous women in Latin America play critical roles in community economies and environmental conservation. Still, many face structural hurdles that limit their involvement in political systems and enable them to own land (Zamora, 2021). Development intervention that ignores these interrelated dimensions will likely maintain the same inequalities they try to address. Therefore, intersectional analysis is critical to shaping inclusive policies that respond to the varied lived experiences of marginalized communities.

Cultural values heavily influence the perceptions, justifications, and challenges of inequality. In the way of thinking, hierarchical social systems—like patriarchy, caste systems, and others—are so deeply embedded in the beliefs and practices of those systems that they are regarded as natural and divinely sanctioned, justifying power and resources being unequally divided (OpenStax, 2021). On the other hand, culture also serves as a resource for resistance and change. For example, African feminist movements have deployed cultural symbols and vernacular idioms to contest gender violence and economic exclusion (Salami, 2013). Indigenous rights movements, likewise, have invoked traditional ecological values in their struggle for land rights and environmental justice (Reytar et al., 2024).

Economic inequalities are based on unequal power relations that determine how resources are distributed, who can access opportunities and who makes the rules and decisions. This is due to the historical hierarchies, political agendas, and social structures that privilege powerful groups over others (Brown et al., 2019). Power finds expression through explicit structures, like government and concealed structures, like norms and patronage. Land reforms designed to improve equity can, for example, be captured by local elites to deprive the intended beneficiaries of benefits (Dabla-Norris et al., 2015). These inequalities must be addressed by employing redistributive policies and structural changes, and widening access to power, resources, and representation in governance affairs.

EDUCATION AND DEVELOPMENT AS TOOLS FOR SOCIAL EQUITY

Equitable development is about more than the incremental expansion or even radical transformation of the structural and economic—ranging from increase green space in urban neighborhoods to the creation of affordable housing but ignores the primal majesty of our surroundings; it is also about the affective and educational dimensions that produce ethically rooted, reflective, contemplative citizens who move with both humility and pride through their neighborhoods and respectfully guard ecosystems that existed long before us, and here long before us more than we can fathom. Singha (2024a) states that engaging in service learning through compassion and mindfulness allows students to script civic duty. It encourages self-discovery and emotional literacy—critical skills in navigating the complex, interdependent world. This cross-disciplinary pedagogy facilitates transformative learning and nurturing of value-based developmental ethos, enabling learners to evolve into socially responsible agents.

Intellectual, emotional and ethical growth is central to the new educational models for inclusive development. Building on service learning, Singha (2024) argues that when mindfulness and compassion become part of the academic curriculum through reflective and experiential learning, higher education could be one of the greatest social justice platforms, ethical leadership, and emotional maturity platforms. These practices develop student dispositions that reflect the Sustainable Development Goals (SDGs), especially those to promote peaceful, just, and inclusive societies (SDG 16) as well as to ensure inclusive and equitable quality education, and promote lifelong learning opportunities for all (SDG 4). These approaches tackle root causes of alienation, inequality and disengagement that are widely recognized to undermine conventional development models by providing students with the tools of empathic engagement.

INSTITUTIONAL FAILURES AND POLICY GAPS

Institutions have a special role in steering the broader chariot of internal economic relations towards a socially fair and equitable development. However, weakness, corruption, resource shortage, and bias in institutions often translate into worsening inequality. Failings of institutions may cover poor provision of public services, impunity and biased legal infrastructures (National Academies of Sciences, Engineering, and Medicine, 2017). Some schemes, like developmental programs, are doomed due to mismanagement and elite capture and do not benefit the lower rungs of society. To demolish the bedrock of economic, social, and poverty, and eradicate violence, the potential of transparency, decentralized networking and inclusive governance is undoubtedly needed.

The urban–rural divide and the regional inequality are key structural dimensions of inequality. Urban places have better physical and social capital, job creation, human development indices and basic services than rural places, where they are trailing behind, resulting in uneven development (Ponattu et al. 2019). Uneven development policies and distribution of resources drive these inequalities. "Closing the gap" needs more balanced regional development, prioritizing rural development while basic public services are accessible to all, no matter where one lives.

For participatory development, the community's voice, experience, and power will remain the focus of the development process. Unlike conventional top-down models, it is grounded in active local participation at every phase — acknowledging that people have invaluable experiences. Decisions are more likely to be appropriate, responsive and sustainable when local, affected communities participate in the decision-making process. Such initiatives include community-based management of water in South Asia and participatory budgeting in Latin American cities.

Traditional knowledge systems are generations-old teachings and environmental care. Applying this knowledge will help achieve fairer and more locally relevant development. Combining traditional agriculture and healing _ has also enhanced sustainability and health care among indigenous people (Gorjestani, 2000). Respecting indigenous knowledge undermines epistemic injustices and invites recognition of the rights of indigenous peoples to retain their cultural identities.

POLICY RECOMMENDATIONS FOR SUSTAINABLE AND INCLUSIVE GROWTH

Policies should be grounded in equity, sustainability, and justice to have development for all. Lessons learned from anthropology and evidence-based research could inform more effective and inclusive development approaches as follows:

Embed Governance of Participation: Formalise processes of community consensus, participatory planning, and local governance. Allow those marginalized populations, especially women, indigenous people and youth, to participate in the decision-making. Participatory governance implies that development is accountable to the interests of every stakeholder (UNDP, 2021).

Decentralized Planning Control: Abandon the concept of centralized planning in allocating resources and authority to the regions and competitors in the market. This permits locally-appropriate programmes that respond to local needs and priorities. The local people's welfare through decentralization is better off (UNDP, 2004).

Honour and Protect Indigenous Rights: Bring development in line with international frameworks such as the UN Declaration on the Rights of Indigenous Peoples. Take actions that address legal recognition of rights, cultural practices and traditional governance systems, including land rights (UNDP, 2014).

Facilitate capacity development: Improve local communities' technical, organizational, and financial capacities to manage their growth. That includes access to education, vocational training, and digital literacy. For example, UNDP's Digital Capacity Lab focuses on practical ways to improve digital skills.

Bridge the Rural-Urban gap: Focus on public investment in rural infrastructure, education, health, agro-based industries and decentralized renewable energy to boost rural employment and economic diversification. Spatial inequality is key to promoting balanced regional development.

Adopt Alternative Indicators of Progress: Go beyond GDP-centric indicators toward HDI, GDI, and indicators of social cohesion, ecological sustainability, and community well-being. These indicators can measure a more complex interpretation of development outcomes (UNDP, 2024).

Ensure Policy Accountability and Transparency: Establish feedback and grievance redressal mechanisms that enable local communities to hold institutions accountable for development results. The Stakeholder Response Mechanism of UNDP provides a timely problem-solving mechanism for stakeholders affected by development activities' social and environmental impacts.

Development is not just a technical challenge but a political and ethical one. Policymakers and practitioners can build paths that alleviate economic inequality and nourish sustainable, dignified, and holistic human well-being by reorienting development around people, culture, and justice.

DISCUSSION

The entanglement of development and economic inequality and the conjuncture describes a terrain structured by more than one complexity and asymmetry of power and a culturally embedded system. It reinforces that development is not a neutral or uniform good. Instead, it is highly contextually specific, shaped by history, structure, and culture, and serves to shed light on who wins and who loses.

One of the most important lessons of this exercise is to accept that inequality is not just about statistical differences in income; it is a question of daily life based on the availability — or unavailability — of resources, decision-making power and dignity. Economic anthropology reminds us of the social norms, historical injustices and institutionalized biases that build and sustain those differences. Interventions to stimulate development that fail to take account of these dimensions risk simply entrenching the problems they are trying to address.

The analysis of development as a double-edged sword shows that the most benign efforts can be exclusionary if they do not contend with local realities. Studies from India and Africa demonstrate that grand projects, if not implemented with the involvement of the relevant communities, can lead to displaced populations, the destruction of traditional economies, and even dependency, not empowerment. By contrast, participatory and community-based initiatives demonstrate that by engaging people, development becomes more inclusive and sustainable.

The significance of local knowledge systems is one of the most crucial and commonly neglected factors. These systems are built on centuries of ecological, agricultural and social knowledge, and their response mechanisms are flexible and adaptable to resource management and conflict resolution. In doing so, policymakers are not just letting down their cultural heritage but also acting strategically and materially naïve — solutions borrowed from others are not context-specific and inappropriate. It is not a return to a bygone era but a sensible instrument for inclusive development.

The second is intersectionality, which enriches the analysis, showing that inequality is multiple. An Indigenous woman could then be disadvantaged economically not just because of her class standing, but also because of her gender, as well as ethnicity. These intersecting vulnerabilities mean no community can be treated as a big homogeneous lump. That is why development approaches must reflect this. The IOM (2024) report situates these global migration trends in the larger context of climate change, food insecurity, and human mobility. It is of indispensable worth to interpreting these intricacies of migration today.

In this regard, economic inequality results from structural factors like institutional failure, asymmetrical power relations, and the urban-rural divide. Due to uniform centralized governance, policy interstices, and elite capture, public goods remain out of reach for far-flung areas and sections of people. These inequities persist, suggesting that technical fixes are not the only thing needed; structural change, political will, and a moral imperative are equally necessary.

Lastly, the conversation on inclusive development pathways offers optimistic predictions. That participatory objectives, cultural respect, and distribution of power and resources are not Utopian but rather eco-industrial must-haves. Drawing on anthropological knowledge in policy and planning allows development to be reimagined as something that empowers rather than impoverishes, that heals rather than hurts.

In general, this exchange goes to the heart of the argument that development should be based on justice, participation and the valorization of local knowledge. Only then can it be a fundamental tool for reducing economic inequality and creating the fairer, more resilient world we need.

RECOMMENDATIONS AND SOLUTIONS

Particular attention to economic inequality's enduring and pervasive nature in development settings calls for a holistic, inclusive, and culturally informed approach. Economic anthropology –with its attention to economic life's cultural, structural and historical nature– provides beneficial ingredients for an alternative, participatory, just, and empathic development model. From these anthropological roots, this chapter suggests that development can be reframed not as a top-down, technocratic exercise but as a justice-oriented venture that recognizes the importance of community agency and social/cultural knowledge. GROOTS propose that a fundamental approach should be to make participatory development an organizational procedure by law, ensuring local communities, especially excluded groups such as women, indigenous people and ethnic minorities, are included in all development life cycle phases. It entails having local development councils or village assemblies that have decision-making power over priorities and resources so that development reflects the needs of the grassroots and not the interests of the elite. Acknowledging and incorporating local knowledge systems into traditional ecological methods, indigenous health systems, and regional governance structures is equally important. Such knowledge should not be judged as outdated or unprofessional but treated as knowledge of value, actively documented, verified in one way or another and incorporated in co-learning and co-creation ideas that merge different types of knowledge, knowledge of the past with that of the present. It is also necessary to tackle the structural and policy-level barriers by which power and authority have been decentralized through fostering transparent and accountable institutional mechanisms and instituting equity-based reforms in education, health, and land. Further, taking intersectional policy approaches is required to recognize and address the many dimensions of discrimination experienced by marginalized populations, such as Dalit women, Indigenous youth, persons with disabilities, and migrant workers, whose exclusion is perpetuated by intersecting systems of discrimination. The capacity building of institutions and leadership from below is necessary to maintain this inclusive development – training in participatory planning, conflict resolution, digital literacy and M&E, and support for community-owned enterprises and grassroots innovation 'labs'. Efforts to narrow the urban-rural gap and lessen regional disparities required governments to prioritize balanced regional development, focusing on rural infrastructure, agro-based industries, renewable energy and decentralized public services, complemented by tax relief or subsidies for backwards regions. The same is true of going beyond narrow economic indicators such as GDP to embrace broader, more comprehensive indicators like HDI, GEI , and indicators of cultural resilience, environmental sustainability and community well-being. Interdisciplinary task forces should work together to engage a broad range of stakeholders across government, civil society, academia and community to bring multidisciplinary knowledge into the process of creating ethical cores, which must also be integrated into every facet of our development practice, including through required social impact assessments and cultural audits, to safeguard justice, dignity, and human rights. Third, we should think of development as not a once-and-for-all prescription but an ongoing dialogic process in and through which constant engagement, storytelling, and mutual learning among all the actors involved continue to evolve. These complementary recommendations allow development to be a fundamental driver for social justice, resilience and empowerment rather than exclusion and inequality.

FUTURE RESEARCH DIRECTIONS

Future studies of development and economic inequality from an economic, anthropological standpoint will need to question prevailing models and seek ways for equity and justice specific to local contexts. The first is so long that ethnographic studies follow the effects of development interventions on the communities at risk in the long term. This kind of research can show how power dynamics, cultural changes and structural shifts have changed over the last few decades, affecting inequality directly and indirectly.

Second, researchers should also apply comparative, cross-cultural analysis to participatory development, exploring what works, where and for which reasons. This might support a compendium of best practices based on what works locally rather than externally imposed. Learning how communities from different sociocultural environments manage the challenges without development agendas can provide valuable insights for more flexible and adaptive policy designs.

Third, it will be necessary for future research to engage more directly with the convergence of digital transformation and inequality in development settings. As technology becomes a critical avenue for access to information, services, and income, it is essential to explore for whom digital inclusion works and does not, especially among rural, Indigenous, and non-literate populations.

Another key trend is incorporating Indigenous and ecological information into mainstream development and sustainability discourse. Researchers can scrutinize how such knowledge systems can add to environmental resilience, food security and cultural continuity and how these can be legitimized and protected within policy contexts.

It would be beneficial to investigate more how the politics of youth, gender, and identity impact economic opportunities and social mobility. This includes researching how young people, particularly women and those from marginalized identities, are generating alternative development discourses through activism, social enterprise and digital platforms.

There is an increasing demand for applied policy research that can relay anthropological findings into practical policy advice for governments, NGOs and international development organizations. Mediating between theory and practice, such research will be based on principles of co-authorship, co-creation and collaboration with members of local communities to produce grounded and ethical knowledge effectively.

Future research must be multisectoral, participatory, and justice-oriented to deepen our knowledge of how development can be reconceived as a more culturally specific, collective and just process.

CONCLUSION

Economic inequality is still a complex and intractable global problem involving massive historical baggage, cultural movements, systematic structures and development routines. The author has engaged in this chapter against the notion of development as the panacea to poverty and underdevelopment worldwide . It has treated development as engendering and even deepening inequality when it ignores the local matrix, power relations and cultural diversity.

The chapter has shown that inequality is also a sociocultural and political product originating from marginalization, local knowledge marginalization, institutional collapse, and regional imbalance. Development is in danger of becoming the tool of the elite for resource exploitation and social exclusion if carried out without inclusion and care. However, development can be a transformative process that promotes equity, empowerment and sustainability when guided by participatory principles and grounded in indigenous knowledge systems.

Reimagining development as more than economic growth, a multidimensional process in which justice, dignity, equality, and community well-being are prioritized, is necessary to chart a more inclusive course forward. Policies should be grounded in the life experiences of those marginalized, adaptable to local conditions and dedicated to addressing the structural causes of inequality. Anthropology provides the critical instruments for deconstructing dominant development narratives and revealing alternative pathways framed by cultural dignity, collective capacity, and social accountability.

Closing economic gaps is not simply a matter of redistribution of wealth in the economic pie but rather a shift in the ontology of development. By adopting such culturally sensitive, participatory, politically informed methods, societies can work towards a future where development is not for the few but for all. It implies that inclusive development is a policy target and a moral commitment to social justice, resilience and shared prosperity.

REFERENCES

Brown, A. F., Ma, G. X., Miranda, J., Eng, E., Castille, D., Brockie, T., Jones, P., Airhihenbuwa, C. O., Farhat, T., Zhu, L., & Trinh-Shevrin, C. (2019). Structural interventions to reduce and eliminate health disparities. *American Journal of Public Health, 109*(S1), S72–S78. DOI: 10.2105/AJPH.2018.304844 PMID: 30699019

Cernea, M. M. (2000). Risks, safeguards and reconstruction: A model for population displacement and resettlement. In Cernea, M. M., & McDowell, C. (Eds.), *Risks and reconstruction: Experiences of resettlers and refugees* (pp. 11–55). The World Bank., https://documents.worldbank.org/en/publication/documents-reports/documentdetail/947311468739277702/risks-and-reconstruction-experiences-of-resettlers-and-refugees

Crenshaw, K. (1989). Demarginalizing the intersection of race and sex: A Black feminist critique of antidiscrimination doctrine, feminist theory and antiracist politics. *University of Chicago Legal Forum, 1989*(1), 139–167. https://chicagounbound.uchicago.edu/uclf/vol1989/iss1/8/

Dabla-Norris, E., Kochhar, K., Suphaphiphat, N., Ricka, F., & Tsounta, E. (2015). *Causes and consequences of income inequality: A global perspective*. International Monetary Fund. https://www.imf.org/en/Publications/Staff-Discussion-Notes/Issues/2016/12/31/Causes-and-Consequences-of-Income-Inequality-A-Global-Perspective-42986

Escobar, A. (2012). *Encountering development: The making and unmaking of the Third World*. Princeton University Press., https://www.degruyterbrill.com/document/doi/10.1515/9781400839926/html?lang=

Escobar, A. (2018). *Designs for the pluriverse: Radical interdependence, autonomy, and the making of worlds*. Duke University Press., DOI: 10.1215/9780822371816

Ferguson, J. (1994). *The anti-politics machine: "Development," depoliticization, and bureaucratic power in Lesotho*. University of Minnesota Press. https://www.upress.umn.edu/9780816624379/anti-politics-machine/

Ferguson, J. (2006). *Global shadows: Africa in the neoliberal world order*. Duke University Press., DOI: 10.1215/9780822387640

Frank, A. G. (1967). *Capitalism and underdevelopment in Latin America: Historical studies of Chile and Brazil*. Monthly Review Press. https://nyupress.org/9780853450931/capitalism-and-underdevelopment-in-latin-america/

Fraser, N. (2008). *Scales of justice: Reimagining political space in a globalizing world*. Columbia University Press., https://cup.columbia.edu/book/scales-of-justice/9780231146807

Fricker, M. (2007). *Epistemic injustice: Power and the ethics of knowing*. Oxford University Press., DOI: 10.1093/acprof:oso/9780198237907.001.0001

Furtado, C. (2022). *Development and underdevelopment*. University of California Press. https://www.ucpress.edu/books/development-and-underdevelopment/paper

Gadgil, M., Berkes, F., & Folke, C. (1993). Indigenous knowledge for biodiversity conservation. *Ambio*, *22*(2/3), 151–156. https://www.jstor.org/stable/4314060 PMID: 33566330

Geertz, C. (1973). *The interpretation of cultures: Selected essays*. Basic Books. https://web.mit.edu/allanmc/www/geertz.pdf

Gorjestani, N. M. (2000). *Indigenous knowledge for development: Opportunities and challenges* (World Bank Working Paper No. 24869). World Bank Group. https://documents.worldbank.org/pt/publication/documents-reports/documentdetail/574381468765625385/indigenous-knowledge-for-development-opportunities-and-challenges

Halladay, P., & Gilmour, D. A. (Eds.). (1995). *Conserving biodiversity outside protected areas: The role of traditional agro-ecosystems*. IUCN – The World Conservation Union, AMA – Andalucía, & Centro de Investigación F. González-Bernáldez. https://portals.iucn.org/library/sites/library/files/documents/FR-013.pdf

Harvey, D. (2005). *A brief history of neoliberalism*. Oxford University Press., https://global.oup.com/academic/product/a-brief-history-of-neoliberalism-9780199283279?cc=in&lang=

IOM (International Organization for Migration). (2024). *World migration report 2024*. IOM Publications. https://publications.iom.int/books/world-migration-report-2024

Konwar, J. G., & Das, K. (2012). Creating ethnic identity: A movement of Koch Rajbonshis of Assam. *International Journal of Humanities and Social Sciences, 2*(3), 301–310. Research India Publications. https://www.ripublication.com/ijhss/ijhssv2n3_11.pdf

Lévi-Strauss, C. (1962). *The savage mind* (G. Weidenfeld & Nicholson, Trans.). University of Chicago Press. (Original work published 1962) https://web.mit.edu/allanmc/www/levistrauss.pdf

Marx, K. (1990). *Capital: A critique of political economy. Volume I* (B. Fowkes, Trans.). Penguin Books. (Original work published 1867). https://www.penguinrandomhouse.com/books/261069/capital-by-karl-marx-translated-by-ben-fowkes-introduction-by-ernest-mandel/

Marx, K., & Engels, F. (1848). *Manifesto of the Communist Party* (S. Moore, Trans.). Marxists Internet Archive. (Original work published 1848) https://www.marxists.org/archive/marx/works/download/pdf/Manifesto.pdf

Milanović, B. (2018). *Global inequality: A new approach for the age of globalization*. Harvard University Press. https://www.hup.harvard.edu/books/9780674984035

Ministry of Education. (2025). *Mizoram achieves full functional literacy*. Press Information Bureau, Government of India. https://www.pib.gov.in/PressReleasePage.aspx?PRID=2130080# National Academies of Sciences, Engineering, and Medicine. (2017). *Communities in action: Pathways to health equity*. https://www.ncbi.nlm.nih.gov/books/NBK425845/

Odora Hoppers, C. A. (2009). Education, culture and society in a globalizing world: Implications for comparative and international education. *Compare: A Journal of Comparative Education*, *39*(5), 601–614. DOI: 10.1080/03057920903125628

OECD (Organisation for Economic Cooperation and Development). (2021). *Bridging digital divides in G20 countries*. OECD Publishing. https://doi.org/DOI: 10.1787/35c1d850-en

OECD (Organisation for Economic Cooperation and Development). (2023). *Development Cooperation Report 2023: Debating the Aid System*. OECD Publishing. https://doi.org/DOI: 10.1787/f6edc3c2-en

OpenStax. (2021). *Introduction to Sociology 3e*. https://openstax.org/books/introduction-sociology-3e/pages/9-1-what-is-social-stratification

Piketty, T. (2014). *Capital in the twenty-first century* (A. Goldhammer, Trans.). Belknap Press of Harvard University Press. https://www.hup.harvard.edu/books/9780674430006

Polanyi, K. (2001). *The great transformation: The political and economic origins of our time*. Beacon Press. https://www.beacon.org/The-Great-Transformation-P46.aspx

Ponattu, D., Schmidt, J., & Schmidt, S. (2019). *The urban-rural divide and regionally inclusive growth in the digital age* [Policy brief]. Global Solutions Initiative. https://www.global-solutions-initiative.org/publication/the-urban-rural-divide-and-regionally-inclusive-growth-in-the-digital-age/

Prebisch, R. (1950). *The economic development of Latin America and its principal problems*. United Nations. https://repositorio.cepal.org/handle/11362/29973

Redvers, N., & Blondin, B. (2020). Traditional Indigenous medicine in North America: A scoping review. *PLoS One*, *15*(8), e0237531. DOI: 10.1371/journal.pone.0237531 PMID: 32790714

Reytar, K., Veit, P., & von Braun, J. (2024). *Protecting biodiversity hinges on securing Indigenous and community land rights*. World Resources Institute. https://www.wri.org/insights/indigenous-and-local-community-land-rights-protect-biodiversity

Rodney, W. (1982). *How Europe underdeveloped Africa* (Rev. ed.). Howard University Press., https://monoskop.org/images/8/81/Rodney_Walter_How_Europe_Underdeveloped_Africa_rev_ed_1981.pdf

Sabharwal, N. S., & Sonalkar, W. (2015). Dalit women in India: At the crossroads of gender, class, and caste. *Global Justice: Theory Practice Rhetoric, 8*(1). https://doi.org/DOI: 10.21248/gjn.8.1.54

Salami, M. (2013). A brief history of African feminism. *MsAfropolitan*. https://msafropolitan.com/2013/07/a-brief-history-of-african-feminism .html

Santos, B. de S. (Ed.). (2007). *Cognitive justice in a global world: Prudent knowledges for a decent life* (1st ed.). Lexington Books., https://www .bloomsbury.com/us/cognitive-justice-in-a-global-world-9781978790339/

Scott, J. C. (1998). *Seeing like a state: How certain schemes to improve the human condition have failed*. Yale University Press., DOI: 10.2307/j. ctvxkn7ds

Sen, A. (1999). *Development as freedom*. Oxford University Press., https://global.oup.com/academic/product/development-as-freedom-9780198297581

Sharma, A., & Gupta, A. (Eds.). (2006). *The anthropology of the state: A reader*. Blackwell Publishing. https://voidnetwork.gr/wp-content/uploads/ 2016/10/The-Anthropology-of-the-State-edited-by-Aradhana-Sharma-and -Akhil-Gupta.pdf

Singha, R. (2024). Empathy and compassion as fundamental elements of social cognition. In Shanker, A., & Kumar, V. (Eds.), *Principles and clinical interventions in social cognition* (pp. 22–38). IGI Global., DOI: 10.4018/979-8-3693-1265-0.ch003

Singha, R. (2024a). Fostering mindfulness and compassion: Strategies, benefits, and challenges. In Narayan, P., & Sharma, A. (Eds.), *Applications of service learning in higher education* (pp. 40–60). IGI Global., DOI: 10.4018/979-8-3693-2133-1.ch004

Smith, L. T. (2021). *Decolonizing methodologies: Research and Indigenous Peoples* (2nd ed.). Zed Books (Bloomsbury Publishing). https:// www.bloomsbury.com/us/decolonizing-methodologies-9781786998125/

Stiglitz, J. E. (2012). *Globalization & its discontents*. Penguin India. https://www.amazon.in/Globalization-its-Discontents-Joseph-Stiglitz/ dp/0143417819

Tsing, A. L. (2005). *Friction: An ethnography of global connection*. Princeton University Press., https://archive.org/details/frictionethnogra0000tsin

UNDESA. (United Nations, Department of Economic and Social Affairs). (2023). *World social report 2023: Leaving no one behind in an ageing world*. United Nations Publications. https://desapublications.un.org/publications/world-social-report-2023-leaving-no-one-behind-ageing-world

UNDP. (2004). *Decentralized governance for development: A combined practice note on decentralization, local governance and urban/rural development*. https://www.undp.org/sites/g/files/zskgke326/files/publications/DLGUD_PN_English.pdf

UNDP. (2014). *Implementing the UN Declaration on the Rights of Indigenous Peoples: A handbook for parliamentarians*. https://www.undp.org/sites/g/files/zskgke326/files/publications/es/RightsOfIndigenousPeoples-HandbookForParliamentarians-EN.pdf

UNDP. (2021). *UNDP Strategic Plan 2022–2025*. https://www.undp.org/sites/g/files/zskgke326/files/2022-07/UNDP%20Strategic%20Plan%20 2022-2025.pdf

UNDP. (2024). *Human Development Report 2023/2024: Breaking the gridlock*. https://hdr.undp.org/system/files/documents/global-report-document/hdr2023-24reporten.pdf

UNDP (United Nations Development Programme). (2016). *Human development report 2016: Human development for everyone*. UNDP. https://hdr.undp.org/content/human-development-report-2016

United Nations. (2015). *Transforming our world: The 2030 Agenda for Sustainable Development*. https://sdgs.un.org/2030agenda

Visvanathan, S. (1997). *A carnival for science: Essays on science, technology and development*. Oxford University Press., https://archive.org/download/TheCarnivalOfScience-ShivVishvanathan/shiv-carnival-science.pdf

Zamora, A. (2021). *How local and ethnic women in Latin America are transforming their communities' economies*. Rights and Resources Initiative. https://rightsandresources.org/blog/how-local-and-ethnic-women-in-latin-america-are-transforming-their-communities-economies/

KEY TERMS AND DEFINITIONS

Cultural Dimensions: Refers to how cultural beliefs, practices, and values influence economic behaviours, social relations, and perceptions of inequality within and across communities.

Development Anthropology: A subfield of anthropology that studies how development policies affect communities, emphasizing local participation, cultural context, and the unintended impacts of interventions.

Economic Inequality: The unequal distribution of wealth, income, and resource access among individuals, groups, or regions is often influenced by historical, structural, and cultural factors.

Inclusive Development: Development that ensures equal access to opportunities, resources, and decision-making, prioritizing the needs and rights of marginalized and vulnerable groups.

Local Knowledge Systems: Community-based understandings, practices, and innovations developed through experience and tradition are often overlooked in mainstream development planning.

Participatory Approaches: Development strategies that actively involve community members in decision-making, fostering ownership, accountability, and culturally appropriate outcomes.

Structural Determinants: Institutional, political, and systemic factors—like governance, laws, and policies—shape access to resources and perpetuate or reduce inequality.

Chapter 6
Digital Economies and Marginalized Communities in North-East India:
Labor, Identity, and Resistance in the Digital Age

Vishal Jain
https://orcid.org/0000-0003-1126-7424
School of Engineering and Technology, Vivekananda Institute of Professional Studies - Technical Campus, New Delhi, India

Archan Mitra
https://orcid.org/0000-0002-1419-3558
Amity University, Mumbai, India

Sanchita Paul
https://orcid.org/0009-0006-6437-3991
Neil Patel Digital India, India

DOI: 10.4018/979-8-3373-1260-6.ch006

ABSTRACT

This chapter examines how digital economies are transforming the lives of marginalized communities in North-East India, a region characterized by socio-cultural diversity and economic vulnerability. It will focus on how digital platforms like gig work applications, e-commerce, and digital micro-entrepreneurship integrate with or disrupt traditional labor practices, such as artisanal crafts and subsistence economies. The study will highlight ongoing socio-economic challenges, including algorithmic biases, digital illiteracy, and labor commodification, which exacerbate existing inequalities. Simultaneously, it will explore how marginalized groups actively adapt to these challenges by leveraging digital tools to preserve cultural identity and create alternative economies. Through ethnographic fieldwork and case studies in Assam, Manipur, and Meghalaya, the chapter will provide insights into the complex interplay between digital inclusion, cultural resilience, and systemic exclusion.

1. INTRODUCTION

1.1 Background and Context

1.1.1 The Rise of Digital Economies Globally and in India

Over the past two decades, digital economies have emerged as a transformative force globally, reshaping traditional industries, labor systems, and governance structures. Digital platforms, ranging from e-commerce and fintech to gig work applications, have created new economic opportunities while also deepening existing structural inequalities (Montgomery & Baglioni, 2021; Nathan, Kelkar, & Mehta, 2022). In India, the government's ambitious "Digital India" initiative has driven rapid technological expansion, aiming to connect remote regions, promote digital financial inclusion, and create employment through digital infrastructure. However, this national push often overlooks regional disparities, especially in areas like the North-East, where infrastructural limitations, ethnic diversity, and historic marginalization challenge the seamless implementation of digital integration (Kikhi & Gautam, 2023; Ziipao, 2023). While digital transformation promises productivity and empowerment, its uneven rollout tends to reproduce existing hierarchies, particularly in regions with fragile connectivity, low digital literacy, and limited platform representation (Chaka, 2022; Gruber, 2023). As India deepens its engagement with the global digital economy, understanding how marginalized regions are included, or excluded, becomes critical for equitable development.

1.1.2 North-East India's Socio-Cultural Uniqueness and Historical Marginalization

North-East India, comprising eight states and over 200 distinct ethnic groups, represents a region of immense cultural richness and socio-political complexity. Historically isolated by geography and geopolitics, the region has often been relegated to the periphery of national development narratives (Kikhi & Gautam, 2023; Mishra, 2025). Postcolonial policies, militarization, and economic neglect have resulted in systemic underinvestment in infrastructure and education. This marginalization is compounded by limited digital infrastructure and poor platform representation, leading to digital exclusion (Ziipao, 2023). Despite this, communities in the region have sustained vibrant traditional economies, centered on artisanal crafts, agriculture, and local barter systems, deeply intertwined with cultural and ecological knowledge (Nongbri et al., 2021). While India's Look East Policy and Startup Northeast missions aim to integrate the region into broader economic circuits, these initiatives often adopt a top-down model that overlooks local contexts and needs (Mishra, 2025). Consequently, there is a need for grounded research that foregrounds community voices and examines how the digital economy intersects with identity, resistance, and empowerment in North-East India (Kumar, 2023).

1.1.3 Traditional Labor Systems: Artisanal Crafts, Agriculture, Barter and Subsistence Economies

The traditional labor systems in North-East India are anchored in artisanal, agricultural, and barter-based economies that prioritize community over capital. Handloom weaving, bamboo craft, and pottery, especially among women, are not merely economic activities but also repositories of cultural identity (Gogoi, Bhuyan, & Boruah, 2025). In Assam, for example, women-led weaving communities like those engaged in the Swarnirbhar Naari initiative have turned centuries-old craft knowledge into microenterprises, especially post-2020 (The Indian Express, 2024). Similarly, in Manipur, youth-run digital collectives such as Foodwifi and Teakore are leveraging the digital economy while rooted in traditional entrepreneurial ethics (Rest of World, 2024). Subsistence agriculture remains a dominant livelihood, especially in Meghalaya, where communities engage in foraging, terrace farming, and ecological stewardship passed down through generations. These practices resist commodification and challenge capitalist modes of productivity, often aligning with indigenous knowledge systems (Nongbri et al., 2021; Swu & Roy, 2025). However, the encroachment of digital labor regimes, gig work platforms, and algorithmic governance threatens to displace these practices or reduce them to market commodities (Altenried, 2022; Yin, 2024). A nuanced understanding of how traditional labor is adapting, or resisting, this shift is essential to understanding the full impact of digital economies in the region.

1.2 Problem Statement

Despite growing digital penetration across India, the North-East remains digitally marginalized due to structural inequalities and limited representation. Digital platforms, while offering new avenues for income and mobility, often disrupt established labor systems rooted in community, culture, and sustainability. This disruption is rarely neutral, it introduces algorithmic biases, market-driven imperatives, and exploitative labor models (Cini, 2023; Ziipao, 2023). Furthermore, digital capitalism tends to homogenize labor, often erasing cultural specificity and undervaluing indigenous knowledge (Chaka, 2022). In this context, the integration of digital technologies into local economies requires critical examination. Are these technologies genuinely inclusive, or do they replicate and deepen existing exclusions? How do communities in Assam, Manipur, and Meghalaya navigate these tensions between economic opportunity and cultural survival? Addressing these questions is crucial for building equitable and culturally grounded digital futures in the region.

1.3 Research Objectives

- To analyze labor transformation, digital inclusion/exclusion, and cultural resilience in North-East India.
- To explore adaptive strategies used by marginalized communities to navigate digital disruptions.
- To examine how traditional labor systems integrate with or resist platform-based digital economies.
- To identify region-specific challenges such as algorithmic bias, connectivity gaps, and policy misalignments.

1.4 Research Questions

- How are digital platforms reshaping traditional labor in North-East India?
- What challenges do marginalized communities face in accessing or benefiting from digital economies?
- In what ways do these communities resist, adapt, or reclaim identity in the digital space?

1.5 Scope and Significance

This study focuses on Assam, Manipur, and Meghalaya, three culturally distinct states in North-East India with varying degrees of digital engagement. By combining ethnographic insights with case-based analysis, the research highlights how digital economies intersect with labor, identity, and marginality. It examines digital artisans and women-led enterprises in Assam, youth gig workers and e-commerce platforms in Manipur, and digital knowledge preservation in Meghalaya. The findings contribute to interdisciplinary debates in media studies, development anthropology, and digital labor economics. This work not only fills a gap in scholarship on the digital periphery but also provides grounded frameworks for inclusive technology and policy design that center local knowledge and community agency.

2. LITERATURE REVIEW

2.1 Digital Economies and Labor Precarity

Platform-based digital economies promise flexibility but often entrench precarious labor conditions, particularly in marginalized regions like North-East India. Platform capitalism—where data-driven apps mediate economic exchange—has reconfigured work into task-based gigs rather than stable employment (Khalid, 2025; Montgomery & Baglioni, 2021). While advocates of this model tout entrepreneurial freedom and low entry barriers, critics argue it operates in a regulatory grey zone that enables worker exploitation and algorithmic control in lieu of formal labor rights (Cini, 2023; Nathan et al., 2022). Workers are effectively reduced to data points managed by opaque algorithms, with little say over wages, hours, or performance evaluations (Vogel, 2023). This gig paradigm breeds widespread "precarity"—income instability, lack of workplace protections, and minimal bargaining power—especially among those already on the margins of the global economy.

In India, platform jobs through services like ride-hailing and e-commerce (e.g., Ola, Amazon) disproportionately accrue to urban, tech-savvy workers, leaving peripheral states such as Assam, Manipur, and Meghalaya with limited benefits (Ziipao, 2023). The North-East's infrastructural gaps, linguistic diversity, and cultural distance from metropolitan norms further hinder the integration of gig platforms. In Manipur, for instance, homegrown apps like Foodwifi and My Cabs have emerged to serve local needs but struggle against frequent internet shutdowns, funding shortfalls, and lack of algorithmic visibility on larger networks (Rest of World, 2024). These cases echo global patterns of gig workers teetering between autonomy and exploitation, with additional burdens in regions that lack robust digital infrastructure or political stability. Recognizing these labor dynamics is crucial for assessing the true promises and pitfalls of digital inclusion in North-East India.

2.2 Digital Inequality and Algorithmic Bias

Despite India's rapid connectivity growth, deep digital inequalities persist and are compounded by algorithmic biases that disproportionately affect regions like North-East India. Digital inequality is multilayered: it encompasses not only infrastructural and affordability gaps but also deficits in digital literacy and relevant local-language content (Chaka, 2022). In North-East India, geographic isolation and decades of underinvestment have produced chronically low broadband penetration and digital literacy rates, entrenching a regional digital divide (Kikhi & Gautam, 2023; Ziipao, 2023).

Algorithmic bias in dominant platforms further skews digital opportunity. Far from neutral, algorithms carry their creators' cultural and economic assumptions, which can systematically disadvantage users from peripheral communities (Cini, 2023; Rizzi et al., 2021). For example, e-commerce search rankings and gig-work task allocations often favor urban language fluency and proximity to high-demand areas, penalizing those operating on the margins (Chaka, 2022; Nathan et al., 2022). As a result, many marginalized users experience algorithmic invisibility – their participation in online platforms generates little reward or recognition, reinforcing their exclusion (Chaka, 2022).

In North-East India, these digital injustices are not abstract—they manifest daily. In Manipur, local ride-hailing and delivery startups like Teakore and Foodwifi struggle for visibility, in part because ranking algorithms sideline content from smaller regions (Rest of World, 2024). Similarly, Assamese women who market handloom products via Instagram and WhatsApp find their reach limited by algorithms tuned to metropolitan aesthetics and dominant languages (Gogoi et al., 2025; The Indian Express, 2024). Major platforms offer little support for indigenous languages such as Khasi (Meghalaya) or Mizo (Mizoram), effectively excluding many potential users and content creators (Nongbri et al., 2021). These inequities complicate the narrative of "Digital India" as an equalizer: without deliberate efforts toward algorithmic fairness and culturally inclusive design, digital expansion risks reinforcing the very divides it aims to bridge.

2.3 Economic Anthropology of Indigenous Labor

Indigenous labor in North-East India is grounded in communal values and ecological knowledge, a paradigm that diverges sharply from the profit-driven logic of digital capitalism. In these traditional systems, work is understood not merely as an economic activity but as a social practice tied to collective well-being, customary rights, and cultural continuity (McCormack, 2022; Nongbri et al., 2021). Activities such as handloom weaving, bamboo crafting, foraging, and subsistence farming often operate through barter, reciprocity, or self-help networks, embedding value in relationships and heritage rather than in monetary profit. Labor, in this context, is inseparable from identity and land, intertwined with rituals and stewardship of local ecologies (Swu & Roy, 2025).

Yet platform capitalism's emphasis on individual productivity and algorithmic efficiency directly clashes with these indigenous labor ethics (Altenried, 2022; Vogel, 2023). This clash raises fears that digitizing traditional practices will strip away their cultural meaning, reducing community-based labor to commodified tasks. However, some initiatives seek to bridge these worlds: for instance, Assam's Swarnirbhar Naari project has moved artisanal weaving into online marketplaces while still honoring its cultural context, showing that digital tools can be adapted to support rather than erase indigenous practices (The Indian Express, 2024). Moreover, Northeastern communities have long upheld models of self-reliance—such as cooperative grain banks and clan-managed commons—that demonstrate the resilience of communal labor values (Dana et al., 2023; Gogoi et al., 2025). These examples underscore the importance of shielding community-centric economies from being subsumed under exploitative platform models masquerading as "empowerment" (Ziipao, 2023).

2.4 Identity, Resistance, and Cultural Resilience

Digital platforms can be a double-edged sword for cultural identity: while they often homogenize diverse voices, marginalized communities in North-East India are leveraging these same technologies for cultural resilience and resistance. On one hand, the algorithm-driven tendencies of online capitalism can flatten distinct ethnic identities into generic, click-friendly content (Cini, 2023; Jereza, 2021). On the other, communities are appropriating digital media to preserve and celebrate local identities in ways that mainstream platforms usually overlook (Chaka, 2022; Magarelli, 2025). In Meghalaya, for example, community-led projects have embraced digital storytelling: the NESFAS "Eat Different" podcast records Khasi food traditions and The Forgotten Folklore Project digitizes tribal folktales for younger generations (NESFAS, 2023; Syllad, 2023). Such efforts reclaim digital spaces as repositories of memory and culture rather than sites of erasure.

Cultural resistance also takes collective and entrepreneurial forms. In Assam, women-led handloom cooperatives use WhatsApp and Instagram to bypass exploitative middlemen, merging digital entrepreneurship with cultural sovereignty (Gogoi et al., 2025). In conflict-prone Manipur, despite recurring internet shutdowns, youth-led platforms like Foodwifi and Teakore have built local gig networks grounded in community values and regional identity (Rest of World, 2024; Ursa & Arunkumar, 2023). These grassroots innovations demonstrate that digital inclusion is not just about access, but about agency – the ability of marginalized groups to adapt technology to local needs and values. As issues of land, language, and labor rights intersect with the digital sphere, Northeastern communities are forging hybrid models of resistance that challenge both state neglect and corporate commodification (Kumar, 2023; Swu & Roy, 2025).

3. THEORETICAL FRAMEWORK

3.1 Economic Anthropology and Subsistence Theory

Economic anthropology provides a lens to understand labor not simply as a market commodity but as a culturally embedded practice. In North-East India, traditional economies, such as weaving, foraging, or subsistence farming, are guided by logics of reciprocity, barter, and communal stewardship (McCormack, 2022; Gogoi et al., 2025). These practices often carry symbolic value tied to identity, kinship, and ecological balance. The monetization of such labor through digital platforms introduces tensions between relational labor ethics and extractive platform logics. For example, women artisans in Assam using Instagram for handloom sales gain visibility but also risk commodifying their cultural expressions under algorithmic imperatives (The Indian Express, 2024). Digitization, while offering new markets, also shifts value from community validation to external metrics like likes, views, and sales (Nongbri et al., 2021). This transformation can erode the symbolic and ecological significance of indigenous labor, necessitating frameworks that recognize cultural economies as distinct from capitalist models.

3.2 Digital Sociology and Platform Capitalism

Digital sociology examines how technologies restructure labor, identity, and power. Platform capitalism, a term coined to describe the dominance of firms like Uber, Amazon, or Meesho, represents a new mode of economic control wherein data is commodified and labor is algorithmically governed (Montgomery & Baglioni, 2021; Nathan et al., 2022). Central to this model is surveillance capitalism, where platforms extract behavioral data from users to predict and monetize future actions (Vogel, 2023; Gruber, 2023). Workers are rated, ranked, and often rendered invisible if they fall outside desirable algorithmic profiles (Cini, 2023).

In North-East India, this invisibilization is compounded by infrastructural and cultural marginality. For instance, gig workers in Manipur report being sidelined due to internet disruptions or lack of geographic prioritization by platforms (Rest of World, 2024). Digital labor governance, framed around metrics and efficiency, clashes with regional practices rooted in relationality and adaptation. By analyzing these dynamics, digital sociology reveals how platform economies reproduce social inequalities under the guise of innovation.

3.3 Postcolonial and Decolonial Frameworks

Postcolonial theory critiques how colonial legacies continue to shape political, economic, and epistemic hierarchies. North-East India, long treated as a strategic frontier rather than an integral part of the Indian polity, exemplifies internal colonialism, marked by neglect, militarization, and policy paternalism (Mishra, 2025; Kikhi & Gautam, 2023). Digital development initiatives often replicate this pattern by imposing techno-centric models without acknowledging indigenous knowledge or self-determined priorities.

Decolonial frameworks push beyond critique, emphasizing epistemic disobedience and borderland identities (Chaka, 2022; Swu & Roy, 2025). They argue for the validation of alternative worldviews, including those where labor is relational, land is sacred, and data is not merely extractive. For instance, the Meghalaya Traditional Knowledge Portal documents indigenous wellness systems not to commodify them, but to protect collective rights and promote cultural continuity (SP News Agency, 2024). In this view, digital participation is not merely about access, but about resisting erasure and asserting ontological pluralism. Postcolonial and decolonial theories thus provide tools to interrogate who defines value, whose knowledge counts, and how digital futures can be made more just.

3.4 Cultural Resilience Theory

Cultural resilience refers to a community's ability to maintain and adapt its identity, practices, and values in the face of external pressures. In the context of digital economies, cultural resilience underscores how marginalized communities resist homogenization through creative adaptation (Magarelli, 2025; Dana et al., 2023). Digital storytelling, podcasts, and localized content platforms enable communities to document oral traditions, preserve endangered languages, and engage younger generations in cultural transmission (Syllad, 2023; NESFAS, 2023).

In Meghalaya, projects like The Forgotten Folklore and "Eat Different" exemplify this process, reviving indigenous narratives and culinary knowledge through digital formats (Syllad, 2023; NESFAS, 2023). These initiatives challenge dominant narratives of progress and reframe digital tools as mediums of memory and continuity rather than rupture. Cultural resilience theory also recasts communities as active agents who negotiate modernity on their own terms, rather than as passive recipients of development. This framework aligns closely with grassroots efforts in Assam and Manipur, where digital artisans and youth-led platforms maintain cultural specificity even as they enter the digital marketplace (Gogoi et al., 2025; Rest of World, 2024). Thus, cultural resilience becomes both a method and a vision for equitable digital futures.

3. RESEARCH METHODOLOGY

3.1 Research Design

This study adopts a qualitative, interpretive research design grounded in ethnographic and case-based approaches. Given the research objectives, to explore labor transformation, digital inclusion/exclusion, cultural resilience, and adaptive strategies, the methodology emphasizes contextual depth over numerical generalization. The study is rooted in economic anthropology and digital sociology, aiming to understand lived experiences, socio-cultural dynamics, and power asymmetries within North-East India's evolving digital economy.

3.2 Field Sites and Participant Selection

The research focuses on three states, Assam, Manipur, and Meghalaya, each selected for their distinct socio-cultural, economic, and digital engagement profiles:

- **Assam**: Known for its handloom heritage and women-led micro-enterprises. Focus will be on digital artisans using platforms like Instagram and WhatsApp.
- **Manipur**: A hub for youth-driven gig work and local e-commerce startups. The focus will include gig workers and founders of community-based digital services like Foodwifi and Teakore.
- **Meghalaya**: Renowned for efforts in cultural and ecological preservation through digital storytelling and indigenous knowledge platforms like the Meghalaya Traditional Knowledge Portal and NESFAS.

Participants will include digital entrepreneurs, platform workers, traditional artisans, cultural storytellers, and cooperative members. Snowball sampling and purposive sampling techniques will be used to ensure community representation across gender, age, and economic roles.

3.3 Data Collection Methods

- **Semi-structured interviews**: With approximately 30–40 participants across the three states to gather narratives of digital engagement, labor experiences, and identity negotiations.
- **Digital ethnography**: Analysis of online content (e.g., Instagram shops, YouTube channels, podcast episodes, community websites) to explore digital storytelling, platform use, and algorithmic visibility.
- **Document analysis**: Government reports, NGO publications, platform policies, and local media stories will be examined for policy discourse and contextual framing.

3.4 Data Analysis Strategy

Data will be analyzed using a combination of inductive thematic analysis and narrative analysis. Thematic analysis will involve open and axial coding to identify recurring patterns related to digital labor, platform governance, identity assertion, and cultural resilience. NVivo software will be used to manage and visualize coded data from interview transcripts and online content. Narrative analysis will help interpret how participants frame their digital experiences, such as shifts in self-perception, community belonging, or resistance to platform exploitation. Attention will be paid to both manifest themes (e.g., access to online markets) and latent meanings (e.g., symbolic loss or pride linked to digital work). These insights will be interpreted through the study's theoretical lenses to link empirical patterns with broader structural dynamics.

3.5 Limitations

The study may face several limitations. First, limited internet access in some rural areas may restrict digital ethnography or participant recruitment. Second, linguistic diversity could affect the clarity and depth of interviews, particularly where local dialects dominate and translation nuances arise. Third, socio-political instability, as seen in Manipur's recent internet shutdowns, can disrupt data collection and limit real-time platform observations. Fourth, the qualitative nature of the study prioritizes depth over breadth, which may restrict generalizability to broader populations or other states. Finally, remote fieldwork due to travel constraints might limit the ability to triangulate findings through direct community immersion or participant observation. These limitations will be mitigated through careful sampling, contextual interpretation, and transparency in methodological reflexivity.

4. DATA ANALYSIS

4.1 Mapping Emerging Themes of Digital Engagement and Cultural Labor

Table 1. Thematic Codes and Descriptions

Theme	Sub-Themes	States Covered
Labor Transformation	Gig work, digital microenterprises, hybrid economies	Assam, Manipur
Platform Challenges	Algorithmic bias, platform opacity, discoverability issues	All three
Cultural Resilience	Folklore digitization, language revival, food sovereignty	Meghalaya, Assam
Digital Inclusion/ Exclusion	Literacy gaps, infrastructural barriers, youth-led innovations	Manipur, Meghalaya
Adaptive Strategies	Social media marketing, local platforms, digital cooperatives	Assam, Manipur, Meghalaya

Table 1 outlines the key thematic codes that emerged from the data analysis, offering definitions that structured both intra-state and cross-state comparisons.

4.2 Assam: Craft Heritage Meets Platform Economy

Interviews with women weavers using platforms like Instagram and WhatsApp (e.g., "Aalok Handlooms") revealed how traditional labor is transitioning into microenterprises. Artisans reported increased income, design experimentation, and pride in cultural preservation. However, they also highlighted challenges in reaching wider audiences due to lack of SEO knowledge and language barriers on platforms dominated by metro-centric algorithms.

Figure 1. Instagram Reach vs. Local Sales for Assamese Weavers

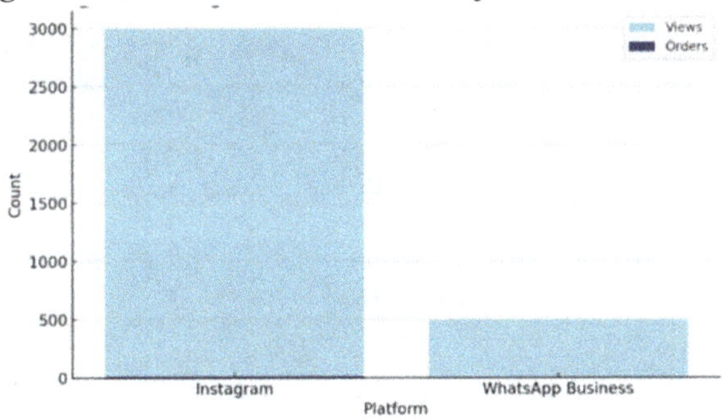

Figure 1 illustrates how Assamese women artisans using Instagram generate significantly higher visibility and sales compared to those relying solely on WhatsApp Business, highlighting the unequal but strategic use of platform affordances

Table 2. Comparative Reach and Order Metrics of Assamese Women Entrepreneurs on Instagram vs. WhatsApp Business

Platform Used	Average Monthly Views	Orders per Month	Language Used
Instagram	3,000	8–15	English/Assamese
WhatsApp Business	500	5–8	Assamese

Table 2 shows Assamese women using Instagram report significantly higher monthly views and order volumes compared to those using

WhatsApp Business, suggesting that visual-centric, multilingual platforms offer expanded economic visibility.

4.3 Manipur: Youth Innovation and Gig Precarity

Startups like Foodwifi and Teakore were analyzed using digital ethnography and interviews with founders. Workers cited flexibility and empowerment, especially during COVID-19, but also reported exploitative ranking systems and high vulnerability during internet blackouts.

Figure 2. Challenges Reported by Manipur Gig Workers (n=12)

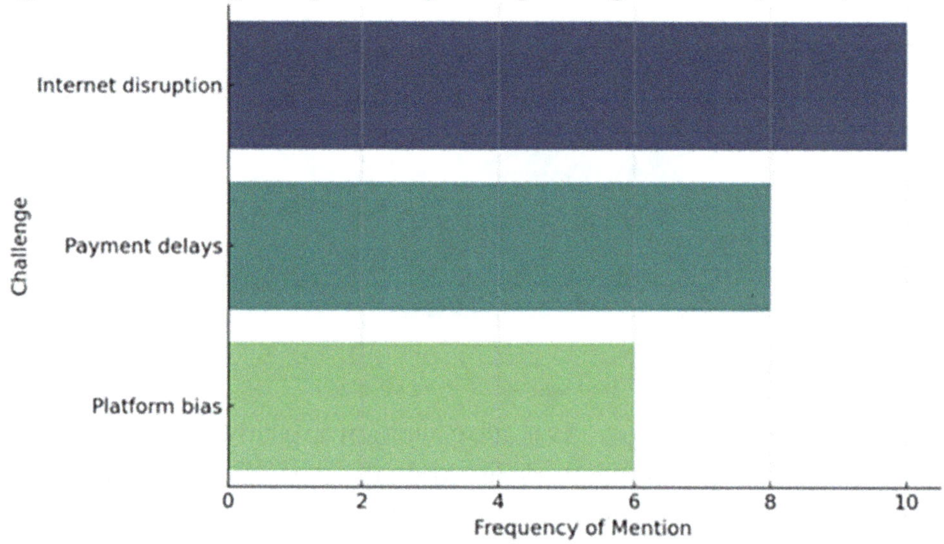

Figure 2 shows Manipur's gig workers identified internet disruption, payment delays, and algorithmic bias as the top three obstacles impacting the reliability and fairness of platform-based employment.

Table 3. Key Challenges Reported by Gig Workers in Manipur's Platform Economy

Challenge	Frequency of Mention
Internet disruption	10
Payment delays	8
Platform bias (location/language)	6

Table 3 shows gig workers in Manipur most frequently reported challenges such as internet disruption, delayed payments, and platform bias based on location and language, reflecting both infrastructural and algorithmic precarity.

4.4 Meghalaya: Digitizing Indigenous Knowledge and Identity

Analysis of content from the Meghalaya Traditional Knowledge Portal and NESFAS podcast series (e.g., "Eat Different") shows digital tools being used to archive indigenous recipes, herbal knowledge, and folktales. Interview narratives highlighted pride in cultural expression and youth engagement. However, concerns about cultural appropriation and sustainability funding were expressed.

Table 4. Digital Platforms and Content Types in Meghalaya

Initiative	Digital Format	Content Focus
Meghalaya TK Portal	Website/Database	Medicinal knowledge
The Forgotten Folklore Project	Storybooks/eBooks	Tribal folktales
NESFAS "Eat Different" Podcast	Audio series	Foraging and food culture

Table 4 highlights how different digital platforms in Meghalaya serve as repositories of indigenous knowledge, from medicinal practices and tribal stories to foraging traditions, thereby supporting cultural preservation through multimedia formats.

4.5 Cross-Regional Narratives: Identity, Inequality, and Innovation

- **Digital Labor and Identity**: Participants often framed digital work as a tool for reclaiming dignity and community value. For instance, Assamese women described weaving as "a way to show who we are, not just earn."
- **Platform Dependence**: All regions highlighted dependence on fragile digital infrastructures and opaque algorithms, leading to cycles of vulnerability.
- **Localized Innovation**: Despite challenges, communities are building adaptive strategies, from gig cooperatives in Manipur to culturally specific e-commerce in Assam and heritage preservation in Meghalaya.

4.6 Regional Distribution of Themes: NVivo Analysis

Figure 3. Frequency of Codes Across States

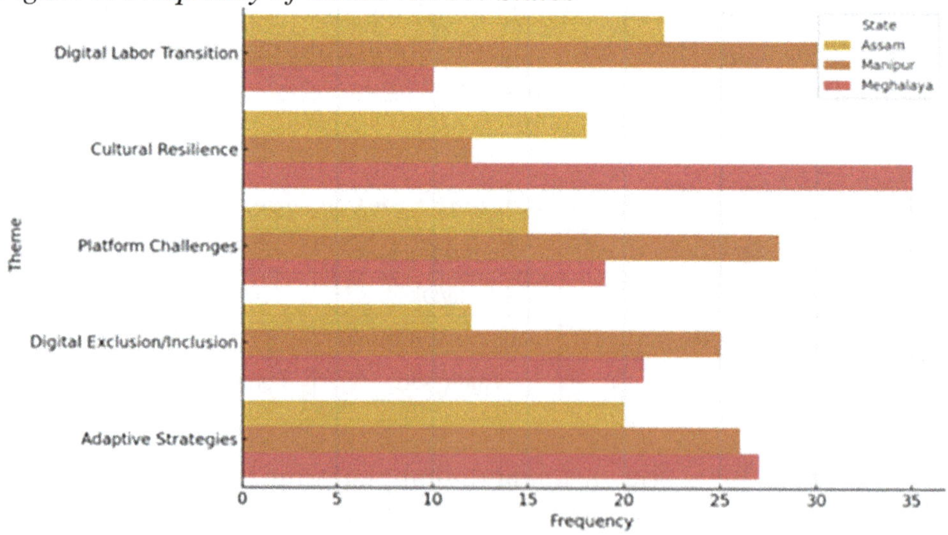

Figure 3 compares the thematic code frequency across Assam, Manipur, and Meghalaya, indicating how different digital experiences are shaped by localized socio-cultural and infrastructural contexts.

Table 5. Frequency of Thematic Codes by State

Theme	Assam	Manipur	Meghalaya
Digital Labor Transition	22	30	10
Cultural Resilience	18	12	35
Platform Challenges	15	28	19
Digital Exclusion/Inclusion	12	25	21
Adaptive Strategies	20	26	27

Table 5 presents the distribution of key themes identified across Assam, Manipur, and Meghalaya, showing that while Manipur had the highest frequency in digital labor and platform challenges, Meghalaya emerged strongest in cultural resilience and adaptive strategies.

6. FINDINGS AND DISCUSSION

6.1 Digital Labor as Transformation and Tension

In Assam and Manipur, digital platforms are reshaping traditional labor into new economic forms. Women weavers in Assam have transitioned into micro-entrepreneurs, using Instagram and WhatsApp to market handloom products, reflecting a fusion of cultural heritage and platform economy (Gogoi, Bhuyan, & Boruah, 2025; The Indian Express, 2024). Participants expressed increased autonomy and visibility but also reported constraints such as SEO illiteracy, language bias in search algorithms, and unfamiliarity with digital marketing tools. Similarly, in Manipur, gig economy platforms like Foodwifi have created localized employment for youth. Founders emphasized agency and flexibility, while gig workers revealed anxieties around algorithmic ranking and dependence on unstable digital infrastructures (Rest of World, 2024).

6.2 Precarity and Algorithmic Governance

Across all three states, platform-based work is marked by systemic precarity. Workers and entrepreneurs consistently cited challenges related to payment delays, sudden algorithmic visibility drops, and lack of formal protections. In Manipur, workers described platform labor as "disappearing work", when internet is down, so is income (Rest of World, 2024). Algorithms mediate not just work allocation but reputation and earnings, often using opaque metrics that fail to account for regional limitations such as connectivity gaps or local dialect usage (Cini, 2023; Rizzi et al., 2021).

Algorithmic governance also reinforces marginality. In Assam, artisans noted that hashtags or captions in Assamese were less likely to trend, forcing them to communicate in English, sometimes uncomfortably. This subtle but persistent erasure of linguistic diversity reflects broader issues of epistemic exclusion (Chaka, 2022). While workers have embraced digital tools, the platforms themselves rarely accommodate the cultural and linguistic contexts of North-East India, resulting in algorithmic invisibilization.

6.3 Cultural Resilience in the Digital Realm

Unlike dominant narratives that view digital transformation as uniformly homogenizing, this research highlights how communities actively preserve and adapt their cultural identities online. In Meghalaya, initiatives like The Forgotten Folklore Project and the NESFAS podcast series demonstrate how oral traditions, foraging knowledge, and indigenous values are being archived and disseminated through digital media (Syllad, 2023; NESFAS, 2023). Youth participation in these initiatives shows that digital storytelling can bridge generational gaps and support cultural continuity.

This aligns with Magarelli's (2025) argument that digital storytelling is not just a communication tool but a mode of cultural mediation. The act of curating stories in digital form enables communities to resist both cultural erasure and misrepresentation. Moreover, as cultural producers, these communities shift from being mere 'content consumers' to agents of narrative control.

Cultural resilience, in this context, is not nostalgic preservation but adaptive innovation. In Assam, women artisans reinvent traditional motifs for digital audiences while maintaining symbolic meanings. In Manipur, platforms like Teakore integrate local products into e-commerce while embedding regional aesthetics and ethics into the user experience.

6.4 Digital Inequality and the Limits of Inclusion

Despite the promise of democratized opportunity, the study reveals layered forms of exclusion. Infrastructural challenges remain significant, particularly in rural Meghalaya and parts of Manipur. Interviewees cited limited mobile connectivity, unreliable broadband, and lack of access to digital devices. Even when infrastructure exists, digital literacy varies greatly by age, gender, and geography.

Platform design and governance further reinforce inequality. For instance, Assamese artisans described how Instagram's aesthetic norms privilege urban, minimalist visuals that often marginalize traditional or vernacular designs (Gogoi et al., 2025). Similarly, Manipur's local platforms, though innovative, struggle to gain visibility on national search engines or app stores due to algorithmic ranking systems (Ziipao, 2023).

Moreover, national-level digital policy often fails to account for these nuances. Government schemes like Startup India and Digital India have limited penetration in the region due to both logistical and epistemic gaps (Mishra, 2025; Kumar, 2023). These gaps suggest that digital inequality is not merely a question of access, but of design, representation, and recognition.

6.5 Localized Innovation and Hybrid Economies

One of the most striking findings of the study is the rise of hybrid economic models that blend traditional values with digital tools. In Assam, cooperatives and SHGs use WhatsApp Business not only to sell but also to coordinate production schedules and manage collective finances (Gogoi et al., 2025). In Manipur, founders of Foodwifi and Teakore described building platforms that are culturally responsive, integrating delivery patterns with local festivals, and providing services in Manipuri and English.

These innovations illustrate a bottom-up model of digital transformation that challenges the top-down technocentric approaches embedded in much of India's digital governance. They also resonate with the idea of platform cooperativism, where community-owned platforms resist corporate extraction and reinvest in local development (Dana et al., 2023).

Such models offer pathways toward sustainable digital inclusion. They validate indigenous knowledge, diversify economic participation, and build infrastructures of care and reciprocity, qualities often missing in corporate-led platform economies (Nathan et al., 2022; Khalid, 2025).

6.6 Synthesis: Resistance and Reinvention at the Margins

The findings suggest that North-East India is not a passive recipient of digitalization but a site of critical negotiation. From digitized folktales in Meghalaya to gig worker cooperatives in Manipur and handloom enterprises in Assam, communities are actively reshaping how labor, culture, and technology interact.

Drawing from postcolonial and decolonial frameworks, this study sees these practices as forms of epistemic disobedience (Chaka, 2022; Swu & Roy, 2025). They question dominant narratives of productivity and modernity, offering alternate visions of what a digital economy can look like. By embedding labor within community, platforms within culture, and data within memory, these actors resist both infrastructural exclusion and symbolic erasure.

Thus, digital transformation in North-East India is not linear or uniform. It is a contested, situated process marked by tension and creativity. Future policies and platforms must recognize these complexities to foster equitable, culturally grounded digital futures.

7. POLICY IMPLICATIONS AND RECOMMENDATIONS

7.1 Infrastructure and Digital Inclusion

To address infrastructural inequality and digital exclusion, policymakers must prioritize region-specific strategies for connectivity and access. Despite the expansion of Digital India, many rural areas in Manipur and Meghalaya remain disconnected due to topography and historic underinvestment (Ziipao, 2023; Mishra, 2025).

First, region-specific broadband infrastructure subsidies should be implemented, targeting remote clusters, especially those involved in cultural preservation and artisanal production. Second, community Wi-Fi zones and digital access centers should be developed in coordination with cooperative institutions and self-help groups. Third, multilingual user interfaces must be integrated into both private and public digital platforms, with a focus on tribal languages such as Khasi, Garo, Ao, and Bodo, thereby enabling inclusive participation (Nongbri et al., 2021). Such interventions must be co-created with local communities to ensure relevance, usability, and sustained adoption.

7.2 Algorithmic Fairness and Representation

Given the documented bias in platform visibility and labor allocation, regulatory frameworks must ensure that algorithmic governance does not reinforce digital marginalization.

First, platforms should be mandated to disclose how visibility, ranking, and content moderation systems operate, particularly in their treatment of rural and linguistic minorities (Rizzi et al., 2021; Cini, 2023). Second, design protocols must require the inclusion of regional aesthetics, culturally significant branding, and vernacular language functionality, thereby enabling Assamese, Manipuri, and tribal artisans to engage without erasing their identities (Gogoi et al., 2025). Third, platforms should be subject to independent audits and provide grievance redressal mechanisms to address algorithmic discrimination, especially in gig work and digital retail spaces (Montgomery & Baglioni, 2021).

7.3 Community-led Digital Models

The study found multiple grassroots innovations, including women's cooperatives in Assam using WhatsApp for business and youth-led platforms in Manipur navigating political instability through adaptive strategies (Rest of World, 2024; Dana et al., 2023).

First, state-backed micro-grants and infrastructure subsidies must support the growth of digital cooperatives and locally owned platforms that integrate indigenous knowledge systems. Second, culturally contextualized digital literacy campaigns, delivered by peer educators in local languages, should target digitally excluded demographics such as rural women, elders, and youth. Third, public–civil society collaborations must be formalized to facilitate the digital documentation and dissemination of oral traditions, foraging practices, and cultural histories via community archives and storytelling apps (Syllad, 2023; NESFAS, 2023).

7.4 Holistic Digital Economy Frameworks

Current digital economy policies in India tend to prioritize GDP growth, start-up output, and monetization metrics, overlooking aspects such as cultural sustainability, community self-reliance, and social justice. The findings from this study call for a broader, more inclusive digital development framework.

First, policy discourse must recognize cultural labor, including handloom weaving, herbal medicine, storytelling, and food foraging, as legitimate economic activities that contribute to both livelihoods and collective identity (Swu & Roy, 2025; Kumar, 2023). Second, digital development indices must be expanded to include cultural sustainability indicators, such as preservation of linguistic diversity, intergenerational knowledge transfer, and ecological stewardship. These would complement standard metrics like productivity or user count and align with Sustainable Development Goals (SDGs) such as SDG 5 (Gender Equality), SDG 10 (Reduced Inequalities), and SDG 11 (Sustainable Communities).

Third, a decentralized governance framework should be developed that empowers local institutions, including village councils, tribal bodies, and cooperative networks, to co-create digital policies. This approach resonates with Kikhi & Gautam's (2023) vision of decentralized marginality and calls for the inclusion of epistemic diversity in national development discourses.

Finally, such a framework must move beyond a technocratic logic to integrate values of self-rule (Swaraj), collective participation (Lokniti), and memory-centered knowledge systems. In doing so, it would acknowledge not only the economic contributions of North-East India but also its philosophical potential to redefine the digital economy on more ethical, pluralistic, and sustainable terms (Nathan et al., 2022; Khalid, 2025).

8. CONCLUSION

This research has explored how digital economies are reshaping labor, identity, and cultural resilience across Assam, Manipur, and Meghalaya. By grounding the study in economic anthropology, digital sociology, and postcolonial theory, it has illuminated how communities in North-East India are navigating the promises and pitfalls of digital transformation. The findings demonstrate that while digital platforms offer new avenues for income generation, visibility, and cultural expression, they also reinforce systemic inequalities through algorithmic bias, infrastructural exclusion, and epistemic marginalization.

The study revealed how artisans in Assam, gig workers in Manipur, and indigenous knowledge holders in Meghalaya are creatively engaging with platforms like Instagram, WhatsApp, and community archives to both adapt and resist. These communities are not passive recipients of digital change but active agents reshaping the contours of participation, labor, and representation. Their strategies reflect a deeper cultural logic rooted in self-reliance, reciprocity, and identity preservation, values often excluded from mainstream digital economy frameworks.

The policy recommendations derived from this study advocate for infrastructural equity, algorithmic fairness, culturally embedded digital literacy, and a holistic approach to digital development. Importantly, these must be implemented through participatory governance structures that acknowledge the unique socio-political histories and epistemologies of North-East India. Without such recognition, digital inclusion risks reproducing colonial hierarchies in new technological forms.

Future research should build on these findings by examining longitudinal changes in platform usage, economic outcomes, and cultural expression in these regions. Further investigation into the role of AI, big data, and algorithmic governance in shaping the labor experiences of marginalized populations will also be critical as India's digital infrastructure deepens.

Ultimately, this study underscores the need to rethink digital transformation not merely as technological expansion, but as a cultural, political, and ethical process, one that must center the voices and aspirations of those historically left at the margins of development.

REFERENCES

Altenried, M. (2022). Platforms, labour, and mobility: migration and the gig economy. In *The Routledge handbook of the gig economy* (pp. 180–189). Routledge.

Chaka, C. (2022). Digital marginalization, data marginalization, and algorithmic exclusions: A critical southern decolonial approach to datafication, algorithms, and digital citizenship from the Souths. *Journal of e-Learning and Knowledge Society, 18*(3), 83-95.

Cini, L. (2023). How algorithms are reshaping the exploitation of labour-power: Insights into the process of labour invisibilization in the platform economy. *Theory and Society*, *52*(5), 885–911.

Dana, L. P., Sharma, N., Kumari, S., Tripathy, K. K., Pillai, B. P., & Jayalaxmi, R. (Eds.). (2023). *Cooperatives as a Catalyst for Sustainability: Lessons Learned from Asian Models* (Vol. 12). World Scientific.

Gogoi, N., Bhuyan, S., & Boruah, S. (2025). Empowering Women through Handloom Weaving: A Focus on Northeast Indias' Heritage and Opportunities for Sustainability. *Women Empowerment in Agriculture: A Pathway Towards. Sustainable Development*, •••, 296.

Gruber, J. (2023). *The Relevance of Algorithm Skills for Digital Inequality* (Doctoral dissertation, University of Zurich).

Jereza, R. (2021). Corporeal moderation: Digital labour as affective good. *Social Anthropology. Anthropologie et Sociétés*, *29*(4), 928–943.

Khalid, N. (2025). The Economic Impacts of India's Gig Economy: Navigating Productivity, Inequality, and Market Dynamics. In *Immersive Technology for the Gig Economy: Transformative Business Practices* (pp. 1-32). IGI Global Scientific Publishing.

Kikhi, K., & Gautam, D. R. (Eds.). (2023). *Marginality in India: Perspectives of Marginalisation from the Northeast*. Taylor & Francis.

Kumar, S. (2023). Empowering Bharat: Role of the Northeast in the Indian Vision of Development. *Available at SSRN* 4842098.

Magarelli, E. (2025). Narrating Survival: Digital Storytelling as a Tool for Language Mediation Practices. *Cross-Media Languages. Applied Research. Digital Tools and Methodologies*, (3), 87–98.

McCormack, F. (2022). Commentary on the special issue: Anthropology and the labour theory of value. *Dialectical Anthropology*, *46*(1), 73–84. PMID: 35282139

Meghalaya, S. I. R. (n.d.). *Syllad*. Syllad.

Mishra, M. (2025). The Northeast and India's Look East Policy: A Critical Analysis of Driven Development Model and Challenges. *South Asian Journal of Social Studies and Economics*, *22*(5), 152–161.

Montgomery, T., & Baglioni, S. (2021). Defining the gig economy: Platform capitalism and the reinvention of precarious work. *The International Journal of Sociology and Social Policy*, *41*(9/10), 1012–1025.

Nathan, D., Kelkar, G., & Mehta, B. (2022). Platform economy, techno-nationalism, and gig workers in India. In *The Routledge Handbook of the Gig Economy* (pp. 374–391). Routledge.

Nongbri, T., Bhargava, R., & Nongbri. (2021). *Materiality and Visuality in North East India*. Springer Singapore.

P, S. K., & Punit, I. S. (2024, December 10). This Indian state wants to be a tech hub. But the government keeps shutting down the internet. *Rest of World*.

Rizzi, A., Kessler, A., & Menajovsky, J. (2021). The stories algorithms tell: Bias and financial inclusion at the data margins. *Center for Financial Inclusion, Accion (2021), 35*.

Swu, N., & Roy, S. (2025). Land, Identity, and Economic Stability: Examining the Shift from Community to Private Ownership in Naga Society. *Heritage & Society*, •••, 1–22.

Ursa, T., & Arunkumar, M. C. (2023). Residents' Perceptions and Outcomes of Community-Based Tourism in Andro Village of Manipur. *Dera Natung Government College Research Journal*, *8*(1), 169–179.

Vogel, Y. A. (2023). Neo-commodification of persons: exploitation of personal data and impact on the sharing economy.

Yin, S. (2024). Situating platform gig economy in the formal subsumption of reproductive labor: Transnational migrant domestic workers and the continuum of exploitation and precarity. *Capital and Class*, *48*(1), 119–133.

Ziipao, R. R. (2023). Out of coverage area: Tribes and digital exclusion in North-east India. *Journal of Development Policy and Practice*, 24551333231163930.

Chapter 7
Nonprofit Governance:
When the Private Sector Controls

Gwyneth Edwards
https://orcid.org/0000-0002-5450-4250
HEC Montréal, Canada

ABSTRACT

Using longitudinal case research methods, this paper demonstrates how a for-profit public firm controls a nonprofit organization, using the specific case of Intrawest Corporation, a Canadian property developer, and its timeshare program, Club Intrawest. The research demonstrates how the governance structure allows the for-profit firm to control the assets and revenue streams of the nonprofit organization, while passing on the costs and risk to the timeshare consumers. This chapter exposes this non-standard governance relationship, questioning both the legality and ethics of such a structure.

INTRODUCTION

In 2016, Gretchen Morgenson of the *New York Times* published a story entitled "The Timeshare Hard Sell Comes Roaring Back" (Morgenson, 2016), which described the sales mechanisms employed by many of North

DOI: 10.4018/979-8-3373-1260-6.ch007

America's timeshare developers. Although the notion of the high-pressure timeshare sale was not new, the article touched upon a fundamental component of the timeshare business model: developer control of the nonprofit homeowners' association (HOA), the legal entity created by the developer that is charged to maintain and operate the timeshare program. The control of the HOA by the developer is documented in the timeshare program instruments, but is not explained to the end consumer in typical high-pressure timeshare presentation.

A typical timeshare sale is performed under a time constraint (e.g. 90 minutes), in absence of the detailed developer contract and HOA documents, all of which can run up to hundreds of pages in length. As a result, consumers may believe that they are purchasing an appreciating asset that they own and control when, in fact, they are purchasing access to a commodity (e.g. room nights) that loses its value immediately upon purchase and comes with significant constraints that make the item worthless on the secondary market.

In 2020, the National Association of Attorneys General reminded the public once again of the fraudulent nature of timeshares (Ordonez & Mée, 2020), followed by warnings from the Federal Bureau of Investigation in 2024 (Smith, 2024). And yet, timeshares persist; in 2023, Arizton Advisory & Intelligence (2023) projected a compound annual growth rate of 7–8% to 2028 (a market value of US$15.3 billion).

This paper demonstrates that the developer controls the HOA and the associated revenue streams through a set of legal documents that are created by the timeshare developer itself, and involve several different developer-owned entities (e.g. developer, manager, and declarant). As part of the developer sales process, the timeshare plan is identified as a standalone nonprofit operation (run by the HOA) that is controlled by those who have purchased the timeshares. However, the HOA is not actually independent. Due to an intricate set of rules and guidelines, the developer controls key aspects of the program and therefore retains material control. In both research and practice, however, this little-known phenomenon is not well understood. Nonprofit governance research has focused primarily on charitable fund-raising, social good, and public service organizations, for example. Government regulations also continue to treat for-profits and nonprofits as distinct and separate entities (Delaware General Corporation Law, n.d.).

This paper therefore investigates the phenomenon of why and how for-profit firms control nonprofit organizations, looking at the historical case of Intrawest Corporation (the developer, "Intrawest") and its timeshare program, Club Intrawest (the HOA, "the Club"). The following section explains the research methods used to perform the analysis, which are based on rigorous qualitative case study methods. Following, the history on how Intrawest created the Club is presented, along with the strategies employed to ensure developer control. The for-profit / nonprofit interlocking business model is then presented in detail, expanding upon the roles of each entity and identifying the mechanisms of control. Two legal cases are then presented, to further illustrate the legal issues related to the timeshare program and developer control. The paper concludes with a summary of key legal and ethical issues.

RESEARCH METHODS

The project was undertaken as an inductive qualitative research initiative. An analysis of the corporate governance literature in both the management and public administration domains shows no evidence of researchers studying the relationship between legally independent nonprofit and for-profit entities. Although some research focuses on hybrid profit/nonprofit entities, defined as "organizations in which there is a combination of public and private organizing logics, through mission-driven businesses, social enterprises, cross-sectoral collaboration, and public-private partnerships of various kinds" (Jay, 2013, p. 1), in this developer/HOA case, there is no evidence of organizing for mutual benefit. The research therefore used historical methods and narrative analysis in support of inductive methods. The intent was to identify the emergence of this type of governance arrangement and to theorize on its role within the realm of market-based industries.

The case study was longitudinal in nature, where the primary unit of analysis was the developer-HOA governance relationship. Using an event analysis and temporal mapping (Langley, 1999), firm decisions were analyzed within the context of the governance relationship, to determine types and levels of control. In addition, documents published by other industry actors, including developers, HOAs, government organizations, and industry organizations were incorporated into the analysis, for a total of over 1000 documents, as outlined in APPENDIX 1. The analysis of US legislation and the American Resort Developer Association (ARDA) (including their timeshare lobbying efforts), for example, made it possible to understand industry structure, competitive dynamics and the relationship between developers and the HOAs.

The governance relationship between the for-profit firm, Intrawest and the nonprofit entity, the Club, was then analyzed within the context of the industry. The Club was a nonprofit HOA created in late 1993 by the developer, Intrawest. and trademarked as Club Intrawest (Intrawest Resort Ownership Corporation, 1994)[1]. Intrawest was the developer of the HOA up until January 2016. As such, the analysis was performed on the period from the inception of the club (1993) to the announcement of the sale (2015). The analysis was performed on the HOA, with a focus on the role that the developer, Intrawest, played over time. Formally, the Club is an association formed under the laws of Delaware.

The analysis focused on Club operations to determine the role of the developer and its relationship with various entities. This analysis included a review of both developer and Club financials to understand what was reported, by whom and how. Board decisions and historical events were analyzed to see who made decisions, how they were made and the impact that the decisions had on both the developer and the Club. The analysis also looked at the establishment and operation of the trusts that held the property, to include transfers into the trusts, along with property swaps and additions. Finally, legal documents were also incorporated into the analysis, including (1) the facts and decisions reported through Canada Revenue Agency's (CRA) action against the Club ("the GST case"), where the CRA argued (and won) that the Club was not an agent of the members but rather a stand-alone entity and therefore required to pay Goods and Services Tax (GST) on the annual service fee collected from the timeshare members[2] and (2) the ongoing Quebec Class Action against Intrawest.[3]

THE CREATION OF THE CLUB BY THE DEVELOPER (INTRAWEST)

In 1993, Intrawest, of British Columbia, Canada, managed several different for-profit businesses. To launch the timeshare plan, they created Intrawest Resort Ownership Corporation (IROC).

> *IROC differs from traditional timeshare companies in that it offers equity ownership in the club through an innovative point-based membership system... After constructing a club location, IROC transfers ownership of the vacation units, free and clear of all encumbrances, to a trustee for the Intrawest Resort Club ("Resort Club"), a non-profit, non-stock corporation. In return, IROC receives the right to sell points (vacation time) to the general public in the Resort Club accommodation. Each individual purchasing points becomes a member in the Resort Club with the entitlement to stay at any Resort Club location or at international resorts through an affiliation with one of the major exchange agencies... Each accommodation type at each Resort Club location is assigned a point value for each day of the year. The point value assigned to each day depends on the day of the week and season, with higher demand times carrying a higher point value. The selling price per point is exclusively controlled by IROC depending upon market conditions. A member of the Resort Club receives an annual allotment of points in perpetuity... Points may be sold, transferred or bequeathed, subject to IROC's right of first refusal to purchase such points. (Intrawest Corporation, 1998, p. 52)*

Keith Thompson, a real estate and financing lawyer, was contracted to establish the Club.

> *I first started doing work for Intrawest Corporation in 1993. At that time, Intrawest had made the decision that they wanted to develop a timeshare program for use in their resorts across North America.* **They had named one of their officers, a fellow called Jim Gibbons, to head up that program.** *And Mr. Gibbons contacted me initially in 1993 and asked what I knew of timeshare. I responded to Mr. Gibbons at the time that I knew almost nothing about timeshare, and he asked me to review materials. I met with him several times over the next two weeks*

> *and at the end of that time, he and I took a trip to Miami Florida, and attended a meeting of the* **American Association of Resort Developers** *in Miami and met a number of people involved in the timeshare industry in North America and learned a fair amount there with respect to the kinds of timeshare programs being offered across North America. We came back to Vancouver, and at that time, I was retained by Intrawest to review with them, and look at a number of timeshare models that they may wish to consider in the development of their resort properties. (Thompson, 2014, p. 40, emphasis added)*

> *At the end of the summer of 1993 Intrawest decided to or elected to proceed on the basis of forming a point -based vacation Club,* **and I was instructed to act on their behalf,** *to incorporate the necessary components and to prepare the requisite documentation in order to give effect to that timeshare plan. (Thompson, 2014, p. 65, emphasis added)*

On November 9th, 1993, Thompson, with the assistance of a US law firm that specialized in creating timeshare organizations, created the nonprofit, non-stock corporation in Delaware.[4]

> *... it turned out that in British Columbia the Society Act at the time was extremely old. And it hadn't been amended, it hadn't been modified for a number of years and it was impossible to have -- to have two classes of members with different voting rights. It did not work. And I had talked to Ingersoll and Bloch about the initial problem and they suggested using a mutual benefit non- stock company out of Delaware because Delaware law did give a* **tremendous amount of flexibility** *with regards to how an entity could be structured. And that's why a Delaware company was used. (Thompson, 2014, p. 162, emphasis added).*

As Intrawest's consultant, Thompson: (1) created an extra provincial nonprofit organization in British Columbia (effective January 20th, 1994) to manage the Club's operations; (2) prepared a prospectus, under the British Columbia Real Estate Act, which he submitted on behalf of Intrawest Corporation; (3) under the direction of Intrawest, wrote the Club documents, which were attached as tables to the prospectus (see Table 1); and, (4) worked with Intrawest to establish trusts, in which the property was reportedly deposited (Thompson, 2014, p. 62-72). Thompson explained that he represented Intrawest, the developer, and at no time represented the Club (Thompson, 2014, p. 130). Thompson also explained how he updated the prospectus to add that the Club was an agent of the members, to meet certain regulatory changes.[5]

Table 1. Timeshare Program Documents (2015 Disclosure) – Evidence of Developer Control

Document	*Title*	*Description*
Disclosure	Club Intrawest Disclosure	Filed by the developer in each jurisdiction where points are sold; filed document includes following Tables, which collectively establish the Club structure.
Table 1	Declaration	Declares the rules and regulations of the program. Provides rights to declarant to control. (2015 version is 19th restated declaration dated May 2012)
Table 2	Trust Agreements	Entities are the bare trustee, the developer and the Club. Developer controls all additions and substitutions.
Table 3	Vacation Homes & Amenities	Describes the type of vacation homes in the trusts and (non-trust) amenities (e.g. pools) that are owned by the developer but funded by the Club.
Table 4	Flow Chart of the Club Structure	Outlines flow of points between Developer and Club.
Table 5	Legal Descriptions	Lists the strata and lot numbers of each vacation home in trust.
Table 6	Guidelines	Outlines the rules by which members can use their points.
Table 7	Equipment and Furnishings List	Provides a list of the equipment made available in the resort accommodations (not an inventory).
Table 8	Purchase Agreements	Lists the contractual items that are agreed upon at purchase (between developer and consumer), including terms and conditions of Club membership.
Table 9	Annual Operating Budget	Aggregate Club budget, set by the manager (developer).
Table 10	Management Agreement	Establishes the terms and conditions of the management contract.
Table 11	ExtraOrdinary Escapes Agreements	Exchange program that is owned and operated by the developer.

continued on following page

Table 1. Continued

Document	*Title*	*Description*
Table 12	Calendar and Total Resort Points	Declarant controls assignment of points to room nights (total points cannot increase without adding occupancy).
Table 13	Bylaws and Certificate of Incorporation	In the bylaws, all power is given to the President of the board; the president is a developer employee. Certificate of incorporation identifies power of the board. Board is controlled by declarant. Declarant is the developer.
Table 16	Club Intrawest Repurchase Program	The terms and conditions under which the developer will repurchase a membership.

Once the Club was established, it began operations with a set of property that had been transferred into a trust by the developer. In return for use of the property, the Club issued points to the developer, which the developer could then sell to consumers. These points would provide consumers access to room nights at the property (a process explained in detail in the following section). During this time, and all future additions of property, the Club was overseen by a board of five directors. Initially, the board members were all employees of the developer, Intrawest. (Thompson, 2014, p. 132-133). Soon after, a member replaced one of the Intrawest employees as board member, who stayed on the board for 22 years and whose company did the Club's taxes for a portion of time. From 1994 to 2015, at least three (of the five) directors were employees of the developer.[6]

As of December 31st, 2015, the trusts included 484 units across North America (see Table 2), for a total of 4,151,643 points issued to the developer (Club Intrawest, 2015). At an estimated average sale price of $150[7] per point, the total initial point sale value is approximately $670 million (notably, points are recycled back to the developer – *not* the Club – who can sell them again). According to the municipal roles, the value of the property in 2015 was about $200 million.[8]

Table 2. Properties in trust as of Dec 31, 2015

Location	*Number of Vacation Homes*
Blue Mountain, Ontario, Canada	62
Panorama, Alberta, Canada	22
Tremblant, Quebec, Canada	53
Ucluelet, British Columbia, Canada	10
Vancouver, British Columbia, Canada	29
Whistler, British Columbia, Canada	114
Palm Desert, California, USA	66
Sandestin, Florida, USA	59
Zihuantanejo, Mexico	69

Source: Club Intrawest (2015) *Financial Report* [Internal Club document]

THE INTERLOCKING BUSINESS MODEL: HOW THE FOR-PROFIT CONTROLS

This section explains the interlocking business model that demonstrates the relationship between the developer (for-profit) and the Club (nonprofit). As shown in Figure 1, the relationships allow for the developer to control the trusts, the sales process, the transfer of membership into the Club, the board of the Club and the management of the Club. Although the developer is noted as one entity in the figure, each of the entities (developer, declarant, manager; by country, and in some instances, by location) were subsidiaries of Intrawest. Following is an overview of each of the business model components, denoted by numbers corresponding to the steps in Figure 1.

Figure 1. The Developer-Club Interlocking Business Model

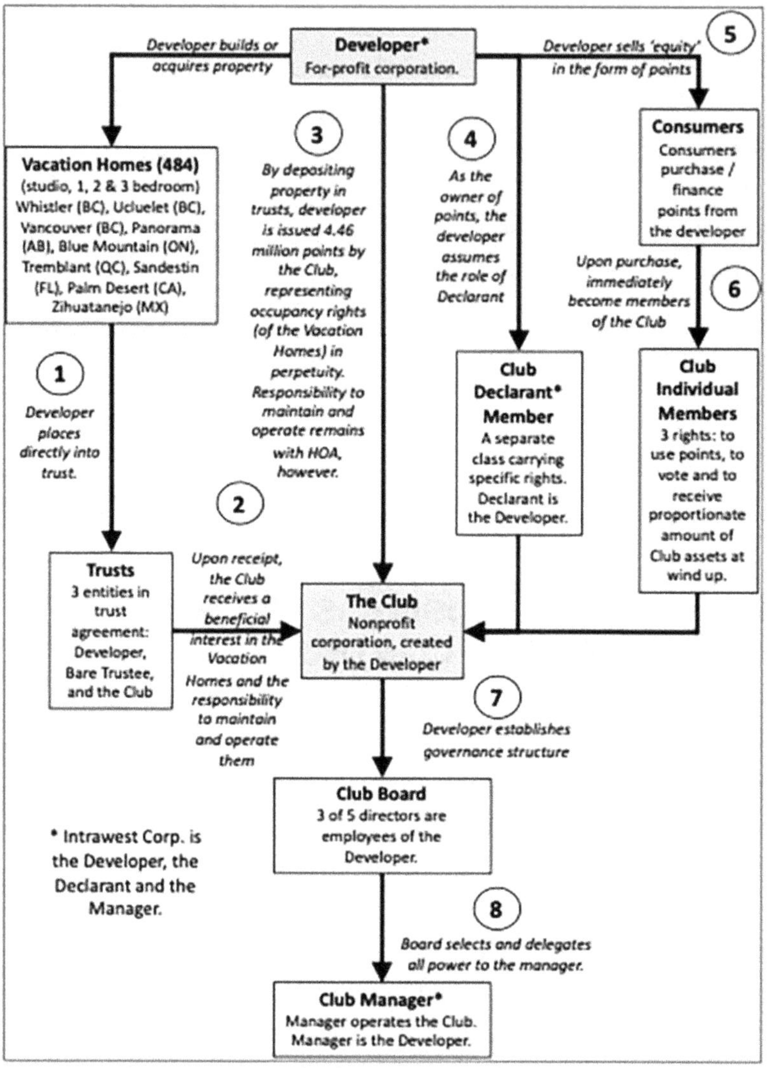

1. The Property and the Trusts

To launch the timeshare plan, Intrawest developed property and deposited the property into trusts (by country and, in some instances, by US state).[9] Each trust includes three legal entities: the developer (Intrawest), the Club (Club Intrawest) and the bare trustee. The municipal land roles list the bare trustees as the owners. The bare trustees take direction from the board of the Club and are accountable to pay the property taxes. This transfer of properties from the developer to the bare trustee is performed outside the boundaries of the Club; that is, there is no evidence that the property was ever directly transferred to the Club. Instead, the property was deposited into the trusts directly, by the developer. In Intrawest's 2015 Disclosure (Intrawest Corporation, 2015b, hereafter "2015 Disclosure"), the property in the trust is referred to as "resort accommodation", defined as follows:

> *A portion of a Project (including the Equipment), consisting of either personal property (such as a motor home or a houseboat), or a leasehold, fee simple or other interest in real property, including a condominium suite or, unit, a hotel suite, a cabin, a house or other facility or interest, including a timeshare interval or interest, which is owned or leased by the Club or by the Trustee on behalf of the Club for the use of the Members and all rights and privileges belonging or in any manner appertaining thereto, now or hereafter submitted to this Declaration, as it may lawfully be amended or supplemented from time to time. (2015 Disclosure, Table 1, §1.50)*

Each of the timeshare resort locations are referred to as "projects", whereby parts of the property are in the trusts, but not all. For example, at the Mont Tremblant, Quebec, Canada, location, of the three parcels of land that make up the timeshare project, two contain resort accommodations that are listed in the trusts, while the third parcel is owned by the developer (Municipalité de Montréal-Tremblant, 2014). This third parcel includes the registration desk, the sales offices, the gym and entertainment services, the pool, the tennis courts and the fire pit.

When the developer indicates its intention to put property in the trust (a right that they have in perpetuity), the Club, in turn, issues points to the developer, representing the occupancy rate of the properties (which is established by the developer); that is, a value is placed on the occupancy rate, not the property itself. The issuance of points is recorded through a Club Board Resolution. The property is identified by its municipal lot or strata number in the amended trust agreement (2015 Disclosure, Table 1, §4).

The trust agreement includes three legal entities: the developer, the bare trustee (chosen by the developer) and the Club. The signatures of the developer and the Club on the original trust agreements and amendments are of developer employees. Notably, the Club president has always been a developer employee (from inception to present). The individual members of the Club, that is, the consumers who purchased the points, are not part of the trust agreement. There is no legal agreement that exists between the Club and the members, as it relates to the beneficial ownership, interest or use of the properties held in trust (see 2015 Disclosure, Table 2, for examples).

The points issued to the developer by the Club are occupancy rights that the developer holds in perpetuity. The Club's role in the transaction is to sign the trust agreements and provide occupancy rights (i.e. points) to the developer, who then determines what to do with those occupancy rights (Disclosure 2015, Table 1, §4.) As described by Justice J.A. Dawson, in describing the process from a legal perspective:

> *The Tax Court began its analysis with the Agreed Statement and the Trust Indenture, finding that initially the legal and beneficial interests in the Canadian vacation homes were held by the Canadian developer. The Canadian developer then transferred the legal and beneficial ownership of the Canadian vacation homes to the Club. Simultaneously with its acquisition of the Canadian vacation homes, the Club transferred legal title to the homes to the Canadian bare trustee to hold such title "in trust for and on behalf of the Club" (Article 2.1 of the Trust Indenture). Finally, as consideration for the Canadian vacation homes, the appellant transferred the occupancy rights in the homes in perpetuity to the Canadian developer. (Club Intrawest v. Her Majesty the Queen, 2017, reasons, paragraphs 86-89).*

The same holds for the transfer of property from the vacation homes located in other countries. To allow for the transfer of properties and the sale of points, the developer establishes a set of stand-alone subsidiaries to process the transactions.

To process the transactions financially, the developer considers the points as inventory and carries this inventory on their balance sheet. The inventory is referred to Vacation Ownership Interests (VOIs). There is no direct relationship reported between the value of the property deposited in the trusts and the VOIs. Developer reports of their Club ownership have conflicted with the timeshare marketing and Club documents; over time, both the developer and the Club suggested that they owned the property, as shown in Table 3.

Table 3. Developer declaration of Club relationship

Developer Report (Emphasis added.)
"And Club Intrawest – **our** highend member-based lodging concept – is now expanding across the continent. We believe we're only beginning to see the strategic advantages of **owning a multi-resort network** both in terms of synergistic growth as well as economies of scale." (Intrawest Corporation 1998 Annual Report, p. 8.)
"An Intrawest Resort Club was built, **providing the highest occupancy figures in Tremblant**." (Author note: The occupancy referred to here is of the Club, not an Intrawest-owned property.) (Intrawest Corporation 1998 Annual Report, p. 12)
"Points revenue associated with membership in the vacation ownership business of the Intrawest Resort Club (**which revenue is included in real estate sales**) is recognized when the purchaser has paid the amount due on closing, all contract documentation has been executed and all other significant conditions of sale are met." (Intrawest Corporation 1998 Annual Report, p. 39)
"The Company also builds and operates resort club locations which are marketed as timeshare vacation ownership resorts." (Intrawest Corporation 1997 (November) Prospectus, p. 7)
"**Intrawest also has** resort club facilities in Palm Desert, California and Hawaii." (Intrawest Corporation 1998 (June) Prospectus, p. 27)
"In December 1997 **IROC acquired 4 units** available for **its** members in Kauai, Hawaii." (Intrawest Corporation 1998 (June) Prospectus, p. 53)
"Club Intrawest is **our** unique points-based vacation ownership concept. With seven locations offering five-star accommodation at some of the world's premier four-season vacation destinations and more than 12,000 members, Club Intrawest is at the leading edge of the vacation ownership business… Club Intrawest increased membership by 20 per cent to 12,000 members." (Intrawest Corporation 2002 Annual Report, p. 41)
"Members of **our** vacation ownership club, Club Intrawest, are also discovering a variety of Intrawest resorts, with a new club at our Sandestin Golf and Beach Resort in Florida and another soon to open at Blue Mountain." (Intrawest Corporation 2003 Annual Report, p. 7)
"**An increase of $26.1 million in the book value of resort club properties** mainly due to the new resort club locations under construction at Blue Mountain and Zihuatanejo, Mexico." (Intrawest Corporation 2003 Annual Report, p. 29)

In their early annual reports (1990s), Intrawest listed the Club as one of their primary offices. On the Investor Relations section of their website, up until 2015, Intrawest stated:

> *Presently, Intrawest Resorts Holdings, Inc. offers membership interests through* **its wholly owned subsidiary Club Intrawest.** *Members share ownership of beautifully crafted Vacation Homes across Canada, the United States and Mexico – nine locations in total. In addition, Club Intrawest Members have access to hundreds of partner hotels and resorts around the world. (Intrawest Corporation, 2015a, emphasis added)*

In addition, Club Intrawest Mexico, LLC, and Club Intrawest Mexico, SRL, were listed as wholly-owned subsidiaries of both the Club (Club Intrawest, 2014) *and* Intrawest (Orbis, 2014), which is legally impossible, as no joint ownership exists.

In some cases, land and property at the Club locations are owned by the developer. For example, at the Mont Tremblant project, there are three parcels of land. Two parcels contain the condominiums and are listed on the town's municipal role as being owned by the bare trustee. The third parcel, referred to as the Amenities Centre, is owned by the developer and includes a building that houses both the developer's sales team and the Club registration team, along with a lounge area, small theatre, fitness room, saunas and hot tubs and a pool, valued at $3 million in 2014 (Municipalité de Montréal-Tremblant, 2014). Renovations (operating and capital) to the developer-owned building are funded by the Club, if related to member services.

2. The Club's Beneficial Interest in the Trust(s)

The Club, through the trust agreement established by the developer, is given the "exclusive right to use and occupy" the vacation homes held in trust (Disclosure 2015, §2.2). The Club transfers this right back to the developer when issuing the points to the developer but does not transfer responsibility to the developer to fund the operations or carry any of the risk related to the Club operations; this responsibility and associated risk remain with the Club. As the Club itself (but not the members) is listed in the trust agreement, the Club is responsible for the operations and maintenance of the vacation homes (see judgements *Club Intrawest v. Her Majesty the Queen*, 2016; *Club Intrawest v. Her Majesty the Queen*, 2017). To fund the ongoing operations and maintenance of the Club, the Club documents indicate that the Club is an agent of the members.

> *Subject to any Project Instruments and the Club Instruments, responsibility for the maintenance, repair, replacement, restoration, improvement, operation, and administration of the Resort Accommodations shall be vested in the Club.* **The Club shall act as the agent** *of all of the Members in collecting Assessments and in paying taxes, utility costs, and other Membership Costs. The Club, through its Board of Directors, Officers, the Manager, and other duly authorized agent(s) may exercise any and all rights and powers granted to it by law or by the Club Instruments, as amended or supplemented from time to time. Pursuant to the provisions of the Certificate of Incorporation, the exclusive power to promulgate and amend the Guidelines shall be vested in the Declarant as long as the Declarant is retained as Manager and the Board shall have no power with respect to such Guidelines except as to the enforcement thereof. (2015 Disclosure, § 9.1, emphasis added)*

Thompson indicated that he added the terms "agent" and "agency" to the Club documents three years after the Club was formed, on the advice of an accountant hired by Intrawest (Thompson, 2014, p. 155-6).

Although the developer and Club both persistently said they were an agent of the members, the Tax Court of Canada (TCA) ruled otherwise. The TCA judgement (supported by the Federal Court of Appeal) indicated that evidence suggested only the Club has beneficial ownership in the vacation homes, not the members of the Club (see judgements *Club Intrawest v. Her Majesty the Queen*, 2016; *Club Intrawest v. Her Majesty the Queen*, 2017).

3. Developer Points

Once the Club issues the occupancy rights to the developer, the developer can then either exercise those rights or sell the rights, both of which are done through the points-based currency. Each of the Vacation Homes, depending on occupancy, are assigned a point value for each room-night throughout the year, the total of which cannot surpass the total number of points issued by the Club to the developer. Point values per room night are influenced not only by occupancy rate, but also by holiday periods. The developer controls the points calendar (2015 Disclosure, Table 1, §2.2).

The points thus become the currency of the Club, which members and the developer use to transact. The developer sells points to the consumer, who then moves into the Club structure and can exercise the use of the points on an annual basis. Once the year terminates, the in-year points expire (or carried over for a maximum of one year) and the annual points purchased are renewed for the coming years. The points are sold as points in perpetuity, meaning that, while the Club exists, the points can be used against resort accommodations (i.e. room nights) (2015 Disclosure, §2.1(a)).

The developer also retains the right to use the resort accommodations for business purposes to include sales and management. The developer, as they wrote into the timeshare documents, has the right to sell points on the resort property and to access members through the membership database, which is owned by the manager (who is also the developer, as explained in point 8). The ownership of points by the developer is a specific role within the Club structure called the "Declarant", discussed in point 5, a developer entity (2015 Disclosure, Table 1, §5).

4. The Product and the Sales Process

The developer can sell points to any consumer of their choosing and through any means. During a sales presentation, consumers are presented with the option to buy points that can be used either at the trust properties or exchanged with other timeshare properties, though an exchange program. The exchange program is run by the developer (a separate legal entity), not the Club, but the power of the exchange is based on the points owned by the member. The exchange program is offered to consumers as an adjunct to their purchase; the purchase price and terms and conditions are controlled by the developer at initial purchase and on an ongoing basis (which can change at any time) (2015 Disclosure, §4, Table 11). The point allotment also establishes the member's ability to purchase ad-hoc room nights at the Club locations; for example, if a room night shows available within a 14-day window, the member can book the room night with cash. The developer holds the right to do the same within a 45-day window (2015 Disclosure, Table 1, §5.11).

During the sales process, once the sale transaction occurs, consumers move from the salesperson to a member enrolment representative, both of whom work for the developer, as described by the Robert Reyes, VP Operations of the Club, who was also an Intrawest employee:

> *So when a person decides to purchase it moves from the salesperson to the member enrolment representative, who then goes through the purchase and membership agreement, the summary of key elements and then they -- along with that they present you with the CD-ROM of the Club instruments. (Club Intrawest, 2013a, lines 470-77; in 2002, at least one member received only the summary sheet, not the CD)*

The 'summary' originally stated, "You are buying equity ownership in the Intrawest Resort Club. Your Club is a non-profit corporation that owns the real estate, which is held in trust on its owners' behalf" (Intrawest Corporation, 2002a). In its original form and until 2015, Club documents indicated that consumers were purchasing equity in property, e.g. "The members' assets, including real estate and equipment at Club locations, are held in trust..." (Club Intrawest, 2015a, note 1).

Once the consumer purchases points, a Club member enrollment specialist, who works for the developer, registers the consumer as a Club member (Club Intrawest, 2013a). At some point in time, the member is provided with a copy of the timeshare documentation (created by the developer in the form of a Disclosure and associated tables, as described earlier). Depending on the location of purchase, consumers have between seven to ten days to rescind their purchase. If a consumer has questions on the documents during this period, they are referred to a membership coach (on site or phone) who works for the developer (Club Intrawest, 2013a).

5. The Declarant (also known as the Developer, the for-profit firm)

As explained earlier, the Club was established by the developer in Delaware, USA, on the advice of the US law firm, Ingersoll and Bloch, so there could be multiple classes of members. Aside from the distinction between those who have a yearly versus biyearly allotment of points, there are two separate classes in the Club: the declarant class and the individual member class, which were formed to ensure that the declarant retained control over all club assets (including members). The declarant member (i.e., the developer) sells the points in their original form. The declarant role retains power in the Club through various means, as described in the declaration and highlighted as follows.

Voting Power. The declarant holds 15-times the voting power over members: members have 1/15th of a vote per point, while the declarant has 1 vote per point. As the declarant votes in all matters, depending upon the percentage of total points owned by the declarant, the declarant can carry the vote (Club Intrawest, 2013a). For example, at 4.48 million points, if the declarant owns 280,000 points – which equates to an ownership of 6.2% – the declarant's voting power is greater than 50%. In addition, in some instances, voting items require the support of each class of member; as the declarant is its own class, the declarant vote is a determining vote. As per the Club bylaws, "The Declarant Membership shall cease and be converted to Resort Point Memberships when the Voting Power of the Declarant Member falls below twenty percent (20%) of the Total Voting Power of the Club" (2015 Disclosure, Table 2, §3.6(ii)). At the current point total, the declarant must only hold 75,000 points to meet this criterion; 1.7% of the actual points interest. The declarant role has persisted since inception.

Right of First Refusal. The declarant retains the right of first refusal on the sale of points in the secondary market by Club members. Should a member elect to sell their points on the open market, the declarant must be provided a copy of the sales offer prior to the transaction, to exercise the right of first refusal. If the declarant so chooses, the declarant can purchase the points for the terms and conditions laid out by the member (the seller) (2015 Disclosure, Table 1, §3.5(a)). As part of this right, the declarant also has the right of first refusal on member forfeitures, which occurs when a member does not pay the annual fee within 18 months of the due date. The declarant can take the points back into inventory if they pay the pending annual fee (a fraction of the original cost of the points) (2015 Disclosure, Table 1, §11.1, §12.2, §12.3).This strategy is known in the industry as 'inventory recapture'.

Right to Sell Room Nights. The declarant retains the right to reserve and use room nights with the points in their possession. The declarant, unlike the members, has the right to use the points for business purposes and therefore can advertise the reserved room nights on internet hospitality sites (e.g. Expedia, Booking.com, hotels.com) or their own website, for any price (2015 Disclosure, Table 1, §5.9). Because the declarant also provides cancellation insurance for member bookings, the declarant can use this option for their own points, such that if the reserved room night goes un-booked, the room nights can be returned into member inventory and the points returned to the declarant, up until midnight of the room night date.

Exchange Program. The declarant holds the right to run an exchange program for members and determine the conditions of the exchange program. Participation in the exchange program, as indicated earlier, is considered a privilege, not a right; that is, there is no automatic association between the purchase of points and the exchange program, although this point is not evident in the two-page summary that members received when buying points (Club Intrawest, 2013a). In 2007, the declarant changed the terms of the exchange program: the new rule stipulated that unless members sold their points for a base price (the same as the developer), the exchange program privileges would be eliminated and non-renewable (Club Intrawest, 2012a) - a condition not made clear upon the original purchase of points (Club Intrawest, 2013a). As this change had a material impact on the value of all points purchases prior to 2007, and because the nature of this condition was arguably not presented during the sales process, a class action lawsuit was launched against the original developer, Intrawest, by a Quebec-based member and accepted to proceed (*Martin Robichaud v. Intrawest ULC*, Que. Sup. Ct., discussed later in the chapter).

Points Calendar. The declarant controls the points calendar, which establishes the seasons and the point value of each room night for all Club resort accommodations (2015 Disclosure, Table 1, §2.2.) High season and weekend nights (Friday and Saturday) require the greatest number of points to book. The overall point value for the entire year and all properties is based on the points issued to the developer by the Club, however the Declarant reserves the right to increase point values by 1% per year (2015 Disclosure, Table 1, §2.2.) As the declarant can modify the point value per room night and increase total point values by 1% per year, the 'cost' of booking the same room at the same period, from one year to the next, is variable.

Property Additions, Substitutions and Upgrades. The declarant can add or substitute property in the trust if they are of similar quality, without approval of the board (2015 Disclosure, Table 1, §4.1, §4.8). For example, in 2014, the declarant added ten vacation homes located in Ucluelet, BC, Canada. In return, the developer received 84,773 points (Intrawest Corporation & Club Intrawest, 2014). The current value of the vacation homes is approximately $2 million[10]; the value of the points, at $150 per point (price at the time) was $12.8 million. If the declarant chooses, the declarant can also upgrade a vacation home by increasing the occupancy rate and, in return, receive points (2015 Disclosure, Table 1, §4.9.)

In theory, the declarant can add, substitute or upgrade property in the trust at their sole discretion (or do nothing at all). How this process works in practice, however, is less clear. For example, in 2007, the declarant substituted ten Hawaii units with units located in Palm Desert and Sandestin (Club Intrawest, 2007b). There is neither a financial transaction for this change on the financials of the Club nor a modification of points; that is, the sale of the Hawaii properties and the purchase of the Plam Desert and Sandestin units cannot be traced.

Right of Egress and Ingress. The declarant holds the right to run a business on the property of the Club to include operating and staffing a sales office, holding units for showcases, and performing any other activities related to the declarant's business (beyond Club business), to include the sale of excursions and other items.

> *Subject to any Project Instruments, the Declarant shall have and hereby retains for itself, its successors and assigns, together with its guests, tenants, licensees, and invitees, an easement to maintain one (1) or more model Resort Accommodations and business and sales offices to enable the Declarant or its designee(s) to market and sell Memberships, display signs, and show Resort Accommodations, common areas and amenity centers at all Projects to prospective purchasers, to rent available Resort Accommodations on a transient basis to members of the general public... (2015 Disclosure, Table 1, §5.8(a)).*

Reservation System. The declarant holds the right to own the reservation system of the Club, which is how and where the Club points inventory is managed.

> *The Club hereby acknowledges that the Declarant shall own and operate and have exclusive control over the Reservation System and that the Club shall have no legal or beneficial interest in the Reservation System, provided that, in the event the Declarant is terminated as Manager, the Club shall be entitled to the data required to operate a reservation system for its members subsequent to such termination, as shall be further provided in the Restated Management Agreement. (2015 Disclosure, Table 1, §12.4).*

Board Structure. The declarant is the developer, and the developer controls the disclosure. The disclosure determines the structure of the Club's board of directors, including the assignment of an independent director position (non-declarant voting). The declarant, therefore, determines who sits on the board and who controls the board. As indicated earlier, individual members have one vote for each 15 points that they hold, while the declarant has one vote for each individual point (2015 Disclosure, §3.9(c)).

Protection. The declarant is protected from any action taken by members against the declarant that would impact the declarant's business. For example, if members were to attempt to gather on a property to protest the declarant's behaviour, the declarant would have recourse in protecting itself.

> *Notwithstanding any provision of the Club Instruments to the contrary, for so long as the Declarant holds for sale in the ordinary course of its business one (1) or more Memberships, the Club shall not take any action which would be detrimental to the sale by the Declarant of Memberships so long as the Declarant is in compliance with all provisions of the Club Instruments; provided, however, that an increase in Resort Fees without discriminating against the Declarant shall not be deemed to be detrimental to the sale of Memberships. (2015 Disclosure, Table 1, §5.10)*

6. The Club's Individual Members

When a consumer purchases points from the developer, they immediately become part of the individual class of members of the Club, as per the disclosure, "Any person who is issued a Membership Certificate shall automatically be a Member of the Club in accordance with the provisions of the Club Instruments" (2015 Disclosure, §6.1(e)). A consumer who purchases points, therefore, is automatically a member of the Club and must comply with the Club rules and regulations, without knowing what those rules and regulations are prior to the purchase. As part of the membership, the purchasers are issued the following rights:

> *Individuals who purchase Resort Points from [the developer] pursuant to this Disclosure Statement receive Membership Certificates evidencing their Membership in the Club and ownership of the purchased Resort Points. Club Members use their Resort Points to: (i) reserve and occupy Vacation Homes on an annual basis; (ii) vote at Club meetings; (iii) participate in exchanges; and (iv) receive their proportionate share of the net value of the Club assets on the wind up and dissolution of the Club. (2015 Disclosure, Table 1, §2.1(b))*

The right to reserve and occupy Vacation Homes on an annual basis. Members can use their annual allotment of points each year, in perpetuity. They can carry over their points for a maximum of one year (known as 'banking') or pull points from the following year in-year, if the annual service fee is paid on all points. Unless points are banked for the following year four months before expiration (in year), the points are lost to the member (2015 Disclosure, §3.2(g)). Terms and conditions on how reservations are made are outlined in the Club Guidelines, which are written and controlled by the declarant. In other words, the developer determines the rules of the Club, not the Club itself:

> *Pursuant to the provisions of the Certificate of Incorporation, the exclusive power to promulgate and amend the Guidelines shall be vested in the Declarant as long as the Declarant is retained as Manager and the Board shall have no power with respect to such Guidelines except as to the enforcement thereof. (2015 Disclosure, Table 1, §9.1)*

The right to vote at Club meetings suggests that there are meetings, including an Annual General Meeting (AGM). Aside from the first meeting, the Club's board (controlled by the developer) cancelled each and every AGM and instead, held the voting of directors by post or internet, citing the Club bylaws as support (2015 Disclosure, Table 13)

The right to participate in exchanges. The exchange program is run by the developer. The right to participate in exchanges is not a right, as the conditions to participate are established outside of the purchase of points. As indicated previously, if a member sells their points on the secondary market below the developer-set base price (i.e. the developer's purchase price or higher), the exchange membership is eliminated and not renewable. This, however, is not evident upon purchase.

> **Shannon Currie** *(Lawyer for the Canada Revenue Agency) But by reading this summary of key elements, a new member wouldn't know that if they sold their membership to someone other than the developer that the new purchaser wouldn't have access to Extraordinary Escapes?*
>
> **Robert Reyes, VP Operations, Club Intrawest**: *Yes, correct.*
>
> (Club Intrawest, 2013a, line 634).

The right to receive a proportion of assets at windup. If 90% of the membership, both the declarant and individual class, independently agree to windup the Club (that is, cease operations), each member is to receive their respective portion of the liquidated assets (based on points held by total number of points) (2015 Disclosure, §2.9(c)). Club properties (assets) are listed in the Club's internal financial statements, but the complete asset list is not provided to members or potential consumers. The Club's 2015 financial statements say:

> *The members' assets, including real estate and equipment at Club Intrawest locations, are held in trust... for Club Intrawest members who are the beneficial owners of the assets. Accordingly, the cost of the real estate and equipment at Club Intrawest locations are not included in these consolidated financial statements. (Club Intrawest, 2015a, note 1)*

Notably, as per the findings of the TCC and FCA Court of Appeal cases, members are not beneficial owners of the property (see judgements *Club Intrawest v. Her Majesty the Queen*, 2016; *Club Intrawest v. Her Majesty the Queen*, 2017). Additionally, given that the statements follow

Generally Accepted Accounting Principles (GAAP), when asked which specific section of the CPA Handbook was relied upon to omit the value of real estate as an asset, the Club Board declined to answer. Club Intrawest's 2007 Annual Report stated that "Assets consists primarily of 2008 Resort Dues collected and receivable and Capital Funds investments" (Club Intrawest, 2007a, p. 6); there is no mention of property and related assets.

Obligations. Membership also comes with an obligation to fund the Club's annual fees, to include maintenance and repairs, insurance, capital reserves, cleaning services, special assessments and any other costs deemed necessary by the board.

> *Subject to any Project Instruments and the Club Instruments, responsibility for the maintenance, repair, replacement, restoration, improvement, operation, and administration of the Resort Accommodations shall be vested in the Club. The Club shall act as the agent of all of the Members in collecting Assessments and in paying taxes, utility costs, and other Membership Costs. The Club, through its Board of Directors, Officers, the Manager, and other duly authorized agent(s) may exercise any and all rights and powers granted to it by law or by the Club Instruments, as amended or supplemented from time to time. Pursuant to the provisions of the Certificate of Incorporation, the exclusive power to promulgate and amend the Guidelines shall be vested in the Declarant as long as the Declarant is retained as Manager and the Board shall have no power with respect to such Guidelines except as to the enforcement thereof. (2015 Disclosure, Table 1, §9.1).*

The annual operating budget is set in the previous year by the manager (who is also the developer); members must pay their fee by the November due date. If a member does not pay the annual fee within an 18-month period, the Club cancels their membership and passes the points back to the declarant.

> *Section 10.6 requires each Member to pay his or her Resort Fees for any calendar year by November 1st of the preceding calendar year or such other time as the Board may determine. If a Member fails to pay all or any part of his or her Resort Fees, interest or legal fees (the "Unpaid Balance") within 18 months of the due date, then the Board may pass a resolution (the "Absolute Forfeiture Resolution") confirming*

> *the Unpaid Balance and absolutely forfeiting the defaulting Member's Membership unless the Unpaid Balance is paid within one hundred and twenty (120) days following the date of the Absolute Forfeiture Resolution (the "Forfeiture Date"). ...* **If the Unpaid Balance is not paid by the Forfeiture Date, then defaulting Member's Membership shall be absolutely forfeited on the Forfeiture Date.** *(2015 Disclosure, Table 1, §10.15(d), emphasis added)*

Regardless of the occupancy, the operating costs are paid for by members, in advance, as determined by the declarant (2015 Disclosure, Table 1, §10.6). The declarant can pay their respective operating costs (based on points owned) monthly or the declarant can subsidize club operations, based on a non-public agreement between the club and the declarant (2015 Disclosure, Table 1, §10.7). Given that operating costs are paid in advance, an empty room night has no negative material impact on Club operations.

Selling the Membership. When the Club launched initially, consumers were told at purchase that they could sell their equity in one of three ways. First, they could redirect their equity towards other Intrawest real estate (e.g. condos and homes) (Intrawest Corporation, 2002b). Intrawest subsequently cancelled this program around 2009. Second, prior to 2013, consumers were told that they could sell their equity back to the club after five years of ownership. To this day, members can put themselves on the developer buy-back list, if no loan exists on the points. As indicated in the instruction on selling a membership, the repurchase program was "designed to provide long-term Members a convenient method of liquidating their Membership" (Club Intrawest, 2012a, p. 3). The details of the program, however, were not provided during the points sale process. These details indicate that the buy-back amount per year is calculated based on 1% of the developer's net point sales, which is an amount not available to the public (Intrawest Corporation, 2008). The disclosure notes in section 3.5(d) that "Intrawest has no obligation to repurchase any Resort points" (2015 Disclosure, §3.5(d)). The third option suggested to members by the developer is to sell their 'equity' (points) on the secondary market. However, as explained earlier, in 2007 Intrawest prevented access to their exchange program on points sold below the developer's base price, effectively eliminating the secondary market. If the member forfeits the membership by not paying the annual dues, the Club indicates in the annual bill that non-payment could result in legal action by the declarant (Club Intrawest, 2015b).

7. The Club Board: Governance and Bylaws

The developer's disclosure stipulates that the board is to consist of five directors, "The officers of the Club are the president, vice-president, secretary and treasurer, all of whom are elected by the Board of Directors and each of whom shall be a member of the Board of Directors" (2015 Disclosure, §3.9(f)). Since inception, three of the five board positions have been held by developer employees, providing the developer with voting control (Club Intrawest, 2013a). The fourth board member of the board (declarant voting, but a Club member) joined the board in 2002 and remained until 2015; the developer voted for this same member every three years. The fifth board member, also a Club member, joined the board soon after the inception of the Club. His position was deemed 'independent' by the developer, as the declarant cannot vote for this position. From 2011 to 2015, the Club declared this fifth board member was also hired by the board to do the Club's taxes (Club Intrawest, 2011a, 2012b, 2013b, 2014, 2015a)

The bylaws outline the roles and responsibilities of the board. The board is given the authority to modify the bylaws at any time. In addition, the "the Bylaws may be amended by resolution of the Board of Directors or upon the affirmative vote or written assent of two-thirds of the Voting Power of each class of Members" (2015 Disclosure, §2.9(b)). The Board therefore has ultimate power over the bylaw modifications, as they control the declarant class vote.

The bylaws define the way in which the Club is governed through the board of directors, including the types of meetings, the way in which business is conducted at the meetings, proxies, special general meetings, and order of business. The Club President carries all power on the conduct of the meetings; he/she can adjourn the meeting at any time, determine or change the rules, limit participation, and propose any motion for vote (2015 Disclosure, Table 13, §3.11).

Board meetings are held four times per year to approve the budget, set the date of the AGM, identify open director positions, approve financial statements (180 days after year-end), select the officers and finalize the member forfeitures. Decisions can also be made outside of board meetings, in the form of resolutions. In the case of the former, minutes must be made available to members within 90 days. In the case of the latter, resolutions must be available within 3 days (2015 Disclosure, Table 13, §3). Board meeting minutes have not always been made available to members. Additionally, it is not possible to track decisions made outside of a meeting, as the type of decision requiring a resolution is not defined in the bylaws.

Every year, the Club Board dispenses with the AGM and holds the election of directors by written ballot. The Club Board defends this decision by claiming that the membership is too dispersed to make an AGM feasible (Club Intrawest, 2013a). New business has therefore never been discussed in an open forum with members. Should an AGM ever be held, the Club president, as per the bylaws, has the ultimate power to stop the meeting at any time (2015 Disclosure, Table 13, §3.11(a)). In 2015, British Columbia instituted the *Societies Act* (2015), applicable to all nonprofit organizations, including extra provincial nonprofits, such as Club Intrawest. Part II of the Act stipulates, amongst other things, that all societies are required to hold an AGM. The Club did not hold an AGM in 2015.

Decisions made during Board meetings are voted on by the five directors, three of whom have always been developer employees and the fourth of which has always been voted in by the declarant (who carries the vote due to their voting power). Since 2009, the board meeting minutes (four per year) were made available to members, while some others were made available through court cases. Examples of decisions are as follows.

In 2004, the Board transferred (sold) the name of the Club "Club Intrawest" back to the developer (the trademark license was owned originally by the Club). The board has not provided documentation of this transaction, or details on the amount (2015 Disclosure, Table 1, §12.5). From 2009 to 2015, the Board meeting minutes listed few updates on a 2002-2008 assessment initiated by the Canadian Revenue Agency (CRA). The Club's 2009 Financial Reports indicated, "The final outcome of this matter cannot be predicted with certainty, and therefore, there can be no assurance that its final resolution will not have a material effect on the Club's financial position or results of operation in future fiscal years" (Club Intrawest, 2009, note 10). In 2011, the Board passed a resolution that indicated that the 2009 and 2010 budgets included "monies which have been or will be used by the Club to pay the GST/HST Assessment and to appeal those Assessments and to pay for the legal fees of the club" and that if any monies remain in the GST/HST fund following settlement with the CRA, that the money shall be retained by the Club as a capital contribution (i.e. not returned to the members) (Club Intrawest, 2011b). In 2013, the Club Board approved a $75,000 subsidy, payable to the developer (Intrawest) to cover losses at one of the properties' restaurants, which was owned and operated by the developer (Club Intrawest, 2013c).

Up until 2013, Thompson, the external counsel hired by the developer to launch the timeshare program and who indicated that he had never worked directly for the Club, attended Club board meetings, at invitation by the Club Board. In some instances, he was the assistant recording secretary (Club Intrawest, 2013d). The Club Board also invited the manager, an employee of the developer, to attend the meetings and report on various issues, including the GST/HST assessment by the CRA. As per the declaration, "All powers, duties and rights of the Club or the Board, as provided by law and herein, may be delegated to a Manager under a Restated Management Agreement" (2015 Disclosure, Table 1, §9.2).

The Board is also responsible to approve the financial statements, prepared by the manager (who is the developer). The statements must be approved by the board within 150 days of the year-end and include a consolidated statement of (1) financial position, (2) operations and change sin fund balances, and (3) cash flows. The financial statement refers to two Mexican Club subsidiaries, which, as noted earlier, were also listed as the developer's subsidiaries in the Orbis (2014) database.

8. The Club Management

The Board of the Club is responsible to appoint a manager to operate the Club, including the Club's reservation system (*emphasis added*):

> **The Club appoints the Manager** *as an independent contractor to provide the full range of services including those described herein and to act as Manager for the Club in carrying out the powers, duties and obligations of the Club as set forth in the Declaration and By-Laws*

consistent with specifications set forth from time to time by the Board of Directors to provide a full range of services including, but not limited to, administrative, operational and financial services to the Club. (2015 Disclosure, Table 1, §2.1)

The Developer is affiliated with the Manager of the Club. *The Manager oversees the day-to-day administration of the Club and the maintenance of a reservation system which Members use to reserve occupancy of the Vacation Homes. The Manager prepares an annual operation budget for the Club and Members pay their proportionate share of the operating expenses of the Club based on their Resort Point holdings. (2015 Disclosure, §2.1(b))*

All powers, duties and rights of the Club or the Board, as provided by law and herein, may be delegated to a Manager *under a Restated Management Agreement. (2015 Disclosure, Table 1, §9.2)*

The manager is paid by the Club on a 10-15% cost-plus basis (2015 Disclosure, Table 10, §5.1). The manager, on behalf of the Board, sets the annual budget and then requests approval by the Board (2015 Disclosure, Table 10, §3.2(a)). The Club then communicates the annual budget to the members in the form of a price per point. In parallel, the disclosure is updated with the most recent budget, in the annual operating budget.

At the end of the year, there is no reconciliation between what members paid and what was spent. If the actual expense is lower, the additional resort fees collected are retained by the Club. If the expenses are higher, the fees are increased the following year. In 1994, the annual fee per point was $3.63; in 2013 it was $7.31 (Club Intrawest 1994, 2013e). When using the Bank of Canada's consumer price index inflation calculator (Bank of Canada, n.d.), the 2013 annual fee per point equates to $5.18. There is no mechanism for members to provide input into the annual operating budget (Club Intrawest, 2013a).

The manager manages the declarant-owned reservation system for the Club, which includes the member contact information and preferences, points held, points used, reservations booked, statement of account (fees) and statement of loans. Given the time sensitive nature of reservations during peak times, the reservation system is the core element of the timeshare program.

Revenue Streams Analysis

Due to the rights given to the declarant and manager, by the developer, the revenue streams for the combined entities (i.e. the developer itself) include (1) the sale of points, (2) the financing of points at a rate set by the developer, (3) loan securitizations, (4) the resale of points obtained through inventory recapture, (5) exchange memberships, (6) exchange fees, (7) management fees, (8) reservation insurance, and (9) excursions. The declarant also has, through the manager, direct access to members for upsells, refinancing of loans, and the sale of any other product of their choosing.

LEGAL CASES

This section reviews two notable legal cases involving the Club and provide conclusions drawn from each case: the Canadian Revenue Agency's (CRA) Goods and Services Tax (GST) case (*Club Intrawest v. Her Majesty the Queen*, 2016; *Club Intrawest v. Her Majesty the Queen*, 2017) and the Quebec Class Action (*Martin Robichaud v. Intrawest ULC*, n.d.). The GST case focuses on the issue of control, through the analysis of the principal-agent relationship between members and the Club. The Quebec Class Action looks at the product itself, and the conditions placed by the developer on the resell of the product on the secondary market.[11]

Canadian GST Case

Around 2009, the CRA assessed the Club taxes, arguing that the Club should have paid GST on the annual resort fees collected from 2002 to 2007. The CRA argued that the annual fee was essentially a service fee that members were required to pay to retain their membership and book room nights. The Club delegated the case to the manager (an Intrawest employee), who (on behalf of the Club) hired McCarthy Tétrault, a Canadian law firm, to appeal the decision to the Tax Court of Canada (TCC).

The GST case focused on two issues: (1) the characterization of the annual fee, suggesting that as the Club itself was acting on the members' behalf, as an agent of the members, the fee was a reimbursement for operating costs, and (2) if the annual fee was in fact considered a service fee and that GST was due, that the method used to calculate the GST should be based on the actual operating costs of the Canadian locations only (not the Canadian percentage of the resort points)[12].

The details of the GST case, and conclusions on the two issues were not made available to members. Rather, the GST was described in the Club financials as a debate on a payment already made:

> *In 2010, the Club paid assessments from the CRA totalling $1,939,464 relating to years 2002-2008. The funds required to make this payment were transferred from the capital Fund to the Operating Fund. (Club Intrawest, 2015, Note 8).*

Throughout the period of the appeal, the Club, on advice of the Manager, collected $12 million from members as contingency for a potential GST payout. As indicated in the previous section, in 2011, the Club's board resolved that any remaining monies collected for the purpose of the potential GST payment would not be returned to members but deposited into the Club's capital fund (Club Intrawest, 2011b). As the manager receives a 15% fee for all financial transactions, analysis suggests that the manager received $1.8 million on the GST collection.

The TCC heard the Club's arguments and dismissed its appeal. The Club's lawyer argued that the Club was an agent of the members, but this argument was denied. The judgment indicated that the Club was not an agent of the members, and that the Club was solely accountable to maintain and operate the properties, and critically that members did not have beneficial ownership of the properties in trust. The judge then ruled that GST was due on all Canadian resort fees, based on the proportion of points assigned.

The Club appealed the TCC decision at the Federal Court of Appeal (FCA). The FCA decision upheld the TCC's conclusion that the Club was not an agent of the members and that members did not have beneficial interest of the properties. The FCA did agree with the Club's argument on the determination of GST payable, that is, to be based on the actual operating costs of the Canadian locations (and not related to points).

The conclusions from the GST case, including appeals and judgments, are twofold. First, it was ruled that the Club is not an agent of the members; rather, it is a stand-alone entity that provides a service to consumers who are required to renew their membership on an annual basis to book room nights at the Club. As indicated in the disclosure, should a member not pay their annual service fee (resort dues), they forfeit their points, so the ability to book room nights is not a right that is received when purchasing points (as the documents claim); rather it is a right that must be renewed annually with the payment of a service fee that is established by the Club itself, without member input. Second, it was ruled that members do not have beneficial ownership of the properties in trust. It is not clear if the Club itself has beneficial ownership or even beneficial interest, aside from the fact that the trusts indentures provide allowance for the Club to use the properties. Regardless, if the Club does have beneficial ownership, the ownership does not transfer to the members; it stops at the Club.

Quebec (Canada) Class Action

The Class Action was launched by Martin Robichaud, a Quebec-based Club member, who argues that the conditions of membership and resell were not made clear to him when he originally purchased the product. The certified class action investigates the following issues (*Martin Robichaud v. Intrawest ULC*, n.d.)

a) Has Intrawest ULC engaged in prohibited trade practices against members?

b) Were the fees claimed from members valid under the CPA?

c) If applicable, should Intrawest ULC reimburse the fees to the members?

d) Considering Intrawest's breaches of the CPA, if any, are members entitled to the reduction of their obligation with regard to the acquisition of the points?

e) If so, what is the reduction?

f) Are members entitled to punitive damages for Intrawest's breaches of the CPA by Intrawest?

g) In the alternative, are the clauses that govern the ability of members to terminate their contractual relationship with Intrawest and the latter's conduct in implementing (sic) them abusive in nature and effect?

The issues in this action appear to have been created by the lack of reasonable disclosure during the sales process confirming the character of the product. Robichaud argues that the purchase price of the product should represent the full price over time and should not be tied to the condition of renewing membership through the payment of an annual service fee. He also argues that the criteria established by the developer regarding the transfer of Extraordinary Escapes (the developer's exchange program) inhibits the resell value of the product. As noted earlier, in 2007, Intrawest imposed a minimum resell price per point to allow for the transfer of the exchange program, consequently the same price as Intrawest's.

The class action is based on Quebec's *Consumer Protection Act* (CQLR c P-40.1). It includes all members who purchased points in Quebec and who did not sell their points prior to 2007, when the conditions were modified by Intrawest. It highlights not only the lack of disclosure during the sales process, but also the ongoing control held by the developer. The exchange program is sold to consumers when they first purchase the points and can be renewed annually. However, during the 90-minute sales process, it is arguably unclear to the consumer that the developer, who owns the program, can change conditions at any time, even conditions related to the product itself (i.e. the points). In this case, the developer changed the conditions under which the exchange product was made available to members, which directly and negatively reduced the value of the points on the secondary market. The case independently argues that the character of the timeshare product purchased by consumers is not equity, as argued by the developer, but is a service that must be renewed on an annual basis, through an annual service fee.

CONCLUSION

The story of Club Intrawest begins with the creation of a nonprofit organization (the Club) by a for-profit firm (the developer, Intrawest). The timeshare program was established by the developer, who guided an external counsel to prepare all related documentation, some of which were submitted by the developer, some of which were submitted by counsel (under developer direction). External counsel, due to his self-reported lack of expertise, engaged a US law firm that specialized in timeshare program creation, along with the expertise of the ARDA. The developer built the properties, placed them into a trust for the beneficial use of the Club (the HOA) that they created, and then proceeded to govern HOA through a developer-controlled board. As per the Club documents, the board delegated all power to the manager, who was paid on a cost-plus basis, and who set the annual operating budget for the Club. In addition, the developer, in the role of declarant member (which owned all the timeshare interests initially), had a 15 to 1 voting power over all other members.

The developer controls all revenue streams while passing on risk to a 3rd party (the Club), who then passes the risk on to individual consumers. As an analogy, the purchase of points from the Club is akin to a golf membership, whereby there is an initiation fee (the purchase price of the points themselves) and an ongoing membership fee (the annual resort fee, which covers the operating costs of the properties). Should a member default on the annual fee, the membership is withdrawn; the initiation fee is a sunk cost, essentially an entry price to join the club, no more. Once in the club, the member has one role, to fund the operations of the club, without any voice. The developer, as the declarant, manager and board, controls *all* decisions, running the nonprofit organization as if it was one of its own wholly owned subsidiaries. Accountability for revenues and profits, through the sale of points and financing, is to the shareholders of the for-profit organization. Control is made possible through the Club documents, specifically through the role of the declarant.

The decision to launch a timeshare program is based, in part, on financial interests. When a developer has real estate available to operate either a hotel or a timeshare, or to sell the property outright, some options are more lucrative than others. In their article on the value proposition of a timeshare, Barreda et al. (2016) argue that vacation ownership is a more lucrative proposition than a hotel, by calculating the 7-year net present value (NPV) of both[13]; the NPV of a Florida timeshare was US $518 million versus US $292 million for a hotel, and the NPV of a Hawaii timeshare was US $1.8 billion versus US $329 million for a hotel.

The timeshare option is more lucrative than a one-time sale of the property, for four reasons. First, the developer sets the price of the product, which is always higher than if the consumer owned the property, even for the same set amount of time; consumers are willing to pay more for one week of holiday than they would if they owned the same property. Second, the timeshare product can be sold repeatedly and financed repeatedly. The original sale will cover the cost of the development, with a healthy profit. Consequently, as the developer can recapture inventory through forfeitures and cheap buybacks, based on the right of first refusal, profits are maximized. Third, the declarant has a captive consumer through the control of the reservation system and ability to sell onsite, allowing the developer to upsell to current members. Finally, the developer receives a guaranteed cash flow as the manager of the club, without risk (cost-plus service contract). In addition to these revenue opportunities, the developer carries no risk, as all the risk sits with the club and, importantly, with its members.

With the developer's material control, why do timeshares persist? As argued in Morgenson's *New York Times* article (2016), the high-pressure sale to potential consumers who are already on holiday tends to incite purchases. A more important and critical reason, however, is the absence of HOA documents during the sales process; sales personnel can essentially say whatever they want during the process, without challenge, as the documents are not available to the consumer. However, the documents are considered binding, so the consumer purchases a product *prior* to receiving the contract itself. Additionally, although there is a rescission period, the timeshare documents are often extremely complex and prefaced with marketing material, making it hard for the consumer to determine the exact nature of the product. And although some consumers attempt to rescind, timeshare organizations can make the process difficult.

In the case of the Club, members not only had to deal with the above aspects of the sales process but also were provided with marketing and sales documentation that said, outright, that members owned property and held equity. The sales process also summarized the advantages of membership in a two-page document that lacked the fine print of each benefit. It would take a careful reading of hundreds of pages to establish that all roads lead back to developer control and that the value of the membership was considerably lower than what was paid for and essentially worthless on the secondary market.

The persistence of timeshares brings into question both ethical and legal questions. Ethically, is it right to sell a product to a consumer under a high-pressured environment, to provide minimal information, to take advantage of their state of mind and to leave them with (eventually) buyer's remorse? Certain provinces and states may argue that it is not ethical and have put in place consumer protection laws that help to prevent such situations. For example, Quebec's *Consumer Protection Act* (CQLR c P-40.1) allows for a 30-day rescission period, putting into question the ability to manipulate and materially change a product after it has been sold (as in this case).

Legally, it is difficult to determine if the developer, in the construction of the program, broke corporate and consumer laws; the Club Board (developer-controlled) declined requests to create certainty amid by-design ambiguity. The company was registered in state of Delaware, as Thompson indicated, because their laws provide a "tremendous amount of flexibility" with regards to how the club could be structured (Thompson, 2014, p. 162). In Title 8, nonprofit fiduciary duty is vaguely defined, and nonprofit requirements are minimal: firms need only file a certificate of incorporation with very basic bylaws.

In this case, the Club is registered as a Delaware nonprofit but operates as an extra-provincial British Columbia (Canada) corporation. Throughout its history, the Club has never reported its operations or financials to any government organization, except for the change of director names. When the Club appears to break nonprofit rules and regulations, or minimally to stretch them (e.g. cancel AGMs without legitimate reason), members have limited individual recourse. Additionally, most legislation in the United States favours the developer, based on lobbying efforts by the ARDA. In Canada, almost no legislation exists, and relevant legal challenges are only now finding their footing. Ultimately, as the case demonstrates, given the current corporate laws in place in North America and the absence of ethical standards, a for-profit firm can create a separate stand-alone nonprofit organization and pass on all the financial risk, while retaining full control and complete access to revenue streams.

REFERENCES

Arizton Advisory & Intelligence. (2023, May). *U.S. vacation ownership market: Industry outlook & forecast 2023–2028*(191 pp.). Arizton Advisory & Intelligence. https://www.arizton.com/market-reports/us-vacation-ownership-market

Bank of Canada. (n.d.). Inflation calculator. https://www.bankofcanada.ca/rates/related/inflation-calculator/

Barreda, A., Murphy, K., Gregory, A., & Singh, D. (2016). Evaluating the value proposition of developing a vacation ownership resort: The case of Florida and Hawaii. *Tourism Review*, *71*(3), 165–179.

Club Intrawest (1994). *Annual dues summary.* [Internal document]

Club Intrawest. (2007a). *Annual report.* [Internal Club document]

Club Intrawest. (2007b). *Financial statements report.* [Internal Club document]

Club Intrawest. (2009). *Financial statements.* [Internal Club document]

Club Intrawest. (2011a). *Financial statements* [Internal Club document]

Club Intrawest. (2011b, September 1). *Board resolution.* [Internal Club document]

Club Intrawest. (2012a, May 2). *Selling your membership.* [Internal Club document]

Club Intrawest. (2012b). *Financial statements*[Internal Club document]

Club Intrawest. (2013b). *Financial statements.* [Internal Club document]

Club Intrawest. (2013c, September 26). *Board meeting minutes.* [Internal Club document]

Club Intrawest. (2013d, April 17). *Board meeting minutes.* [Internal Club document]

Club Intrawest. (2013e). *Annual dues summary.* [Internal Club document]

Club Intrawest. (2014). *Financial statements.* [Internal Club document]

Club Intrawest. (2015a). *Financial statements.* [Internal Club document]

Club Intrawest. (2015b). *Annual dues summary.* [Internal Club document]

Club Intrawest. (2013a, June 27). *Respondent's discovery read-ins, Club Intrawest v. Her Majesty the Queen: Examination for discovery of Robert Reyes,* 2012-3401(GST)G (Tax Court of Canada), lines 413–634.

Consumer Protection Act, CQLR c P-40.1 (Québec).

Database, O. R. B. I. S. (2014, June). *Club Intrawest Mexico, LLC and Club Intrawest Mexico, SRL listings.* Bureau van Dijk. https://www.bvdinfo.com

Delaware General Corporation Law. Tit. 8, § 101 (n.d.). https://delcode.delaware.gov/title8/c001/index.shtml

Federal Court of Appeal. (2017). *Club Intrawest v. Her Majesty the Queen,* 2017 FCA 43 (CanLII). https://canlii.ca/t/gx2v6

Intrawest Corporation. (1998, June). *Prospectus.*

Intrawest Corporation. (2002a). *Summary of key elements of your membership.*

Intrawest Corporation. (2002b). *Selling your membership.*

Intrawest Corporation. (2008, February 21). *Club Intrawest repurchase program, restated February 21, 2008).*

Intrawest Corporation (2015a) Corporate offices, accessed 2015, December 29).

Intrawest Corporation. (2015b, May 15). *Disclosure Statement of Intrawest ULC for Club Intrawest* (including Tables 1 through 14).

Intrawest Corporation & Club Intrawest. (2014, January 15). *Supplemental declaration of annexation for Club Intrawest.*

Intrawest Resort Ownership Corporation. (1994, January 20). *Prospectus of Intrawest Resort Ownership Corporation for Intrawest Resort Club.* Revision: February 8, 1994.

Jay, J. (2013). Navigating paradox as a mechanism of change and innovation in hybrid organizations. *Academy of Management Journal, 56*(1), 137–159.

Langley, A. (1999). Strategies for theorizing from process data. *Academy of Management Review*, *24*(4), 691–710.

Morgenson, G. (2016, January 22). The timeshare hard sell comes roaring back. *The New York Times*. https://www.nytimes.com/2016/01/24/business/diamond-resorts-accused-of-using-hard-sell-to-push-time-shares.html

Municipalité de Montréal-Tremblant. (2014.). *Rôle d'évaluation foncière* (Lot 2803899, Dossier no. 227101).

Ordonez., G. & Matthew du Mée, M. (2020, March 3). *Timeshare obligations, regulations, and challenges. Attorney General Journal*. National Association of Attorneys General. https://www.naag.org/attorney-general-journal/timeshare-obligations-regulations-and-challenges/

Smith, J. (2024, January 11). *FBI New York warns of scams targeting timeshare owners*. Federal Bureau of Investigation – New York Field Office. https://www.fbi.gov/contact-us/field-offices/newyork/news/fbi-new-york-warns-of-scams-targeting-timeshare-owners

Tax Court of Canada. (2016). *Club Intrawest v. Her Majesty the Queen* (2012-3401(GST)G), 2016 TCC 149 (CanLII). https://canlii.ca/t/h2ps9

Thompson, K. (2014, November 24). *Cross-examination by Ms. Burch, in Club Intrawest v. Her Majesty the Queen, No. 2012-3401(GST)G (Tax Court of Canada), transcript of proceedings.*

ENDNOTES

1 Intrawest Resort Ownership Corporation was a subsidiary of Intrawest Corporation

2 The GST case is presented later in the chapter but is referred to throughout. All legal documents on the case were ordered through the Canadian Tax Court of Canada (TCC) and the Canadian Federal Court of Appeal (FCA).

3 This Quebec Class Action is presented later in the report. The author attended 1 of the 2 days where the reasons for the class action were argued before the courts.

4 The HOA certificate of incorporation was faxed by Ingersoll and Bloch, an American law firm. William Boley Ingersoll is one of the five founders of the American Resort Development Association (ARDA). The ARDA directors include corporate officers from major developer (timeshare) corporations, such as Marriot, Disney, Holiday Inn, and Marriott, and lawyers and lobbyists. See www.arda.org

5 During a phone call with the British Columbia (Canada) Office of the Superintendent of Real Estate, the officer indicated that the act of filing a disclosure allowed the corporation to market and sell points, but that the evaluation of the legal structure of the plan was not within the office's purview. Thompson indicated that, between 2004 and 2007, he updated the document on behalf of Intrawest, to comply with new regulations (Thompson, 2014). In 2006, the prospectus was referred to as a disclosure statement, under the revised BC Real Estate and Marketing Act.

6 The names of the board members are listed in the prospectus/disclosures filed from 1994 to 2015, all of which were reviewed to support this statement.

7 All currency in Canadian dollars, unless otherwise indicated.

8 The value of the property is based on average municipal valuations for the condos at the 9 resorts, in Canadian dollars.

9 There are several trusts, based on geography. Trustees differ and have changed over time. (2015 Disclosure, Table 3).

10 The value of lot 13 of the Ucluelet location is reported at $142,000. To calculate the total value of the 10 units, we increased the individual value to $200,000 and multiplied by the 10 units (for a total of $2 million). See the municipal register for lot 13 as an example.

11 In this section, the GST case refers to both the TCA and FCC cases (*Club Intrawest v. Her Majesty the Queen*, 2016; *Club Intrawest v.*

Her Majesty the Queen, 2017) and the Class Action refers to the Quebec-base Class Action lawsuit (*Martin Robichaud v. Intrawest ULC*, n.d.).

12 The documents related to the Tax Court of Canada (TCC) were not made available to members by the Club. The author ordered all documents from the TCA. This review is based on those documents.

13 NPV for the vacation ownership business is based on the price of the VOI plus the maintenance fee, less marketing and sales costs. NPV for the hotel business is based on the present value of the properties, the number of rooms, the average daily rate, the occupancy rate and the total number of days.

APPENDIX

List of Research Documents (Published Between 1994 and 2015)

HOA (Club Intrawest documents

1. HOA instruments: Certification, Master Declaration, Trust Agreements and Bylaws
2. Consolidated financial statements
3. Annual budget summaries
4. Annual dues (service fees) notifications
5. Board meeting minutes and resolutions
6. Board-to-all members communication
7. HOA insurance
8. Trademark registrations
9. Marketing documentation
10. Municipal land titles
11. Board of Directors election material and results

Developer (Intrawest Corporation) documents

1. Project instruments (Club documents but owned by developer): Developer disclosure, Trust indentures, Legal titles of vacation homes, Equipment lists (and other assets), Purchase agreements, Governance flow charts, Annual operating budgets, Management agreement, Interval International agreement, Extraordinary Escapes rules and guidelines, Schedule of total occupancy points, Points calendars, by resort / season, Repurchase program, and Guidelines
2. Municipal land titles of developer-owned property
3. Trademark licenses for "Club Intrawest"
4. Intrawest corporate documentation: SEC filings, analyst presentations, press releases and legal actions and parent document (2008 onwards)

GST Appeal Documents

1. Tax Court Appeal: Judgment, filings, and exhibits, including testimonies
2. Federal Court of Appeal: Judgement, filings, exhibits, recording of hearing.

Industry Documents

1. Corporate documents (SEC filings) from industry competitors/players
2. Industry associations (American Resort Development Association; Canadian Vacation Ownership Association)
3. Academic research on the timeshare industry
4. Analyst reports on the timeshare industry
5. Consulting reports on the timeshare industry
6. News articles on timeshares, including investigative reports
7. Legal actions

Regulatory Documents (timeshare and governance)

1. BC Real Estate Development Marketing Act
2. Consumer protection laws (provincial, Canada)
3. Delaware Code, Title 8 – Corporations
4. Florida Condo and Timeshare regulation
5. California Timeshare regulation

Compilation of References

Abdul Rahman, R., Dahiru Muhammad, A., & Mahayudin, I. (2013). Applicability of the Islamic Micro-Investment Model (IMIM) in Islamic Bank in Malaysia. *World Applied Sciences Journal*, *24*(5), 609–616. DOI: 10.5829/idosi.wasj.2013.24.05.13213

Abubakar, M., Hassan, M. K., & Haruna, M. A. 2019. "Cryptocurrency Tide and Islamic Finance Development: Any Issue?" Pp. 189–200 in *International Finance Review*. Vol. 20.

Adams, M. S., & Mittiga, R. (2020). Material scarcity and scalar justice. *Philosophical Studies*, *178*(7), 2237–2256. DOI: 10.1007/s11098-020-01539-3

Aderemi, A. M. R., & Ishak, M. S. I. (2023). Qard Hasan as a Feasible Islamic Financial Instrument for Crowdfunding: Its Potential and Possible Application for Financing Micro-Enterprises in Malaysia. *Qualitative Research in Financial Markets*, *15*(1), 58–76. DOI: 10.1108/QRFM-08-2021-0145

Agamben, G. (2011). *The Kingdom and the Glory: For a Theological Genealogy of Economy and Government* (Chiesa, L., & Mandarini, M., Trans.). Stanford University Press.

Ahmed, H., & Aassouli, D. (2022). Entrepreneurial Finance, Agency Problems and Islamic Ethics: Complementarities and Constraints. *Venture Capital*, *24*(1), 25–46. DOI: 10.1080/13691066.2022.2067017

Almustafa, E. (2025). Islamic Financing Mechanisms for Renewable Energy Projects: Mapping Research Trends and Future Directions. *International Journal of Energy Economics and Policy*, *15*(3), 453–470. DOI: 10.32479/ijeep.18866

Altenried, M. (2022). Platforms, labour, and mobility: migration and the gig economy. In *The Routledge handbook of the gig economy* (pp. 180–189). Routledge.

Anthroholic. (2023). *Formalist and substantivist debate in economic anthropology. Anthroholic.* https://anthroholic.com/formalist-and-substantivist-debate

Arizton Advisory & Intelligence. (2023, May). *U.S. vacation ownership market: Industry outlook & forecast 2023–2028*(191 pp.). Arizton Advisory & Intelligence. https://www.arizton.com/market-reports/us-vacation-ownership-market

Armstrong, P., & Siddiqui, K. (2019). The case for the ontology of money as credit: Money as bearer or basis of 'value'. *Real-world. Economic Review (Kansas City, Mo.)*, *90*, 98–118.

Austin, J. L. (1962). *How to do things with words*. Clarendon Press.

Ayub, M., & Khan, M. F. (2021). Evolving monetary economics in Islamic perspective. *Journal of Islamic Monetary Economics and Finance*, *7*(2), 317–340. DOI: 10.21098/jimf.v7i2.1372

Badjatya, K. (2024). The Concept of Puru Rtha from the Present Perspective: An Observation. *Journal of Social Sciences and Humanities*. Advance online publication. DOI: 10.53469/jssh.2024.06(08).20

Bandelj, N., Boston, T., Elyachar, J., Kim, J., McBride, M., & Tufail, Z. (2017). Morals and emotions of money. In Bandelj, N., Wherry, F. F., & Zelizer, V. A. (Eds.), *Money talks: Explaining how money really works* (pp. 39–56). Princeton University Press., DOI: 10.23943/princeton/9780691168685.003.0003

Bank of Canada. (n.d.). Inflation calculator. https://www.bankofcanada.ca/rates/related/inflation-calculator/

Baraldi, C., Corsi, G., & Esposito, E. (2021). *Unlocking Luhmann: A keyword introduction to systems theory*. Bielefeld University Press. https://library.oapen.org/bitstream/id/87961f81-6012-4c17-837e-f511b974b9d3

Barreda, A., Murphy, K., Gregory, A., & Singh, D. (2016). Evaluating the value proposition of developing a vacation ownership resort: The case of Florida and Hawaii. *Tourism Review*, *71*(3), 165–179.

Basu, M., & Nag, R. N. (2020). Open Economy Macroeconomics of Commodity Price Fluctuation, Sectoral Inter-Linkage and Employment. *Journal of Economic Studies (Glasgow, Scotland)*, *47*(6), 1467–1494. DOI: 10.1108/JES-11-2018-0399

Baudrillard, J. (1983). *Simulacra, semiotics*. Semiotext(e).

Baxter, H. (2013). Niklas Luhmann's theory of autopoietic legal systems. *Annual Review of Law and Social Science*, *167*, •••. https://scholarship.law.bu.edu/faculty_scholarship/140

Bear, L., Ho, K., Tsing, A., & Yanagisako, S. (2015, March 30). *Gens: A feminist manifesto for the study of capitalism*. Society for Cultural Anthropology. https://culanth.org/fieldsights/gens-a-feminist-manifesto-for-the-study-of-capitalism

Ben Jedidia, K., & Hamza, H. (2024). Does PLS in Islamic Banking Limit Excessive Money Creation? *Journal of Islamic Accounting and Business Research*, *15*(3), 422–442. DOI: 10.1108/JIABR-02-2022-0047

Benmamoun, M., & Sobh, R. (2024). An Islamic Perspective on AI Ethics: A Case Study of Wahed Invest Robo Advisory. *Journal of Business Ethics Education*, *21*, 231–244. DOI: 10.5840/jbee20242114

Bhanot, D., & Verma, S. (2020). Lived experiences of the Indian stigmatized group in reference to socio-political empowerment: A phenomenological approach. *The Qualitative Report*. Advance online publication. DOI: 10.46743/2160-3715/2020.4143

Bhinekawati, R. (2021). Comparing the concept of scarcity: Conventional vs. Islamic economics. Journal of Applied Business and Economics. https://doi.org/DOI: 10.33423/jabe.v23i3.4352

Birch, K., & Muniesa, F. (2020). *Assetization: Turning things into assets in technoscientific capitalism.* The MIT Press., DOI: 10.7551/mitpress/12075.001.0001

Blue, S. A. (2007). The Erosion of Cuban Health Care. *Latin American Research Review*, *42*(1), 161–173. DOI: 10.1353/lar.2007.0011

Bockelmann, E. (2025). *Money: Understanding modern society.* Matthes & Seitz.

Boland, T., & Griffin, R. (2021). Archaic Anthropology: The Presence of the Past in the Present. The Reformation of Welfare. https://doi.org/.DOI: 10.46692/9781529211344.002

Bossone, B. (2025). *Trailblazing visions of money in economic theory. Contributions to Economics.* Springer., DOI: 10.1007/978-3-031-82544-6

Boswell, T. (1989). Colonial Empires and the Capitalist World-Economy: A Time Series Analysis of Colonisation, 1640-1960. *American Sociological Review*, *54*(2), 180. DOI: 10.2307/2095789

Bratoeva, M. (2024). *The Song of Desire (Kāma): If you meet Kāma, don't kill him.* Filosofiya-Philosophy., DOI: 10.53656/phil2024-01-04

Braun, E. (2021). The institutional preconditions of homo economicus. *Journal of Economic Methodology*, *28*, 231–246. DOI: 10.1080/1350178X.2021.1898659

Brown, A. F., Ma, G. X., Miranda, J., Eng, E., Castille, D., Brockie, T., Jones, P., Airhihenbuwa, C. O., Farhat, T., Zhu, L., & Trinh-Shevrin, C. (2019). Structural interventions to reduce and eliminate health disparities. *American Journal of Public Health*, *109*(S1), S72–S78. DOI: 10.2105/AJPH.2018.304844 PMID: 30699019

Budini, S. (2024). The humanistic foundation to sustainability. *Humanistic Management Journal*. Advance online publication. DOI: 10.1007/s41463-024-00172-0

Cagli, E. C., & Dimpfl, T. (2025). Have cryptocurrencies arrived in the system of fiat currencies? An appraisal based on monetary policy uncertainty. *Finance Research Letters, 107993*. Advance online publication. DOI: 10.1016/j.frl.2025.107993

Callon, M. (1999). Actor-Network Theory—The market test. *The Sociological Review*, *47*(1, suppl). Advance online publication. DOI: 10.1111/j.1467-954X.1999.tb03488.x

Carrier, J. G. (Ed.). (2005). *A handbook of economic anthropology*. Edward Elgar Publishing., DOI: 10.4337/9781845423469

Carrillo, F. (2023). From Marx to Now: Exploring collective ownership, classlessness, and the evolving state. *Social Science Chronicle*, *2*(1). Advance online publication. DOI: 10.56106/ssc.2023.011

Cernea, M. M. (2000). Risks, safeguards and reconstruction: A model for population displacement and resettlement. In Cernea, M. M., & McDowell, C. (Eds.), *Risks and reconstruction: Experiences of resettlers and refugees* (pp. 11–55). The World Bank., https://documents.worldbank.org/en/publication/documents-reports/documentdetail/947311468739277702/risks-and-reconstruction-experiences-of-resettlers-and-refugees

Chaka, C. (2022). Digital marginalization, data marginalization, and algorithmic exclusions: A critical southern decolonial approach to datafication, algorithms, and digital citizenship from the Souths. *Journal of e-Learning and Knowledge Society, 18*(3), 83-95.

Chaudhuri, B. (2022). Programmed welfare: An ethnographic account of algorithmic practices in the public distribution system in India. *New Media & Society*, *24*(5), 887–902. DOI: 10.1177/14614448221079034

Chiad, F., & Gherbi, A. (2024). The role of Islamic banks in promoting economic growth and financial stability: Evidence from Saudi Arabia. *Investment Management and Financial Innovations, 21*(3), 357–369. DOI: 10.21511/imfi.21(3).2024.29

Choudhury, M. A., & Hoque, M. N. (2017). The Future of Monetary Reform and the Real Economy: A Problem of Trade versus Interest. *ACRN Journal of Finance and Risk Perspectives, 6*(4), 37–52.

Cini, L. (2023). How algorithms are reshaping the exploitation of labour-power: Insights into the process of labour invisibilization in the platform economy. *Theory and Society, 52*(5), 885–911.

Club Intrawest (1994). *Annual dues summary.* [Internal document]

Club Intrawest. (2007a). *Annual report.* [Internal Club document]

Club Intrawest. (2007b). *Financial statements report.* [Internal Club document]

Club Intrawest. (2009). *Financial statements.* [Internal Club document]

Club Intrawest. (2011a). *Financial statements* [Internal Club document]

Club Intrawest. (2011b, September 1). *Board resolution.* [Internal Club document]

Club Intrawest. (2012a, May 2). *Selling your membership.* [Internal Club document]

Club Intrawest. (2012b). *Financial statements*[Internal Club document]

Club Intrawest. (2013a, June 27). *Respondent's discovery read-ins, Club Intrawest v. Her Majesty the Queen: Examination for discovery of Robert Reyes,* 2012-3401(GST)G (Tax Court of Canada), lines 413–634.

Club Intrawest. (2013b). *Financial statements.* [Internal Club document]

Club Intrawest. (2013c, September 26). *Board meeting minutes.* [Internal Club document]

Club Intrawest. (2013d, April 17). *Board meeting minutes.* [Internal Club document]

Club Intrawest. (2013e). *Annual dues summary.* [Internal Club document]

Club Intrawest. (2014). *Financial statements.* [Internal Club document]

Club Intrawest. (2015a). *Financial statements.* [Internal Club document]

Club Intrawest. (2015b). *Annual dues summary.* [Internal Club document]

Coeckelbergh, M. (2015). Money as medium and tool: Reading Simmel as a philosopher of technology to understand contemporary financial ICTs and media. *Techné: Research in Philosophy and Technology*, *19*(3), 358–380. DOI: 10.5840/techne2015121039

Consumer Protection Act, CQLR c P-40.1 (Québec).

Córdova, G. C. (2020). Notes on the Anthropological Approach to Money and Investment According to Leonardo Polo. *Studia Poliana*, *22*(22), 119–131. DOI: 10.15581/013.22.119-131

Crenshaw, K. (1989). Demarginalizing the intersection of race and sex: A Black feminist critique of antidiscrimination doctrine, feminist theory and antiracist politics. *University of Chicago Legal Forum*, *1989*(1), 139–167. https://chicagounbound.uchicago.edu/uclf/vol1989/iss1/8/

Dabla-Norris, E., Kochhar, K., Suphaphiphat, N., Ricka, F., & Tsounta, E. (2015). *Causes and consequences of income inequality: A global perspective*. International Monetary Fund. https://www.imf.org/en/Publications/Staff-Discussion-Notes/Issues/2016/12/31/Causes-and-Consequences-of-Income-Inequality-A-Global-Perspective-42986

Dana, L. P., Sharma, N., Kumari, S., Tripathy, K. K., Pillai, B. P., & Jayalaxmi, R. (Eds.). (2023). *Cooperatives as a Catalyst for Sustainability: Lessons Learned from Asian Models* (Vol. 12). World Scientific.

Darity, W. (2022). Alternatives to the scarcity principle. *The Journal of Economic Education*, *53*(4), 340–347. DOI: 10.1080/00220485.2022.2111387

Das, N. (2025). *Economic systems: Capitalism, socialism, Communism*. Ilearnlot. https://www.ilearnlot.com/economic-system-capitalism-socialism-and-communism/59995/

Dash, P. (2023). Purusarthas: The Value Paradigms of Human Life (The Bhagavat Gita Perspective). Knowledgeable Research: A Multidisciplinary Journal. https://doi.org/.DOI: 10.57067/kr.v1i12.112

Database, O. R. B. I. S. (2014, June). *Club Intrawest Mexico, LLC and Club Intrawest Mexico, SRL listings*. Bureau van Dijk. https://www.bvdinfo.com

De Soto, H. (2000). *The mystery of capital: Why capitalism triumphs in the West and fails everywhere else*. Basic Books. https://www.hachettebookgroup.com/titles/hernando-de-soto/the-mystery-of-capital/9780465016150/

Delaware General Corporation Law. Tit. 8, § 101 (n.d.). https://delcode.delaware.gov/title8/c001/index.shtml

Derrida, J. (1991). *Given time: I. Counterfeit money*. The University of Chicago Press.

Deshpande, A. (2017). Stigma or red tape? Roadblocks in the use of affirmative action. In The Empire of Disgust. https://doi.org/DOI: 10.1093/oso/9780199487837.003.0002

Devi, S. (2020). HARMONY IN SOCIETY THROUGH PURU ĀRTHAS..

di Somma, E. (2022). Trust, faith, and social imaginary. In Relational Anthropology for Contemporary Economics. https://doi.org/DOI: 10.1007/978-3-030-84690-9_9

Dodd, N. (2015). Redeeming Simmel's money. *HAU*, *5*(2), 435–441. DOI: 10.14318/hau5.2.030

Dorninger, C., Hornborg, A., Abson, D. J., von Wehrden, H., Schaffartzik, A., & Giljum, S.. (2021). Global patterns of ecologically unequal exchange: Implications for sustainability in the 21st century. *Ecological Economics*, *179*, 106824. DOI: 10.1016/j.ecolecon.2020.106824

Dunn, E. C. (2024). Time and space in the work of Katherine Verdery. *Journal of Ethnographic Theory*, *14*(2), 490–493. DOI: 10.1086/731280

Elmawazini, K., Khiyar, K. A., & Aydilek, A. (2020). Types of Banking Institutions and Economic Growth. *International Journal of Islamic and Middle Eastern Finance and Management*, *13*(4), 553–578. DOI: 10.1108/IMEFM-09-2018-0304

Encyclopaedia Britannica. (2025). *Industrial Revolution: Definition, history, dates, summary, & facts*. https://www.britannica.com/event/Industrial-Revolution

Erasmo, V. (2022). *Amartya Sen's earlier conception of economic agents*. Erasmus Journal for Philosophy and Economics., DOI: 10.23941/ejpe.v15i1.596

Escobar, A. (2018). *Designs for the Pluriverse: Radical Interdependence, Autonomy, and the Making of Worlds*. Duke University Press. https://www.dukeupress.edu/designs-for-the-pluriverse

Escobar, A. (2012). *Encountering development: The making and unmaking of the Third World*. Princeton University Press., https://www.degruyterbrill.com/document/doi/10.1515/9781400839926/html?lang=

Escobar, A. (2018). *Designs for the pluriverse: Radical interdependence, autonomy, and the making of worlds*. Duke University Press., DOI: 10.1215/9780822371816

Federal Court of Appeal. (2017). *Club Intrawest v. Her Majesty the Queen*, 2017 FCA 43 (CanLII). https://canlii.ca/t/gx2v6

Ferguson, J. (1994). *The anti-politics machine: "Development," depoliticization, and bureaucratic power in Lesotho*. University of Minnesota Press. https://www.upress.umn.edu/9780816624379/anti-politics-machine/

Ferguson, J. (2006). *Global shadows: Africa in the neoliberal world order*. Duke University Press., DOI: 10.1215/9780822387640

Fernandes, S. (2006). *Cuba represents! Cuban arts, state power, and the making of new revolutionary cultures*. Duke University Press., DOI: 10.1215/9780822388227

Fotaki, M., & Prasad, A. (2015). Questioning Neoliberal Capitalism and Economic Inequality in Business Schools. *Academy of Management Learning & Education, 14*(4), 556–575. DOI: 10.5465/amle.2014.0182

Frank, A. G. (1967). *Capitalism and underdevelopment in Latin America: Historical studies of Chile and Brazil*. Monthly Review Press. https://nyupress.org/9780853450931/capitalism-and-underdevelopment-in-latin-america/

Fraser, N. (2008). *Scales of justice: Reimagining political space in a globalizing world*. Columbia University Press., https://cup.columbia.edu/book/scales-of-justice/9780231146807

Fricker, M. (2007). *Epistemic injustice: Power and the ethics of knowing*. Oxford University Press., DOI: 10.1093/acprof:oso/9780198237907.001.0001

Furtado, C. (2022). *Development and underdevelopment*. University of California Press. https://www.ucpress.edu/books/development-and-underdevelopment/paper

Gadgil, M., Berkes, F., & Folke, C. (1993). Indigenous knowledge for biodiversity conservation. *Ambio, 22*(2/3), 151–156. https://www.jstor.org/stable/4314060 PMID: 33566330

Gangopadhyay, K., Jacob, R. T., & Jayanth, R. S. S. (2020). How effective is theory-based learning of ethics in India? *IIM Kozhikode Society & Management Review, 9*, 55–61. DOI: 10.1177/2277975219889778

Gauliver, C. (2023). Economic anthropology: From cultural norms to social relations and their complexities. *Anthropology; a Guide to First Degree Courses in UK Universities, 11*(3), 1000317. https://www.longdom.org/open-access-pdfs/economic-anthropology-from-cultural-norms-to-social-relations-and-their-complexities.pdf

Geertz, C. (1973). *The interpretation of cultures: Selected essays*. Basic Books. https://web.mit.edu/allanmc/www/geertz.pdf

Gemici, K. (2008). Karl Polanyi and the antinomies of embeddedness. *Socio-economic Review*, *6*(1), 5–33. DOI: 10.1093/ser/mwl034

Ghosh, S. (2022). Time, scarcity, and abundance. *Frontiers in Research Metrics and Analytics*, *7*. Advance online publication. DOI: 10.3389/frma.2022.974706 PMID: 36118014

Gibson-Graham, J. K. (2006). *A postcapitalist politics*. University of Minnesota Press.

Giraud, G. (2023). Economics as Religion and Christianity as oikonomia: Giorgio Agamben and the Homo Sacer. *Religions*. Advance online publication. DOI: 10.3390/rel14121490

Gogoi, N., Bhuyan, S., & Boruah, S. (2025). Empowering Women through Handloom Weaving: A Focus on Northeast Indias' Heritage and Opportunities for Sustainability. *Women Empowerment in Agriculture: A Pathway Towards. Sustainable Development*, •••, 296.

Gorjestani, N. M. (2000). *Indigenous knowledge for development: Opportunities and challenges* (World Bank Working Paper No. 24869). World Bank Group. https://documents.worldbank.org/pt/publication/documents-reports/documentdetail/574381468765625385/indigenous-knowledge-for-development-opportunities-and-challenges

Graeber, D. (2001). *Toward an anthropological theory of value: The false coin of our own dreams*. Palgrave.

Graeber, D. (2011). *Debt. The first 5,000 years*. Melville House Publishing.

Grafov, D. (2022). Informal relations in Indian society. Journal of the Institute of Oriental Studies RAS. https://doi.org/DOI: 10.31696/2618-7302-2022-3-098-111

Grey, M. L., & Suri, S. (2019). *Ghost Work: How to Stop Silicon Valley from Building a New Global Underclass*. Houghton Mifflin Harcourt. https://www.harpercollins.com/products/ghost-work-mary-l-graysiddharth-suri

Gruber, J. (2023). *The Relevance of Algorithm Skills for Digital Inequality* (Doctoral dissertation, University of Zurich).

Gudeman, S. (1986). *Economics as culture: Models and metaphors of livelihood.* Routledge & Kegan Paul.

Gudeman, S. (2001). *The anthropology of economy: Community, market, and culture.* Blackwell.

Gull, I., & Khan, B. A. (2023). *The financial accounting and management of the Dharmarth Trust (1846–1947 A.D.): An insight into the religious affairs of the Dogra State.* International Journal for Multidisciplinary Research., DOI: 10.36948/ijfmr.2023.v05i05.6331

Haberl, H., Fischer-Kowalski, M., Krausmann, F., Martinez-Alier, J., & Winiwarter, V. (2011). A socio-metabolic transition towards sustainability? Challenges for another Great Transformation. *Sustainable Development, 19*(1), 1–14. DOI: 10.1002/sd.410

Halladay, P., & Gilmour, D. A. (Eds.). (1995). *Conserving biodiversity outside protected areas: The role of traditional agro-ecosystems.* IUCN – The World Conservation Union, AMA – Andalucía, & Centro de Investigación F. González-Bernáldez. https://portals.iucn.org/library/sites/library/files/documents/FR-013.pdf

Hart, K. (1973). Informal income opportunities and urban employment in Ghana. *The Journal of Modern African Studies, 11*(1), 61–89. DOI: 10.1017/S0022278X00008089

Hart, K., & Ortiz, H. (2014). The Anthropology of Money and Finance: Between Ethnography and World History. *Annual Review of Anthropology, 43*(1), 465–482. DOI: 10.1146/annurev-anthro-102313-025814

Harvey, D. (2005). *A brief history of neoliberalism.* Oxford University Press., https://global.oup.com/academic/product/a-brief-history-of-neoliberalism-9780199283279?cc=in&lang=

Hasan, R., M. K. Hassan, and M. Rashid. 2021. "Qard Hasan (Interest-Free Loan) as a Tool for Sustainable Development-Global Evidence." Pp. 307–30 in *Islamic Finance and Sustainable Development: A Sustainable Economic Framework for Muslim and Non-Muslim Countries*.

Hassan, M. K., Rabbani, M. R., & Mohd. Ali, M. A. (2020). Challenges for the Islamic Finance and Banking in Post COVID Era and the Role of Fintech. *Journal of Economic Cooperation and Development*, *41*(3), 93–116.

Hinton, A. L. (2005). *Why did they kill? Cambodia in the shadow of genocide*. University of California Press., DOI: 10.1525/9780520937949

Hornborg, A. (2024a). Defetishizing money: Perspectives from economic anthropology. Gudeman Lecture, University of Minnesota, March 20, 2023. *Journal of Ethnographic Theory*, *14*(2), 310–319. DOI: 10.1086/731656

Hornborg, A. (2024b). Limiting money: Redesigning the artifact that shapes modern people. *Sustainability Science*. Advance online publication. DOI: 10.1007/s11625-024-01489-3

Hornborg, A. (2024c). *Liquidate: How money is dissolving the world*. Routledge., DOI: 10.4324/9781032702186

Horváth, M., & Lovász, A. (2024). From the Anthropocene to the Capitalocene and beyond. *The Anthropocene Review*. Advance online publication. DOI: 10.1177/20530196241270703

Humphrey, C. (1991). *The unmaking of Soviet life: Everyday economies after socialism*. Cornell University Press. https://lccn.loc.gov/91118707

Humphrey, C. (1983). *Karl Marx's collective: Economy, society and religion in a Siberian collective farm*. Cambridge University Press., https://www.amazon.com/Karl-Marx-Collective-Cambridge-Anthropology/dp/052127401X

Hydén, G. (1980). Beyond Ujamaa in Tanzania: Underdevelopment and an uncaptured peasantry. University of California Press.https://books.google.co.in/books/about/Beyond_Ujamaa_in_Tanzania.html?id=VGkqAAAAYAAJ&redir_esc=y

Incekara, A., F. Y. Tatoğlu, and M. Ustaoğlu. 2014. "Modeling Islamic Finance and Inclusive Growth for Emerging Markets: Evidence and Roadmap of Turkey and Malaysia." Pp. 74–95 in *Islamic Finance Alternatives for Emerging Economies: Empirical Evidence from Turkey.*

Ingham, G. (2004). *The nature of money.* Cambridge University Press.

Intrawest Corporation & Club Intrawest. (2014, January 15). *Supplemental declaration of annexation for Club Intrawest.*

Intrawest Corporation (2015a) Corporate offices, accessed 2015, December 29).

Intrawest Corporation. (1998, June). *Prospectus.*

Intrawest Corporation. (2002a). *Summary of key elements of your membership.*

Intrawest Corporation. (2002b). *Selling your membership.*

Intrawest Corporation. (2008, February 21). *Club Intrawest repurchase program, restated February 21, 2008).*

Intrawest Corporation. (2015b, May 15). *Disclosure Statement of Intrawest ULC for Club Intrawest* (including Tables 1 through 14).

Intrawest Resort Ownership Corporation. (1994, January 20). *Prospectus of Intrawest Resort Ownership Corporation for Intrawest Resort Club.* Revision: February 8, 1994.

IOM (International Organization for Migration). (2024). *World migration report 2024.* IOM Publications. https://publications.iom.int/books/world-migration-report-2024

Ishak, A. H., Amira Mohamad, S. N., Ab Manan, S. K., Yahaya, M. H., Wan Daud, W. N., & Sharif, D. (2025). The Critical Success Factors of Waqf Land Development for Sustainable Agriculture. *Social Sciences & Humanities Open, 11*. Advance online publication. DOI: 10.1016/j.ssaho.2024.101244

Isomae, J. (2022). Anthropology of Religion. In Weyel, B. (Eds.), *i>International Handbook of Practical Theology</i>*. De Gruyter., DOI: 10.1515/9783110618150-046

Jafar, A., H. Ibrahim, and R. Malik. 2025. "Waqf: From Classical Charitable System to Modern Financial Tool." *International Journal of Ethics and Systems*. doi: .DOI: 10.1108/IJOES-10-2024-0354

Jarbou, S. I., Irimia-Diéguez, A., & Prieto-Rodríguez, M. (2024). Financial Performance of Islamic and Conventional Banks in MENA Region: A GLS Approach. *Journal of Islamic Accounting and Business Research*. Advance online publication. DOI: 10.1108/JIABR-11-2023-0380

Jay, J. (2013). Navigating paradox as a mechanism of change and innovation in hybrid organizations. *Academy of Management Journal, 56*(1), 137–159.

Jeffrey, C. (2010). *Timepass: Youth, Class, and the Politics of Waiting in India*. Stanford University Press.

Jereza, R. (2021). Corporeal moderation: Digital labour as affective good. *Social Anthropology. Anthropologie et Sociétés, 29*(4), 928–943.

Kato, T. 2022. "Islamic and Capitalist Economies: Comparison Using Econophysics Models of Wealth Exchange and Redistribution." *PLoS ONE* 17(9 September). doi: .DOI: 10.1371/journal.pone.0275113

Keerthiraj, M. A., & Vang-Phu, T. (2025). India's BRICS Engagement: A Strategic Lever in South Asia and the Indian Ocean. In A. Gedikli, S. Erdogan, & H. Çalışkan Terzioğlu (Eds.), Changing the Global Political Economy: BRICS Countries and Alternative Relations Strategies (pp. 189-214). IGI Global Scientific Publishing. https://doi.org/DOI: 10.4018/979-8-3693-7393-4.ch006

Khalid, N. (2025). The Economic Impacts of India's Gig Economy: Navigating Productivity, Inequality, and Market Dynamics. In *Immersive Technology for the Gig Economy: Transformative Business Practices* (pp. 1-32). IGI Global Scientific Publishing.

Kikhi, K., & Gautam, D. R. (Eds.). (2023). *Marginality in India: Perspectives of Marginalisation from the Northeast*. Taylor & Francis.

Kipnis, A. B. (2008). Audit cultures: Neoliberal governmentality, socialist legacy, or technologies of governing? *American Ethnologist, 35*(2), 275–289. DOI: 10.1111/j.1548-1425.2008.00034.x

Klamer, A. (2023). An essay on the need to redefine economics. Journal of Philosophical Economics. https://doi.org/DOI: 10.46298/jpe.10887

Knorr Cetina, K., & Bruegger, U. (2002). Global microstructures: The virtual societies of financial markets. *American Journal of Sociology, 107*(4), 905–950. DOI: 10.1086/341045

Konnova, N. (2020). Economics of values and philosophy of economics. *Humanitarium, 23*, 27–37. DOI: 10.15421/172022

Konwar, J. G., & Das, K. (2012). Creating ethnic identity: A movement of Koch Rajbonshis of Assam. *International Journal of Humanities and Social Sciences, 2*(3), 301–310. Research India Publications. https://www.ripublication.com/ijhss/ijhssv2n3_11.pdf

Kumar, S. (2023). Empowering Bharat: Role of the Northeast in the Indian Vision of Development. *Available at SSRN* 4842098.

Langley, A. (1999). Strategies for theorizing from process data. *Academy of Management Review, 24*(4), 691–710.

Latour, B. (2005). *Reassembling the social: An introduction to Actor-Network-Theory*. Oxford University Press.

Ledeneva, A. V. (1998). *Russia's economy of favours: Blat, networking and informal exchange*. Cambridge University Press., https://www.cambridge.org/9780521621748

Lévi-Strauss, C. (1962). *The savage mind* (G. Weidenfeld & Nicholson, Trans.). University of Chicago Press. (Original work published 1962) https://web.mit.edu/allanmc/www/levistrauss.pdf

Li, T. M. (2014). *Land's end: Capitalist relations on an indigenous frontier*. Duke University Press. https://www.dukeupress.edu/lands-end

Love, T. (2022). Scarcity. In Stepmother. https://doi.org/DOI: 10.2307/j.ctv1s5nxzd.9

Luhmann, N. (1984). Die Wirtschaft der Gesellschaft als autopoietisches System. *Zeitschrift für Soziologie*, *11*(4), 366–379.

Luhmann, N. (1988). *Ökologische Kommunikation*. Suhrkamp.

Lushch-Purii, U. (2021). *From homo economicus to homo eudaimonicus*. Anthropological Measurements of Philosophical Research., DOI: 10.15802/ampr.v0i19.235992

Magarelli, E. (2025). Narrating Survival: Digital Storytelling as a Tool for Language Mediation Practices. *Cross-Media Languages. Applied Research. Digital Tools and Methodologies*, (3), 87–98.

Mahmoud, M. A., Umar, U. H., Danlami, M. R., & Ado, M. B. (2025). An Analysis of Islamic Financing Access in Nigeria: Perspectives of MSME Owners. *International Journal of Islamic and Middle Eastern Finance and Management*, *18*(1), 49–67. DOI: 10.1108/IMEFM-02-2024-0072

Mäki, U. (2021). Homo economicus under multiple pressures. In Philosophy of Economics. https://doi.org/DOI: 10.1007/978-981-15-9395-6_18

Malm, A., & Hornborg, A. (2014). The geology of mankind? A critique of the Anthropocene narrative. *The Anthropocene Review*, *1*(1), 62–69. DOI: 10.1177/2053019613516291

Malthus, T. R. (1993). *An Essay on the Principle of Population* (2nd ed.). Oxford University Press. (Original work published 1798)

Martikainen, T., & Brekke, T. (2022). The Rejection of Interest-Based Loans among Muslim Entrepreneurs and Professionals in Finland. *Journal of Muslims in Europe*, *6*(2), 1–17. DOI: 10.1163/22117954-bja10074

Martini, N., Sudarma, M., Purwanti, L., & Adib, N. (2025). The Concepts of Performance Measurement based on the Purposes of the Hindu Religion. Finance. *Theory into Practice*. Advance online publication. DOI: 10.26794/2587-5671-2025-29-1-195-203

Marx, K. (1990). *Capital: A critique of political economy. Volume I* (B. Fowkes, Trans.). Penguin Books. (Original work published 1867). https://www.penguinrandomhouse.com/books/261069/capital-by-karl-marx-translated-by-ben-fowkes-introduction-by-ernest-mandel/

Marx, K., & Engels, F. (1848). *Manifesto of the Communist Party* (S. Moore, Trans.). Marxists Internet Archive. (Original work published 1848) https://www.marxists.org/archive/marx/works/download/pdf/Manifesto.pdf

Maurer, B. (2006). The anthropology of money. *Annual Review of Anthropology*, *35*, 15–36. DOI: 10.1146/annurev.anthro.35.081705.123127

Maurer, B. (2015). *How would you like to pay? How technology is changing the future of money*. Duke University Press., DOI: 10.1215/9780822375173

McCormack, F. (2022). Commentary on the special issue: Anthropology and the labour theory of value. *Dialectical Anthropology*, *46*(1), 73–84. PMID: 35282139

McNeill, D. (2020). *Fetishism and the theory of value: Reassessing Marx in the 21st century*. Palgrave Macmillan.

Meghalaya, S. I. R. (n.d.). *Syllad*. Syllad.

Miku, Marek, and Max Planck. 2014. "Uvođenje Eura i Nacionalna Valuta u Hrvatskoj." 195–210.

Milanović, B. (2018). *Global inequality: A new approach for the age of globalization*. Harvard University Press. https://www.hup.harvard.edu/books/9780674984035

Minch, D. (2021). Pastoral Criticism, Structural Collaboration: The Role of Ecclesial Power Structures in Modernization and Economic Individualization. *Horizons*, *48*, 367–403. DOI: 10.1017/hor.2021.53

Ministry of Education. (2025). *Mizoram achieves full functional literacy*. Press Information Bureau, Government of India. https://www.pib.gov.in/PressReleasePage.aspx?PRID=2130080# National Academies of Sciences, Engineering, and Medicine. (2017). *Communities in action: Pathways to health equity*. https://www.ncbi.nlm.nih.gov/books/NBK425845/

Mishra, D. (2022). Economic Strategy in the Kautilīya Arthaśāstra. .

Mishra, M. (2025). The Northeast and India's Look East Policy: A Critical Analysis of Driven Development Model and Challenges. *South Asian Journal of Social Studies and Economics*, *22*(5), 152–161.

Misra, A. & Keerthiraj. (2025). Integrating Sustainability in India's Tourism Sector: An Uphill Battle. In S. Poddar, B. Paul, & M. Luperi (Eds.), Sustainable Business Ecosystems and Social Perspectives (pp. 359-386). IGI Global Scientific Publishing. https://doi.org/DOI: 10.4018/979-8-3693-8437-4.ch016

Mohamed, A., & Akande, A. E. (2025). *Waqf-Led Buildings and Green Infrastructure Role in Environmental Sustainability: Understanding Critical Gaps in Current Research Landscape*. Management and Sustainability., DOI: 10.1108/MSAR-09-2024-0152

Mondal, S., & Choudry, A. (2024). Dharma in Sri Aurobindo's The Renaissance in India and other essays on Indian culture. Journal of Dharma Studies. https://doi.org/DOI: 10.1007/s42240-024-00176-x

Montgomery, T., & Baglioni, S. (2021). Defining the gig economy: Platform capitalism and the reinvention of precarious work. *The International Journal of Sociology and Social Policy*, *41*(9/10), 1012–1025.

Moore, J. W. (2016). *Anthropocene or Capitalocene? Nature, history, and the crisis of capitalism*. PM Press.

Moran, D. D., Lenzen, M., Kanemoto, K., & Geschke, A. (2013). Does ecologically unequal exchange occur? *Ecological Economics*, *89*, 177–186. DOI: 10.1016/j.ecolecon.2013.02.013

Morgenson, G. (2016, January 22). The timeshare hard sell comes roaring back. *The New York Times*. https://www.nytimes.com/2016/01/24/business/diamond-resorts-accused-of-using-hard-sell-to-push-time-shares.html

Morshed, A., Othman, M. D., & Al-Amarneh, A. (2024). Investigating the applicability of the expected credit loss model to Islamic sukuk: Law aspects. *Corporate Law and Governance Review*, *6*(3), 81–89. DOI: 10.22495/clgrv6i3p9

Municipalité de Montréal-Tremblant. (2014.). *Rôle d'évaluation foncière* (Lot 2803899, Dossier no. 227101).

Nagaraj, N., & Prakash, A. (2021). Digital biometric authentication and citizens' right to food: Neglect of the 'local' in India's Aadhaar-enabled Public Distribution System. *Proceedings of the 14th International Conference on Theory and Practice of Electronic Governance*. https://doi.org/ DOI: 10.1145/3494193.3494239

Nathan, D., Kelkar, G., & Mehta, B. (2022). Platform economy, techno-nationalism, and gig workers in India. In *The Routledge Handbook of the Gig Economy* (pp. 374–391). Routledge.

Nelson, J. (1995). Feminism and economics. *The Journal of Economic Perspectives*, *9*(2), 131–148. 110.1257/jep.9.2.131

Nigam, A., & Chandra, S. (2022). Digital accessibility and information mining of Dharmaśāstric knowledge traditions

Nongbri, T., Bhargava, R., & Nongbri. (2021). *Materiality and Visuality in North East India*. Springer Singapore.

Odora Hoppers, C. A. (2009). Education, culture and society in a globalizing world: Implications for comparative and international education. *Compare: A Journal of Comparative Education*, *39*(5), 601–614. DOI: 10.1080/03057920903125628

OECD (Organisation for Economic Cooperation and Development). (2021). *Bridging digital divides in G20 countries*. OECD Publishing. https://doi.org/DOI: 10.1787/35c1d850-en

OECD (Organisation for Economic Cooperation and Development). (2023). *Development Cooperation Report 2023: Debating the Aid System*. OECD Publishing. https://doi.org/DOI: 10.1787/f6edc3c2-en

OpenStax. (2021). *Introduction to Sociology 3e*. https://openstax.org/books/introduction-sociology-3e/pages/9-1-what-is-social-stratification

Ordonez., G. & Matthew du Mée, M. (2020, March 3). *Timeshare obligations, regulations, and challenges. Attorney General Journal*. National Association of Attorneys General. https://www.naag.org/attorney-general-journal/timeshare-obligations-regulations-and-challenges/

Ortiz, H. (2019). The Political Anthropology of Finance and the Anthropology of Money. *Sociologia & Antropologia*, *9*(3), 773–795. DOI: 10.1590/2238-38752019v933

P, S. K., & Punit, I. S. (2024, December 10). This Indian state wants to be a tech hub. But the government keeps shutting down the internet. *Rest of World*.

Pagano, U. (2014). The Crisis of Intellectual Monopoly Capitalism. *Cambridge Journal of Economics*, *38*(6), 1409–1429. DOI: 10.1093/cje/beu025

Pallesen, T., & Pedersen, K. (2023). Model of Human Fallibility: Traveling Behavioral Assumptions in Public Governance. *Perspectives on Public Management and Governance*. Advance online publication. DOI: 10.1093/ppmgov/gvad001

Parsons, T. (1978). *Action theory and the human condition*.

Pericoli, A. (2025). Islamic Instruments for Refugee Financing: The IsDB and UNHCR Collaborative Approach. *Global Policy*, *16*(S1), 46–56. DOI: 10.1111/1758-5899.13476

Petras, J. F. (2018). Twentieth-Century socialist revolutions and their class components: Russia, China, Cuba, and Vietnam. In *Springer eBooks* (pp. 85–113). https://doi.org/DOI: 10.1007/978-3-319-92354-3_5

Piketty, T. (2014). *Capital in the twenty-first century* (A. Goldhammer, Trans.). Belknap Press of Harvard University Press. https://www.hup.harvard.edu/books/9780674430006

Pires, G. (2024). ONTOLOGICAL ROOTS OF HOMO ECONOMICUS. Interfaces Científicas - Humanas e Sociais. https://doi.org/.DOI: 10.17564/2316-3801.2024v12n2p441-454

Polanyi, K. (2001). *The great transformation: The political and economic origins of our time*. Beacon Press. https://www.beacon.org/The-Great-Transformation-P46.aspx

Polanyi, K. (1957). *The great transformation: The political and economic origins of our time* (2nd ed.). Beacon Press., https://inctpped.ie.ufrj.br/spiderweb/pdf_4/Great_Transformation.pdf

Polanyi, K. (2001). *[1944]. The Great Transformation: The political and economic origins of our time*. Penguin Modern Classics.

Ponattu, D., Schmidt, J., & Schmidt, S. (2019). *The urban-rural divide and regionally inclusive growth in the digital age* [Policy brief]. Global Solutions Initiative. https://www.global-solutions-initiative.org/publication/the-urban-rural-divide-and-regionally-inclusive-growth-in-the-digital-age/

Prebisch, R. (1950). *The economic development of Latin America and its principal problems*. United Nations. https://repositorio.cepal.org/handle/11362/29973

Rabbani, M. R., Bashar, A., Nawaz, N., Karim, S., Ali, M. A. M., Rahiman, H. U., & Alam, M. S. (2021). Exploring the Role of Islamic Fintech in Combating the Aftershocks of Covid-19: The Open Social Innovation of the Islamic Financial System. *Journal of Open Innovation*, *7*(2). Advance online publication. DOI: 10.3390/joitmc7020136

Radhakrishnan, S. (1922). The Hindu Dharma. The International Journal of Ethics, 33(1), 1–22. https://doi.org/DOI: 10.1086/INTEJETHI.33.1.2377174

Raworth, K. (2017). *Doughnut economics: Seven ways to think like a 21st-century economist*. Chelsea Green Publishing. https://www.kateraworth.com/doughnut/

Redvers, N., & Blondin, B. (2020). Traditional Indigenous medicine in North America: A scoping review. *PLoS One*, *15*(8), e0237531. DOI: 10.1371/journal.pone.0237531 PMID: 32790714

Rela, N. L. (2021). Adam Smith's homo oeconomicus. Manuscrito. https://doi.org/DOI: 10.1590/0100-6045.2021.v44n3.nr

Reytar, K., Veit, P., & von Braun, J. (2024). *Protecting biodiversity hinges on securing Indigenous and community land rights*. World Resources Institute. https://www.wri.org/insights/indigenous-and-local-community-land-rights-protect-biodiversity

Ribeiro, R. J. (2022). Scarcity as an alibi: On the false ethical discussions about the war on COVID-19. *Philosophies*, *7*(6), 125. DOI: 10.3390/philosophies7060125

Ricardo, D. (1817). *Principles of Political Economy and Taxation*. Dover Publications.

Rivkin-Fish, M. (2005). *Women's health in post-Soviet Russia: The politics of intervention*. Indiana University Press., https://iupress.org/9780253217677/womens-health-in-post-soviet-russia/

Rizzi, A., Kessler, A., & Menajovsky, J. (2021). The stories algorithms tell: Bias and financial inclusion at the data margins. *Center for Financial Inclusion, Accion (2021), 35*.

Robbins, J. (2020). Theology and the Anthropology of Christian Life. . https://doi.org/.DOI: 10.1093/oso/9780198845041.001.0001

Rodney, W. (1982). *How Europe underdeveloped Africa* (Rev. ed.). Howard University Press., https://monoskop.org/images/8/81/Rodney_Walter_How_Europe_Underdeveloped_Africa_rev_ed_1981.pdf

Roy, A. (2020). Consuming Bollywood. *The Journal of Religion and Film*. Advance online publication. DOI: 10.3726/978-1-4539-1231-7

Sabharwal, N. S., & Sonalkar, W. (2015). Dalit women in India: At the crossroads of gender, class, and caste. *Global Justice: Theory Practice Rhetoric, 8*(1). https://doi.org/DOI: 10.21248/gjn.8.1.54

Sadr, S. K. (2014). Qar asan financing in Islamic banks. *ISRA International Journal of Islamic Finance, 6*(2), 7–20. DOI: 10.12816/0019261

Sahlins, M. (1972). *Stone age economics*. Routledge.

Salami, M. (2013). A brief history of African feminism. *MsAfropolitan*. https://msafropolitan.com/2013/07/a-brief-history-of-african-feminism.html

Santos, B. de S. (Ed.). (2007). *Cognitive justice in a global world: Prudent knowledges for a decent life* (1st ed.). Lexington Books., https://www.bloomsbury.com/us/cognitive-justice-in-a-global-world-9781978790339/

Schneider, B. R., & Soskice, D. (2009). Inequality in Developed Countries and Latin America: Coordinated, Liberal and Hierarchical Systems. *Economy and Society, 38*(1), 17–52. DOI: 10.1080/03085140802560496

Scott, J. C. (1998). *Seeing like a state: How certain schemes to improve the human condition have failed*. Yale University Press. https://archive.org/details/seeinglikestate00jame

Scott, J. C. (1998). *Seeing like a state: How certain schemes to improve the human condition have failed*. Yale University Press., DOI: 10.2307/j.ctvxkn7ds

Searle, J. R., & Vanderveken, D. (1985). *Foundations of illocutionary logic*. Cambridge University Press.

Sen, A. (1999). *Development as freedom*. Oxford University Press., https://global.oup.com/academic/product/development-as-freedom-9780198297581

Sen, A. (2005). *The argumentative Indian: Writings on Indian history, culture and identity*. Farrar, Straus and Giroux.

Shah, G. (2023). Caste, Community, and Crisis Response in India's COVID-19 Lockdown. *Economic and Political Weekly*, *58*(2), 35–42.

Shah, P. (2025). The codependence of Orientalism and the social sciences. *History of the Human Sciences*. Advance online publication. DOI: 10.1177/09526951241306299

Sharma, A., & Gupta, A. (Eds.). (2006). *The anthropology of the state: A reader*. Blackwell Publishing. https://voidnetwork.gr/wp-content/uploads/2016/10/The-Anthropology-of-the-State-edited-by-Aradhana-Sharma-and-Akhil-Gupta.pdf

Simmel, G. (2004) [1900]. *The philosophy of money*. 3.rd enlarged ed. Routledge.

Singha, R. (2024). Empathy and compassion as fundamental elements of social cognition. In Shanker, A., & Kumar, V. (Eds.), *Principles and clinical interventions in social cognition* (pp. 22–38). IGI Global., DOI: 10.4018/979-8-3693-1265-0.ch003

Singha, R. (2024a). Fostering mindfulness and compassion: Strategies, benefits, and challenges. In Narayan, P., & Sharma, A. (Eds.), *Applications of service learning in higher education* (pp. 40–60). IGI Global., DOI: 10.4018/979-8-3693-2133-1.ch004

Smith, J. (2024, January 11). *FBI New York warns of scams targeting timeshare owners*. Federal Bureau of Investigation – New York Field Office. https://www.fbi.gov/contact-us/field-offices/newyork/news/fbi-new-york-warns-of-scams-targeting-timeshare-owners

Smith, L. T. (2021). *Decolonizing methodologies: Research and Indigenous Peoples* (2nd ed.). Zed Books (Bloomsbury Publishing). https://www.bloomsbury.com/us/decolonizing-methodologies-9781786998125/

Smith, A. (1776). *The Wealth of Nations* (Cannan, E., Ed.). Bantam Classics.

Srairi, S., Bourkhis, K., & Houcine, A. (2022). Does Bank Governance Affect Risk and Efficiency? Evidence from Islamic Banks in GCC Countries. *International Journal of Islamic and Middle Eastern Finance and Management, 15*(3), 644–663. DOI: 10.1108/IMEFM-05-2020-0206

Ssorin-Chaikov, N. V. (2003). *The social life of the state in subarctic Siberia*. Stanford University Press., https://www.sup.org/books/asian-studies/social-life-state-subarctic-siberia

Standing, G. (2011). *The precariat: The new dangerous class*. Bloomsbury Academic. https://www.bloomsbury.com/uk/precariat-9781849663512/

Stiglitz, J. E. (2012). *Globalization & its discontents*. Penguin India. https://www.amazon.in/Globalization-its-Discontents-Joseph-Stiglitz/dp/0143417819

Sun, H., & Teichert, T. (2022). Scarcity in today's consumer markets: Scoping the research landscape by author keywords. Management Review Quarterly, 1–28. https://doi.org/DOI: 10.1007/s11301-022-00295-4

Sunandan, K. N. (2022). Caste, knowledge, and power. https://doi.org/DOI: 10.1017/9781009273138

Sun, Z., Wang, Y., Zhou, X., & Yang, L. (2019). The Roundabout from Interest Rates to Commodity Prices in China: The Role of Money Flow. *Resources Policy, 61*, 627–642. DOI: 10.1016/j.resourpol.2018.10.011

Swamy, D., Nagarajan, K., & Babu, N. (2021). Yogic Principles of Artha and Dāna with Reference to Individual and Corporate Social Responsibility. *International Journal of Yoga, 14*, 248–255. DOI: 10.4103/ijoy.ijoy_106_21 PMID: 35017868

Swu, N., & Roy, S. (2025). Land, Identity, and Economic Stability: Examining the Shift from Community to Private Ownership in Naga Society. *Heritage & Society*, •••, 1–22.

Talan, G. (2020). A holistic business model based on South Asian philosophies. In *Contemporary issues in South Asia* (pp. 33–46). Nova Science Publishers, Inc.

Tax Court of Canada. (2016). *Club Intrawest v. Her Majesty the Queen* (2012-3401(GST)G), 2016 TCC 149 (CanLII). https://canlii.ca/t/h2ps9

Thompson, K. (2014, November 24). *Cross-examination by Ms. Burch, in Club Intrawest v. Her Majesty the Queen, No. 2012-3401(GST)G (Tax Court of Canada), transcript of proceedings.*

Thompson, S. P. (2022). *False doctrine, false god, false economy*. The Kenarchy Journal., DOI: 10.62950/vxkla45

Tolbert, C. M., Lyson, T. A., & Irwin, M. D. (1998). Local Capitalism, Civic Engagement, and Socioeconomic Well-Being. *Social Forces*, *77*(2), 401–428. DOI: 10.2307/3005533

Trüeb, R. M., Gadzhigoroeva, A., Kopera, D., Luu, N. C., & Dmitriev, A. (2023). The Problem with Capitalism in the Trichological Sciences. *International Journal of Trichology*, *15*(3), 79–84. DOI: 10.4103/ijt.ijt_15_23 PMID: 38179012

Tsing, A. L. (2005). *Friction: An ethnography of global connection*. Princeton University Press., https://archive.org/details/frictionethnogra0000tsin

Tsing, A. L. (2015). *The mushroom at the end of the world: On the possibility of life in capitalist ruins*. Princeton University Press.

Tuniz, C., & Vipraio, P. T. (2020). Homo oeconomicus. In From Apes to Cyborgs. https://doi.org/DOI: 10.1007/978-3-030-36522-6_11

Uhl, P. (2016). The alternative community as revolutionary avant-garde. In *The Power of the Powerless: Citizens Against the State in Central and Eastern Europe* (pp. 187–188). Routledge. https://doi.org/DOI: 10.4324/9781315487373-15

Umam, K., Ismail, A. G., Tohirin, A., & Sriyana, J. (2021). Islamic endogenous money: Evidence from the Islamic banking system in Indonesia and Malaysia. *Journal of Islamic Monetary Economics and Finance*, *7*(3), 545–560. DOI: 10.21098/jimf.v7i3.1351

UNDESA. (United Nations, Department of Economic and Social Affairs). (2023). *World social report 2023: Leaving no one behind in an ageing world.* United Nations Publications. https://desapublications.un.org/publications/world-social-report-2023-leaving-no-one-behind-ageing-world

UNDP (United Nations Development Programme). (2016). *Human development report 2016: Human development for everyone*. UNDP. https://hdr.undp.org/content/human-development-report-2016

UNDP. (2004). *Decentralized governance for development: A combined practice note on decentralization, local governance and urban/rural development*. https://www.undp.org/sites/g/files/zskgke326/files/publications/DLGUD_PN_English.pdf

UNDP. (2014). *Implementing the UN Declaration on the Rights of Indigenous Peoples: A handbook for parliamentarians*. https://www.undp.org/sites/g/files/zskgke326/files/publications/es/RightsOfIndigenousPeoples-HandbookForParliamentarians-EN.pdf

UNDP. (2021). *UNDP Strategic Plan 2022–2025*. https://www.undp.org/sites/g/files/zskgke326/files/2022-07/UNDP%20Strategic%20Plan%202022-2025.pdf

UNDP. (2024). *Human Development Report 2023/2024: Breaking the gridlock*. https://hdr.undp.org/system/files/documents/global-report-document/hdr2023-24reporten.pdf

United Nations. (2015). *Transforming our world: The 2030 Agenda for Sustainable Development*. https://sdgs.un.org/2030agenda

Upadhyay, S., Sanwal, K., & Goswami, P. (2024). The Concept of Liberation (Moksha) in Indian Philosophy: An Analysis. *African Journal of Biomedical Research*. Advance online publication. DOI: 10.53555/ajbr.v27i4s.6093

Ursa, T., & Arunkumar, M. C. (2023). Residents' Perceptions and Outcomes of Community-Based Tourism in Andro Village of Manipur. *Dera Natung Government College Research Journal*, *8*(1), 169–179.

Verdery, K. (2015). Socialist Societies: Anthropological aspects. In *Elsevier eBooks* (pp. 849–853). https://doi.org/DOI: 10.1016/b978-0-08-097086-8.12147-6

Verdery, K. (1996). *What was socialism, and what comes next?* Princeton University Press., https://press.princeton.edu/books/paperback/9780691011325/what-was-socialism-and-what-comes-next

Visvanathan, S. (1997). *A carnival for science: Essays on science, technology and development.* Oxford University Press., https://archive.org/download/TheCarnivalOfScience-ShivVishvanathan/shiv-carnival-science.pdf

Vogel, Y. A. (2023). Neo-commodification of persons: exploitation of personal data and impact on the sharing economy.

von Mises, L. (1949). *Human Action: A Treatise on Economics* (4th rev. ed.). Liberty Fund.

Wahyudi, H., Lestari, W. R., Said, U. B., Leny, S. M., & Awaluddin, I. (2025). Dynamics of Growth and Stability in the Islamic Financial Services Industry on ECA, GCC, MENA, SSA, and EAP. *International Journal of Economics and Financial Issues*, *15*(3), 448–456. DOI: 10.32479/ijefi.19200

Wahyudi, H., Tubarat, C. P. T., Rodliyah, N., Kusnadi, A., & Leny, S. M. (2025). The Nexus of Crowdfunding and E-Wakaf to Islamic Fintech in Indonesia in the Era of Industrial Revolution 5.0. *Journal of Ecohumanism*, *4*(1), 208–219. DOI: 10.62754/joe.v4i1.4657

Weber, M. (1905). *The Protestant Ethic and the Spirit of Capitalism* (Kalberg, S., Trans.). Roxbury Publishing Company.

Werbach, K. (2018). *The Blockchain and the new architecture of trust.* MIT Press.

Wilk, R. R. (2001). Consuming morality. *Journal of Consumer Culture, 1*(2), 245–260. DOI: 10.1177/146954050100100208

Wray, L. R. (2025). *Understanding modern money theory: Money and credit in capitalist economies*. Edward Elgar.

Yan, Y. (2009). *The individualization of Chinese society*. Berg Publishers. https://www.bloomsbury.com/us/individualization-of-chinese-society-9781847883780/

Yan, Y. (2003). *Private life under socialism: Love, intimacy, and family change in a Chinese village, 1949–1999*. Stanford University Press., https://www.sup.org/books/asian-studies/private-life-under-socialism

Yashodha. (2019). Trust and kinship: Experimental evidence from rural India. Journal of the Economic Science Association, 5(2), 223–237.

Yin, S. (2024). Situating platform gig economy in the formal subsumption of reproductive labor: Transnational migrant domestic workers and the continuum of exploitation and precarity. *Capital and Class, 48*(1), 119–133.

Yurchak, A. (2006). *Everything was forever, until it was no more: The last Soviet generation*. Princeton University Press., https://press.princeton.edu/books/paperback/9780691121178/everything-was-forever-until-it-was-no-more

Yussuf, D. (2024). *Ujamaa: How Julius Nyerere's socialist philosophy evolved in Tanzania*. TRT Afrika Insight. https://www.trtafrika.com/insight/ujamaa-how-julius-nyereres-socialist-philosophy-evolved-in-tanzania-18220801

Zaheer, S., & van Wijnbergen, S. (2025). Sukuk Defaults: On Distress Resolution in Islamic Finance. *Qualitative Research in Financial Markets, 17*(2), 292–311. DOI: 10.1108/QRFM-08-2023-0203

Zamora, A. (2021). *How local and ethnic women in Latin America are transforming their communities' economies*. Rights and Resources Initiative. https://rightsandresources.org/blog/how-local-and-ethnic-women-in-latin-america-are-transforming-their-communities-economies/

Zander, U., Lu, L., & Chimenti, G. (2025). The platform economy and futures of market societies: Salient tensions in ecosystem evolution. *Journal of Business Research*, *189*, 115037. DOI: 10.1016/j.jbusres.2024.115037

Zelizer, V. A. (2017). *The social meaning of money: Pin money, paychecks, poor relief, and other currencies.* Princeton University Press. [1] andrae@zedat.fu-berlin.de https://orcid.org/0000-0002-8586-7812

Ziipao, R. R. (2023). Out of coverage area: Tribes and digital exclusion in North-east India. *Journal of Development Policy and Practice*, 24551333231163930.

Дискурсі, Г. У., & Культурної, З. (2020)... *ГЛОБАЛЬНИЙ КАПІТАЛІЗМ VS ТРАДИЦІЙНА КУЛЬТУРА*, *39*(100), 248–258.

About the Contributors

Bryan Christiansen is an Adjunct Business Professor at Southern New Hampshire University and the Chief Executive Officer of the management consultancy, Soluvex, LLC in New Mexico, USA. He is currently Editor-in-Chief of the IGI Global Book Series, "Advances in Digital Crime, Forensics, and Cyber Terrorism" as well as "Advances in Psychology, Mental Health, and Behavioral Studies". Christiansen is fluent in Chinese, Japanese, and Spanish, and is currently learning Russian. He has presented at several universities in other countries including Oxford University in the United Kingdom. He earned an MBA from Capella University and a BS in Marketing from the University of the State of New York. Christiansen's extensive travels around the world since 1973 have enabled him to produce 50 Reference books on a variety of subjects ranging from cultural studies to organizational sociology. Over 70 percent of these publications have become Scopus- and/or Web of Science-indexed.

John Branch currently teaches a variety of marketing and international business courses at the undergraduate, MBA, and executive levels at the Stephen M Ross School of Business at the University of Michigan's Main Campus in Ann Arbor, Michigan, USA. He also serves as Co-Director of the Yaffe Digital Media Initiative. Previously, he was Academic Director of the School's weekend and evening MBA programs as well as the Director of Educational Outreach at the University's William Davidson Institute. John also holds an appointment at the University's Center for Russian, East European, & Eurasian Studies, and maintains a Research Fellowship at the William Davidson Institute. He holds a Bachelor of

Engineering Science in Electronics from the University of Western Ontario (Canada), a Master of Business Administration from the University of New Brunswick (Canada), a Master of Arts in Education from Washington University in Saint Louis (USA), a Doctor of Philosophy in Marketing from the University of Cambridge (England), a Doctor of Education from the University of Michigan (USA), and a Doctor of Professional Studies from Middlesex University (England).

***

Keerthiraj is currently serving at GFGC Punjalakatte (affiliated to Mangalore University) and has previously served at the School of Law & Liberal Arts, Alliance University, Bengaluru. His journey is one of discovering how knowledge emerges in places the academy rarely sees. Born in a forest village of coastal Karnataka, in a family untouched by formal education, he worked as a coolie, quarry labourer, and salesman to support his studies and family. These were not obstacles but the ground on which his thinking grew. He completed his BA in History, Economics, and Political Science, followed by an MA in Political Science from Mangalore University with distinction. His doctoral research at Kuvempu University focused on Media, Public Policy, Colonial Consciousness, Public Perceptions, and Politics. His work spans ideologies, diplomacy, policy, strategy, and international relations. For him, scholarship is a responsibility—to rethink, unlearn, and make knowledge meaningful.

Gwyneth Edwards is an associate professor of global strategy and international business at HEC Montréal. Prior to academia, she was a senior leader in a global high tech manufacturing firm. She teaches global strategy and cross-cultural management at the bachelors, masters and executive levels. She has a mechanical engineering degree and also does research on the experiences of women in engineering. She can be reached at www.gwynethedwards.com.

Razali Haron obtained his DBA from UKM in 2012, MBA (Finance) from IIUM in 2003 and BBA (Finance) from UiTM in 1994. Prior to joining IIUM in 2003, he had extensive industrial experience for almost

13 years covering the capital market, portfolio management, unit trust industry and merchant (investment) banking in Malaysia. With his vast industry experience, he has been appointed as a member of the IIUM Investment sub-Committee from 2012-2021 and Director of IIUM Shariah Advisory Services Sdn. Bhd from 2019-2020. His area of expertise includes the corporate finance, capital market and portfolio management and has published his research works with reputable international publishers such as the Emerald, Elsevier, Sage, Inderscience and Palgrave Macmillan. Being an active researcher, he has been awarded with - The Best Researcher Award and Best Indexed Journal Article (Department of Finance) in 2014, Highest Citation in Citation Index Journal (Social Science) at the IIUM Quality Day 2015, Top 250 Contributors to IIUM Research Performance 2015-2017, Highest Number of Publications Award (IIiBF - 2019), Top 30 Contributors to IIUM Research Performance at the IIUM Takrim Day 2019, Highest Top Researchers of Joint Publications for 2019-2021 in IIUM, High Impact Responsible Research Award (IIiBF 2020), Journal Article Publication Award (IIiBF 2020), Award for Chapter in Book Publication (2019) in Conjunction with Universiti Malaysia Sabah (UMS) Researcher Award 2019 & 2020, Top 50 Contributors to IIUM Research Performance (Responsible Research & Innovation Appreciation Day 2022), MyRA Quantity and Quality of Research Award (IIiBF 2022), MyRA Professional Services & Gifts (IIiBF 2022), and Highest Citations in Indexed Journal Award (Social Sciences) 2nd Place (Responsible Research & Innovation Appreciation Day 2024). His has also won The Best Research Paper in the 8th ASEAN International Conference in Islamic Finance (2020), held in Tazkia (Bogor, Indonesia) and very recently, The Best Oral Presenter during the 12th ASEAN International Conference in Islamic Finance (2024), held in MSU (Mindanao, the Philippines).His co-authored paper on Bitcoin Currency has been awarded with The Highly Commended Paper in the 2020 Emerald Literati Awards.

Sofia Idris has done MS Gender Studies from University of the Punjab (Pakistan) and M Phil Political Science from Government College University, Lahore (Pakistan). Her areas of interest include Politics, environment, climate change, sustainable development, social media, gender issues, human rights, local politics, local governments, current affairs, political economy, international relations, peace, strategy, terrorism, conflict and conflict resolution, politics, society & social systems, environment, social & cultural issues, social care, women empowerment, women, children and gender issues.

Vishal Jain is presently working as a Professor at the Department of Computer Science & Engineering, School of Engineering & Technology, Vivekananda Institute of Professional Studies - Technical Campus, New Delhi. Before that, he worked as Professor at Sharda University, Greater Noida and Associate Professor at Bharati Vidyapeeth's Institute of Computer Applications and Management (BVICAM), New Delhi. He has associated as a member of the Faculty Board, Board of Planning and Management, Executive Council, Academic Council, Curriculum Development and Review Committee and Academic Audit of various higher education Institutions. He is associated with Kuala Lumpur University of Science and Technology (KLUST), Malaysia, Lincoln University College, Malaysia and Research Institute of IoT Cybersecurity, Department of Electronic Engineering, National Kaohsiung University of Science and Technology, Taiwan for research oriented activities.

Nizar K. is a dedicated educator and researcher with over nine years of experience in teaching Economics. Currently pursuing a PhD at Presidency University, his research focuses on the dynamics and challenges of the informal workforce. He has a keen interest in labour economics, development policy, and social equity.

Early Ridho Kismawadi is a lecturer at the Department of Islamic Banking, Faculty of Islamic Economics and Business IAIN Langsa, Aceh, Indonesia, he has been a lecturer since 2013, he has completed a doctoral program in 2018 majoring in Sharia economics at the State Islamic University of North Sumatra. He was appointed head of the Islamic economics Law study program (2023) Islamic banking study program (2020) and Islamic financial management study program (2019) at Langsa State Islamic Institute (IAIN Langsa), Aceh, Indonesia. His research interests include financial economics, applied econometrics, Islamic economics, banking, and finance. He has published articles in national and international journals. In addition, he is also a reviewer of several reputable international journals such as Finance Research Letters, Financial Innovation, Cogent Business &; Management, Journal of Islamic Accounting and Business Research. He has also presented his papers at various local and international seminars.

Apoorva Misra is a legal scholar specializing in environmental law, international maritime governance, and sustainable development. She holds a Ph.D. in Law from Guru Gobind Singh Indraprastha University and has served as Assistant Professor of Law at Alliance University. Her research bridges legal theory and practice, with publications in peer-reviewed journals and international edited volumes.

Archan Mitra is an Assistant Professor at School of Media Studies (SOMS) at Presidency University, Bangalore. He is the author of two book "Cases for Classroom Media and Entertainment Business" and "Multiverse and Media", he also has other several edited books to his credit. He has done his doctorate from Visva-Bharati Santiniketan, West Bengal in the field of "environmental informatics and communication for sustainability". In addition to that he is a certified Science Communicator and Journalism from Indian Science Communication Society (ISCOS), certified Corporate Trainer with Amity Institute of Training and Development, Certified Social Media Network Analyst. He has a strong interest in environmental communication. He was awarded certificate of merit by PRSI, Kolkata Chapter and Medal of Honor by Journalistic Club of Kolkata. He was working as a research assistant with the World Bank's "Environmental Capacity Building in Southeast Asia" project at IIM Kashipur. He was instrumental in launching the World Bank's Green MBA MOOC, he has also assisted in the research project on Uttarakhand disaster mitigation by ICSSR, the leading research on Uttarakhand disaster.

Sanchita Paul is a dedicated and accomplished content strategist with extensive experience in managing diverse content formats across different digital platforms. With a strong background in content strategy, editing, and UX writing, she has honed her skills in branding, social media management, and technical writing. Holding an MA in Communication and Journalism from Visva-Bharati University, Ms. Paul is proficient in tools like Google Analytics, Canva, and MS Office Suite, making her a versatile professional committed to producing high-quality, impactful content to improve brand visibility.

Dede Ruslan is a Professor/Professor at the Faculty of Economics, State University of Medan (Unimed) with expertise in the fields of Monetary Economics, Finance, and Banking. He has a doctoral education background in Economics from Padjajaran University Bandung and is active in scientific research and publications focusing on monetary policy, financial inclusion, financial technology, and economic dynamics after the Covid-19 pandemic. His works are widely cited and contribute to the development of economics, especially in the context of Indonesia and ASEAN. As an academic, Dede Ruslan also plays an active role in the development of study programs and faculty management, having served as the Head of the Department of Economics at the Faculty of Economics of Unimed. In addition, he is known as a prolific researcher with numerous scientific articles that discuss current issues in the field of monetary and financial economics, including monetary policy analysis, economic stability, and the role of financial technology in the economy. His profile reflects a strong commitment to the development of economics through education, research, and community service, especially in supporting regional and national economic progress through relevant and applicable scientific approaches.

Ranjit Singha is a dedicated Ph.D. Scholar in the Department of Psychology at Christ (Deemed to be University), specializing in addiction research. As the developer of the Multidimensional Addiction Behaviour Scale (MABS), his research unravels the complexities of addiction to inform effective prevention, intervention, and education strategies. With over 10 years of experience as a facilitator, Editor and Reviewer, he has conducted workshops and talks that empower individuals with knowledge and tools for healthier decision-making and addiction awareness programs. Additionally, he has led Art of Writing Skills workshops, helping participants enhance their academic and professional communication. With a solid academic record, he has published 195+ scholarly works, including 81+ Scopus-indexed publications, reflecting his commitment to impactful research and dissemination of knowledge.

Surjit Singha is an academician with a broad spectrum of interests, including UN Sustainable Development Goals, Organizational Climate, Workforce Diversity, Organizational Culture, HRM, Marketing, Finance, IB, Global Business, Business, AI, K12 & Higher Education, Gender and Cultural Studies. Currently a faculty member at Kristu Jayanti College, Dr. Surjit also serves as an Editor, reviewer, and author for prominent global publications and journals, including being on the Editorial review board of Information Resources Management Journal and contributor to various publications. With over 16 years of experience in Administration, Teaching, and Research, Dr. Surjit is dedicated to imparting knowledge and guiding students in their research pursuits. As a research mentor, Dr. Surjit has nurtured young minds and fostered academic growth. Dr. Surjit has an impressive track record of over 150+ publications (SCOPUS Indexed 100+), including articles, book chapters, and textbooks, holds two US Copyrights, one patent granted, and has successfully completed and published two fully funded minor research projects from Kristu Jayanti (Deemed to be University).

Index

www.ingramcontent.com/pod-product-compliance
Lightning Source LLC
LaVergne TN
LVHW081523300926
849161LV00006B/1279